Clinical Dermatology Illustrated

Clinical Dermatology Illustrated

A Regional Approach

by
John R.T. Reeves
Associate Clinical Professor of Dermatology,
University of California, San Francisco
and
Howard Maibach
Professor of Dermatology,
University of California, San Francisco

WILLIAMS & WILKINS AND ASSOCIATES PTY LIMITED
Sydney · Baltimore · London

Clinical Dermatology Illustrated:
A Regional Approach

National Library of Australia
Cataloguing-in-Publication entry

Reeves, John R.T. (John Richard T.), 1942-
  Clinical dermatology illustrated.

  Includes index.
  ISBN 0 86433 031 6.

  1. Dermatology. I. Maibach, Howard I.
(Howard Ira). II. Title.

616.5

First printed in hard bound edition by ADIS Health Science Press 1984

WILLIAMS & WILKINS AND ASSOCIATES PTY LIMITED
43 Herbert Street, Artarmon, NSW 2064, Australia

Printed in Hong Kong by Creative Printing Co. Ltd.

"To Anne, Jessamyn and Amy."

John R.T. Reeves

Acknowledgements for Illustrations

We would like to thank the following physicians for allowing us to use photographs from their collections:

Dr Loren E. Golitz: pp. 7, 234, 269, 270, 293
Dr Steven A. Davis: pp. 53, 107, 245
Dr Axel Hoke: p. 83
Dr Peter Webb: p. 91

List of Contents

Diagnostic Procedures

Formulary

Introduction

Skin conditions have characteristic patterns, locations, and morphologies. The location or pattern leads experienced clinicians to markedly narrow their list of possible diagnoses. We present common skin conditions by anatomic location, starting from the scalp and working down, and outline their treatment.

The Patient Guides, which have been limited to those the authors have found useful in their own experience, are suitable for photocopying, and will help patients understand their disease and its management.

We hope that you will find this manual valuable in daily clinical practice.

University of California
San Francisco

John R.T. Reeves
Howard Maibach

Scalp

Seborrheic Dermatitis

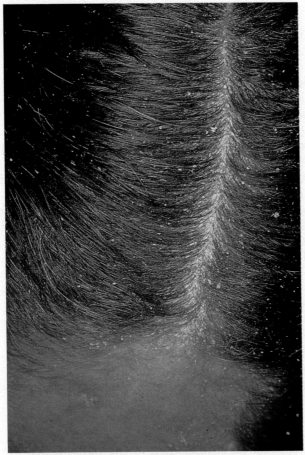

"Dandruff" or excessive scaling of the scalp.
Redness in seborrheic dermatitis is faint, patchy, ill-
defined, and difficult to see even with close
inspection.

Clinical
- Occasional flakes of *dander* on the scalp are normal and should not precipitate attempts at therapy.
- Seborrheic dermatitis consists of excessive scaling, itching and faint inflammation. (Note: *Seborrhea* merely means increased oil flow, and is not synonymous with seborrheic dermatitis).
- Occurs in areas of high oil gland activity: scalp, face, upper chest and, infrequently, axillae and pubis.
- Chronic, but intermittent, frequently flaring with physical and emotional stress.
- More common and severe in fair-skinned individuals.
- Not seen in children. May be seen in infants up to 3-4 months of age because of maternal hormones. Then appears as 'cradle cap', and as red, scaly rash of fold areas of neck, axillae, and groins.

Seborrheic Dermatitis

Treatment
Aimed at reducing scaling and inflammation, either of which may predominate in a given individual.

Shampoos
- Anti-dandruff activity has been demonstrated for shampoos containing
  - ▲ cloroxine
  - ▲ selenium sulfide
  - ▲ sulfur and salicylic acid
  - ▲ zinc pyrithione
- Selenium sulfide (2.5%) and cloroxine shampoos require prescriptions in some countries, but are not more effective than less expensive over-the-counter products containing zinc pyrithione or sulfur and salicylic acid. It is thought, but not proven, that the addition of tar makes a shampoo more effective.
- Shampoos vary considerably with respect to cosmetic texture, ease of lathering and drying effect. Some are now offered with protein added as a conditioner. Patients should try many brands, or be given a variety of samples, and select one which they like.

Dandruff shampoos usually work well. 'Failure' may be due to:
- Infrequent use (may be required once daily to once weekly, often needed every 2-3 days)
- Inadequate duration (may take a week to work)
- Inadequate scalp contact (this is the most common cause of 'failure') — **leave on scalp several minutes**
- Natural fluctuations in disease (shampoos may not suppress all flares).
- These points must be emphasized to the patient. See Patient Guide page 273, for specific instructions.

- If the above regimen is not successful, then the patient may try lathering the scalp, covering it with a plastic shower cap and leaving the shampoo on for 30 minutes before rinsing. This will usually remove even stubborn scale, but may cause slight irritation.
- If dandruff shampoo leaves the hair dry, listless, or with an objectionable odor, the patient may perform a final shampoo with a scented cosmetic product, a rinse, or a conditioner.

Seborrheic Dermatitis

Treatment (continued)

Topical Corticosteroids

- Corticosteroids suppress the inflammatory component of the disease and result in reduced scaling. Mild preparations (hydrocortisone, 1%) are usually adequate. Often only a few applications of the medicine will cause a complete disappearance of the disease for several days or even weeks. If adequate shampooing and keratolytics do not suppress inflammation of the scalp, use a corticosteroid.
- Corticosteroids should be prescribed in a thin solution vehicle, to minimize residue on the hair. Solutions are applied to the scalp in the following manner: the hair is parted in a continuous line along the scalp and one drop of solution is applied every few centimeters along this line and rubbed in. The hair is then parted 2 centimeters parallel to this line and solution is again applied. Parting the hair and applying solution every few centimeters allows application to all areas with minimum residue. This technique is described in the Patient Guide.
- Hydrocortisone solutions are often effective, but more potent steroids provide a brisker response and probably are not injurious to the scalp when used intermittently. Some steroid-containing aerosols are available with a thin nozzle to facilitate the ease of application to the scalp. These are easier to apply, but expensive. *Barseb HC* contains keratolytics and hydrocortisone.

Scale-removing Preparations

- These materials are rubbed into the scalp, left for a prolonged period of time, then shampooed out.
- They remove more scale than do shampoos and are usually effective even in the more severe cases of seborrheic dermatitis, and often in psoriasis.
  - ▲ Mineral oil, 'baby oil', olive oil and other oils facilitate scale removal.
  - ▲ Salicylic acid may be compounded by the pharmacist, 10% in an oil - a commercial product is available in a propylene glycol gel (*Keralyt* gel, p.323).
  - ▲ Tars–*Liquor Carbonis Detergens*, 5% to 10%, compounded in an oil. Tar gels such as *Estar* and *Psorigel* are readily available over the counter (p.323).
- These products are rubbed into the scalp, then shampooed out after several hours. It is convenient to apply them overnight under showercap occlusion (p.311). They may be slightly irritating.

Psoriasis

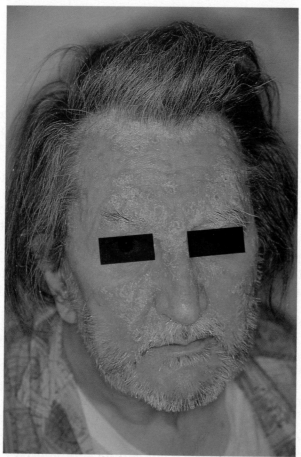

Neglected psoriasis showing marked involvement of the scalp, and the much less common involvement of the face.

Clinical

- Differs from seborrheic dermatitis (p.1) in that
  - ▲ the red areas are clearly demarcated, often elevated, and of a deep red color
  - ▲ the scale is thicker and more profuse
  - ▲ involvement of the face, brows and lashes is less common
- Look for plaques of psoriasis elsewhere (pp.161-170), 'pinking' of the skin of the intergluteal fold (p.163), and nail changes (p.164).

Psoriasis

Treatment
Exactly as for seborrheic dermatitis (p.2) except that
- It is more often necessary to use topical tars, scale-removing oils or corticosteroids, especially under occlusion overnight.
- If the condition is widespread on the body, severe, or disabling, then referral to a dermatologist is indicated for the hospital care, photochemotherapy or treatment with oral anti-metabolites (p.170) which may be required.

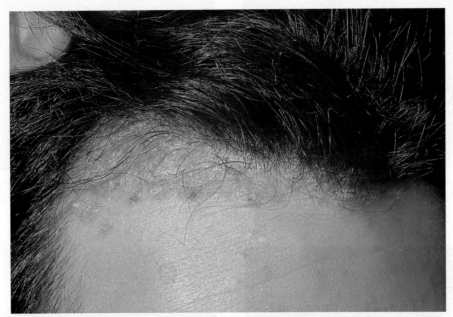

In contrast to seborrheic dermatitis, psoriasis occurs in well-defined plaques, and usually has a thicker, caked scale.

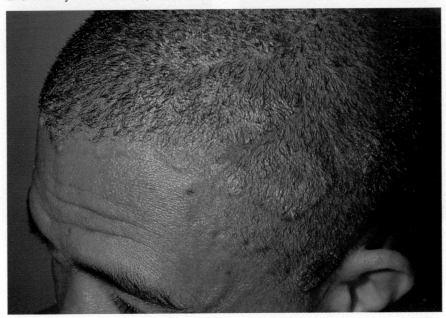

Tinea Capitis

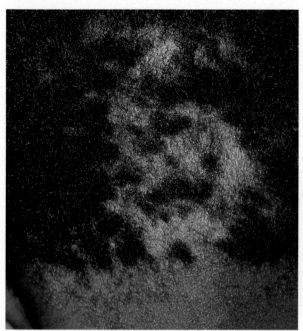

Early, non-inflammatory tinea capitis. Spotty, "moth-eaten" pattern.

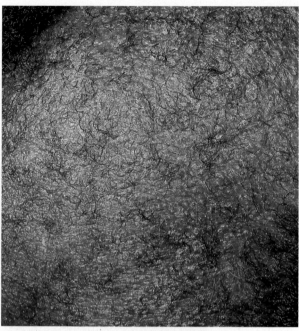

Non-inflammatory tinea capitis causing well-demarcated area of hair loss with residual stumps of broken hairs.

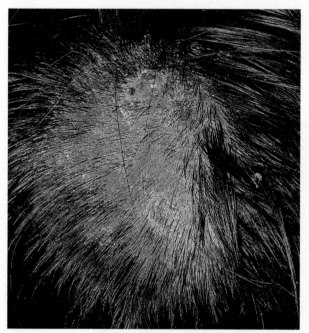

Patch of tinea capitis with broken hair stubs and spots of early inflammation, or kerion formation.

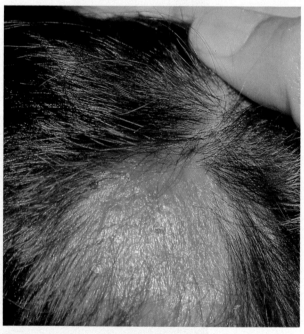

Marked inflammation of kerion in tinea capitis.

Tinea Capitis

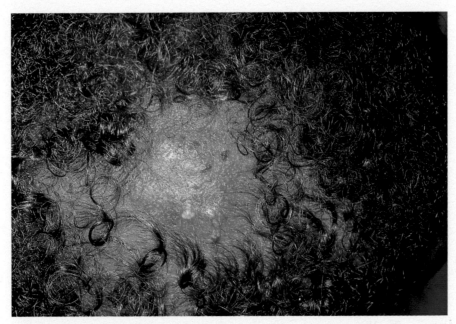

Extreme delayed hypersensitivity to fungal antigens in kerion with inflammatory (sterile) pustules.

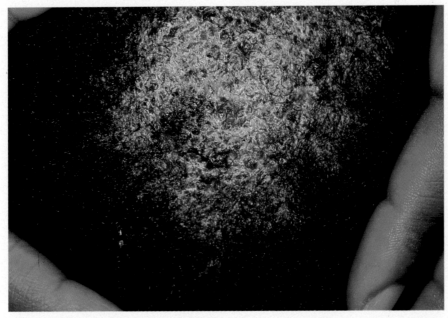

Heavily crusted kerion of long duration.

Tinea Capitis

Clinical

- 'Ringworm' of scalp and hair appears as scattered scaly patches containing broken hairs.
- Asymptomatic to mildly itchy.
- Does *not* result in permanent alopecia.

- After several weeks the lesion may suddenly become inflamed, swollen and even surmounted by pustules.
- This is *kerion*, a delayed hypersensitivity reaction to fungal antigens, similar to a violent purified protein derivative (PPD) reaction. It may result in permanent alopecia.
- Kerion is often misdiagnosed as an acute bacterial process. Bacterial cultures are negative, and antibacterial therapy is ineffective.
- The clinical tip-off is the serenity of the patient. Kerion is mildly symptomatic, whereas the equivalent bacterial folliculitis is exquisitely tender with painful adenopathy.
- Plucking a hair and performing a potassium hydroxide (KOH) examination will confirm the diagnosis. See Diagnosis of Fungal Infections, page 293.

Tinea Capitis

Treatment

- Relapse rate is high with topical therapy because hyphae may grow down into the follicles.
- All patients should receive griseofulvin (p.307). Therapy should continue for 4-8 weeks or at least one week after apparent clearing of the lesion. Alternative regimens which appear to be effective are a single dose of 3g-4g, or 1g daily for 3 days.
  - ▲ Alternative oral antifungal agent is ketoconazole 200mg daily (p.308). It is known to be effective against dermatophytes, but at the time of writing is approved in the US only for generalized candidiasis.
- If griseofulvin cannot be given, refer the patient to a dermatologist for the esoteric treatments (X-ray, oral epilating agents) which may be required.
- See Treatment of Fungal Infections, page 307.

- ■ Griseofulvin is given for kerion, but inflammation will not subside in the first few weeks, because the fungal antigen is still present.
- ■ Kerion inflammation should be treated promptly and vigorously to minimize the likelihood of permanent alopecia. Depot intralesional (p.313) or oral corticosteroids (for 2 weeks) are required to promptly suppress the reaction. Topical steroids are usually ineffective in this deep inflammation.
- ■ Learn to diagnose kerion quickly to avoid frustrating ineffective treatment with systemic antibiotics and incision and drainage, which postpones the administration of appropriate (corticosteroid) therapy.

Head Lice

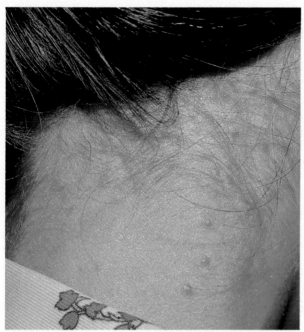

Typical bite papules at nape of neck in pediculosis capitis.

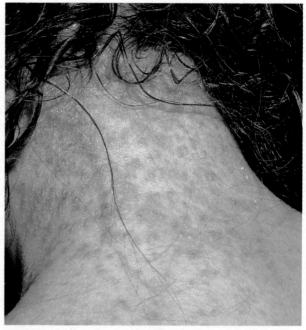

Marked bites with exudation, edema, and possible secondary infection in neglected pediculosis capitis.

Dark (blood-filled) lice on scalp, among bites and excoriations. As a rule, these creatures are not numerous and are hard to find.

Profuse collection of nits attached to hairs in long-standing pediculosis capitis.

Head Lice

Clinical
- Minor to intense itching may occur, especially at occiput, but not uncommonly it is asymptomatic.
- Occasionally an exudative rash is seen.
- Several live adult insects, 2mm in length; several to hundreds of white 1mm nits (ova) adhering to hairs.
- Quite contagious among children.

Treatment
Pediculocides
- Gamma benzene hexachloride (lindane) shampoo is worked into the scalp, left on for five minutes and rinsed out. Repeat shampooing is not necessary to ensure killing of adult lice and nits.
- If shampoo fails, lindane lotion (not shampoo) is left on overnight and rinsed out.
- Equally effective, and available over-the-counter, is pyrethrin solution or gel. It is rubbed into the scalp and shampooed out after 10 minutes.
- Alternative treatments are:
  - ▲ copper oleate-tetrahydronaphthalene
  - ▲ benzyl benzoate

  Lotions are left on the scalp for 15 minutes and then washed out.

Nit Removal
The above treatments kill the nits, but they continue to cling tightly to the hair. Removal may be difficult. The most successful management consists of the following.
- Soak hair in generous amounts of white vinegar diluted 1:1 with water, keep under shower cap or towel occlusion for 30 minutes.
- Immediately comb dripping hair with a fine-toothed flea comb (purchased in pet store), then shampoo with mild shampoo.
- May need to repeat this procedure daily for a few days.
- **Note:** child may return to school even if nits are present after adequate pediculocide treatment.

Preventing Reinfestation and Contagion
- Adult organisms may contaminate hats, collars, high chairbacks, bedclothes, combs and brushes.
- Wash, dry-clean, or hot-iron hats, coats, shirts, blankets, sheets and pillow-cases.
- Thoroughly wash combs and brushes in hot, soapy water.
- Vacuum or otherwise clean beds, pillows, and upholstered furniture used by the patient.
- See Patient Guide page 280.

Hair Loss (Alopecia)

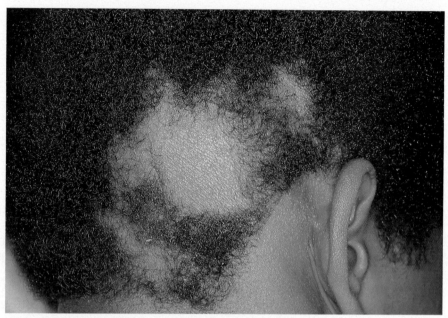

Typical well-defined areas of complete hair loss in alopecia areata.

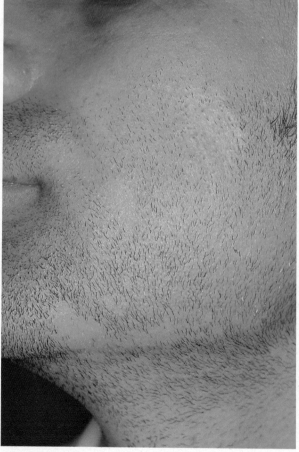

Any hair-bearing site can be affected.

Hair Loss (Alopecia)

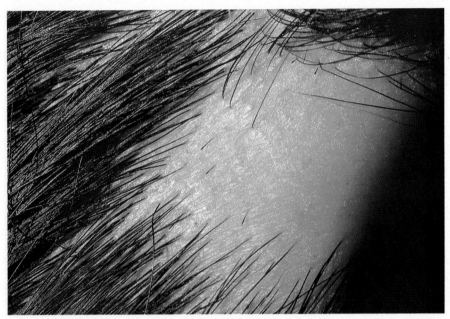

Short, blunt-ended, loose "exclamation-point hairs" may be seen at the edge of the bald area.

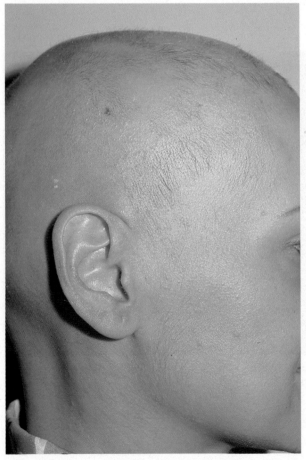

Alopecia can be extensive, which has a poor prognosis.

Hair Loss (Alopecia)

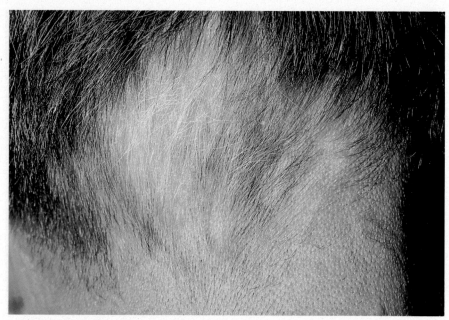

Early re-growth in alopecia areata is often with non-pigmented hairs. Later growth has normal pigmentation.

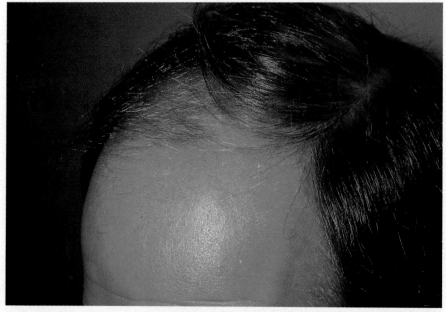

Androgenetic alopecia (male balding) has a temporo-frontal pattern with fine, wispy hairs at the margin.

Hair Loss (Alopecia)

Ascertain whether the patient's symptom is increased shedding of hair (most noticeable when combing or washing) or thinning and balding.

Thinning and Balding

Patchy Hair Loss (Bald Spots)

● Well circumscribed patches of complete baldness with a normal scalp is *alopecia areata*.
   ▲ short, constricted blunt-tipped 'exclamation point' hairs may be seen at the periphery of the bald area
   ▲ white hairs may remain when pigmented hairs fall out
   ▲ may involve brows, lashes, beard, body hair
   ▲ usually regrows spontaneously in several months, but may remain or progress to permanent alopecia
● Other.
   ▲ if inflamed, may be folliculitis or tinea capitis (p.6)
   ▲ a mass may indicate a cyst or metastatic lesion
   ▲ vague scattered small areas of thinning may be 'moth-eaten' alopecia of secondary syphilis
   ▲ an area of short, blunt stubble on an otherwise normal scalp is trichotillomania, the nervous habit of pulling hair

---

Treatment of Alopecia Areata

■ Corticosteroids

   ■ Potent topical preparations under occlusion are occasionally effective.
   ■ Intralesional injection of triamcinolone acetonide, 5mg/mL, or other repository preparation (see page 313 for technique) is usually at least temporarily effective. Repeat at monthly to bimonthly intervals.
   ■ Systemic corticosteroids are occasionally given long-term, often on alternate days, to patients with total or disfiguring alopecia. Refer these patients to a specialist for such management.
   ■ Scalp irritative treatments such as sensitization to and application of a contact allergen, or psoralen-ultraviolet-light therapy are showing promise. Both have practical and theoretical drawbacks.

Hair Loss (Alopecia)

Diffuse Thinning of Hair

● Thinning or bald patches at temples and crown are due to 'androgenetic' alopecia, or inherited pattern balding.

▲ In men this occurs at temples and crown

▲ In women diffuse thinning of entire top of scalp is usually seen

▲ Immature, fine, short, tapering hairs are present at edges of thinning area

---

Treatment of Hereditary Baldness

■ Medication, vitamins, massage, and ultraviolet light are without benefit.

■ Creative hairstyling may minimize the appearance of thinning.

■ Wigs today are lightweight, cool, and stay glued on in all conditions.

■ Scalp plug transplants or flaps improve appearance in selected patients.

Increased Shedding of Hair

● 'Telogen effluvium' occurs 2-3 months after childbirth, fever, severe illness, injury or surgery. Occasionally it occurs after or during drug therapy (thyroxine, Vitamin A, anti-cancer drugs).

▲ Intact hairs, with tiny white bulbs present on their proximal ends, are shed profusely

▲ Scalp is normal

Treatment of Telogen Effluvium

■ No treatment is necessary – regrowth is bound to occur.

■ Follicles are not damaged, just temporarily synchronized in a resting phase.

■ Shedding occurs because new hairs are pushing out old ones.

■ Growth will proceed at normal rate of about 12mm per month.

Face and Neck

Seborrheic Dermatitis

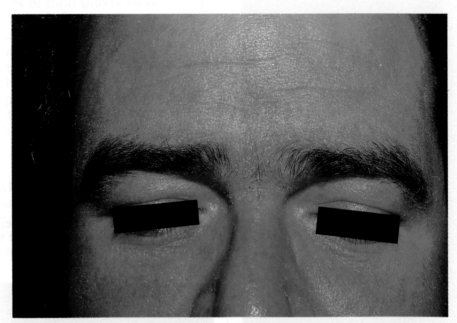

Mild redness and scaling between and in the eyebrows, and on the cheeks. The typical centro-facial distribution of seborrheic dermatitis.

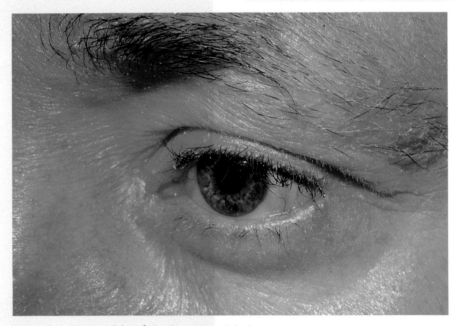

Seborrheic dermatitis of the brows and lashes.

Pityriasis Alba

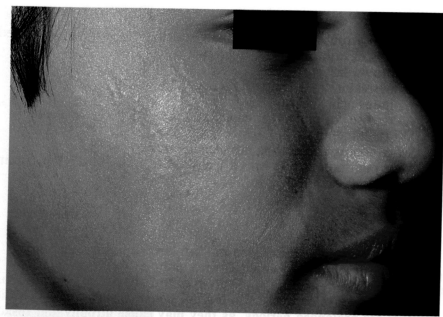

Poorly-defined areas of faint hypopigmentation, often with mild scale, on the face and/or arms in pityriasis alba.

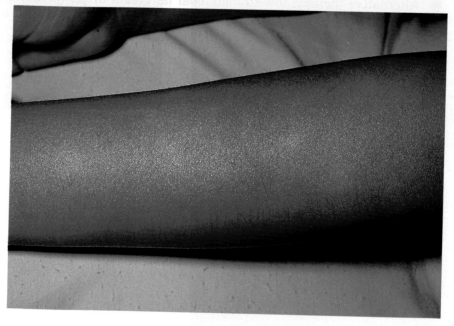

Pityriasis Alba

Clinical

- Usually faint, poorly defined areas of hypopigmentation, often with fine, shiny scale, or slightly glazed surface. The skin may be generally dry or chapped.
- On the cheeks, occasionally on the forehead, neck and upper arms.
- Occurs in children and young adults, much more noticeable in the dark-skinned.
- Asymptomatic.
- Occurs in dry climates, more often during the dry times of the year (winter in temperate zones, when central heating lowers humidity).
- Hypopigmentation is due to mild inflammation, a manifestation of dry, chapped skin. More common in atopic people and individuals with dry skin. Usually resolves at puberty when oil production starts.

Treatment

- Possibly can be prevented or minimized by washing infrequently with mild soap, and using lubricants (see Management of Dry Skin, p.147).
- Mild corticosteroid cream or ointment (hydrocortisone 1-2.5%) twice daily, especially after washing. Repigmentation is not noticeable for at least 4-6 weeks, so **encourage persistence**.
- Total repigmentation may not occur in all patients.

Contact Dermatitis

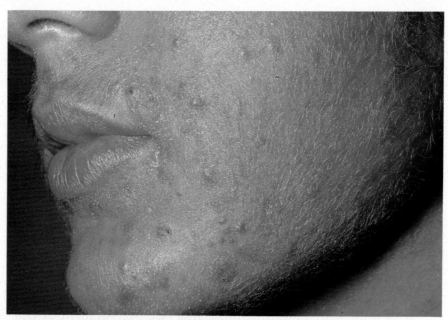

"Dishpan face", or irritant contact dermatitis. Dry, irritated skin from excessive washing with an acne soap.

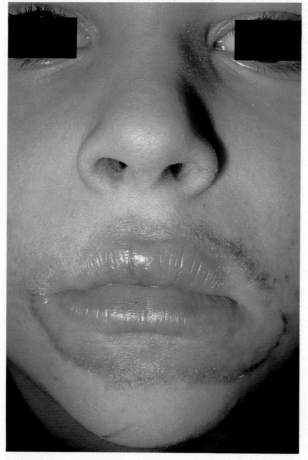

Irritant dermatitis from saliva in child with compulsive licking habit.

Contact Dermatitis

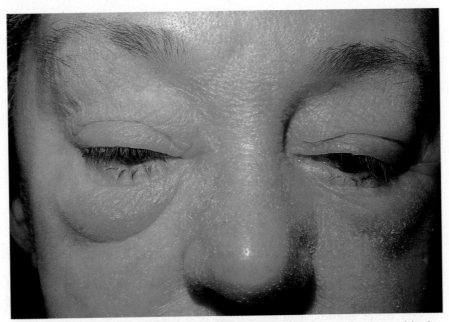

Allergic contact dermatitis from over-the-counter topical medication rubbed over congested sinuses.

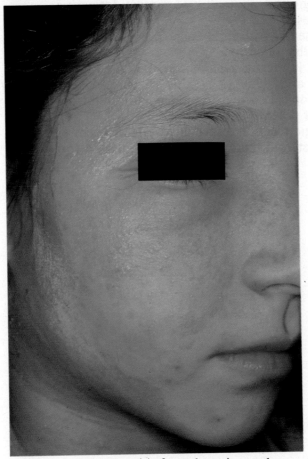

Allergic contact dermatitis from the poison oak plant.

Contact Dermatitis

Clinical
- **Irritant** dermatitis – skin irritated by excessive washing with any type of soap or detergent, astringents, strong medications (eg: benzoyl peroxides for acne), industrial exposure or cosmetics.
- **Allergic** dermatitis – occasional allergy to cosmetics (especially on the eyelids), perfumes, tanning lotions, medications (topical antibiotics, anesthetics), industrial agents. Hair dye allergy usually involves the face and ears as well as the scalp.
- Because of the thinness of eyelid and facial skin, it may react exclusively when there is general exposure to an allergen. *Rhus* (poison ivy, oak) dermatitis is a common example.

Treatment
- Take extensive history for above exposures. Remember that allergic reactions may not occur for up to a week after exposure.
- Irritant dermatitis from cosmetics is more common than allergy. Recommend that individuals go back to a previously safe brand, or try other brands, and encourage less usage.
- If the problem persists or recurs, referral to a dermatologist is necessary for more extensive investigations, including patch testing to rule out allergic and photoallergic contact dermatitis.
- General measures
  - ▲ wash infrequently with mild soap (p.149)
  - ▲ stop all possible offending agents
  - ▲ use a simple lubricant, such as mineral oil
- If inflammation and itching is significant, cool soaks (p.318), or mild to potent topical corticosteroids as indicated (for a few days or weeks only, if potent).
- For severe allergic reaction, especially if also present elsewhere, systemic corticosteroid therapy is usually indicated (p.159).

Photodermatitis

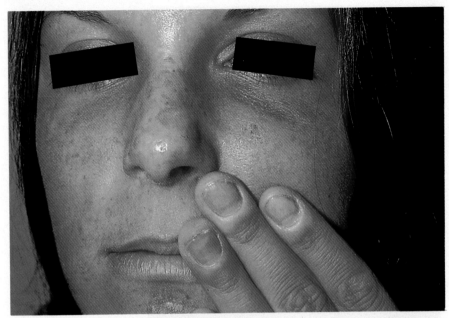

Phototoxic reaction in patient taking tetracycline, with increased sunburn sensitivity and onycholysis (separation of nail plates from nail beds).

Clinical
● Rash
  ▲ occurs on forehead, nose, malar eminences, upper lip, point of chin, ears, sides and back of neck, V-area of upper chest, and backs of hands and arms.
  ▲ spares hair-bearing scalp, eyelids and area under brows, nose, lower lip, and chin (shaded).
● Causes are
  ▲ idiopathic, or 'polymorphous light eruption' ('sun allergy')
    ■ onset a few hours after exposure
    ■ polymorphous lesions – may be dermatitis, papules, plaques, vesicles
    ■ usually itchy
    ■ may or may not recur with each exposure, or be triggered only by intense exposure
  ▲ drug photosensitivity
    ■ 'toxic' or dose-related – such as with tetracyclines (especially demeclocycline) or psoralens – looks like a severe sunburn
    ■ allergic – thiazides, thiazines, sulfa drugs, nitrofurantoin, and many others – itches, looks like dermatitis.
  ▲ internal disease
    ■ lupus erythematosus – may be discoid (purely cutaneous) or systemic – varying degrees of redness, vasculitis, scarring
    ■ dermatomyositis – characteristically also causes 'heliotrope' (violet edema of eyelids)
    ■ porphyria (cutanea tarda, especially) is leathery and hyperpigmented on face, fragile blisters on hands
    ■ pellagra – leathery and hyperpigmented

Photodermatitis

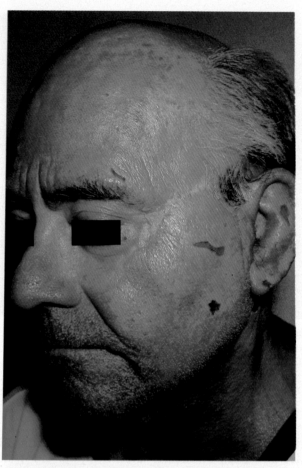

(Same patient). Long-standing, severe idiopathic
photosensitivity of polymorphous light eruption of
face and hands.

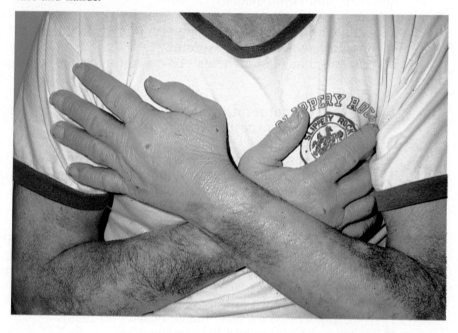

Photodermatitis

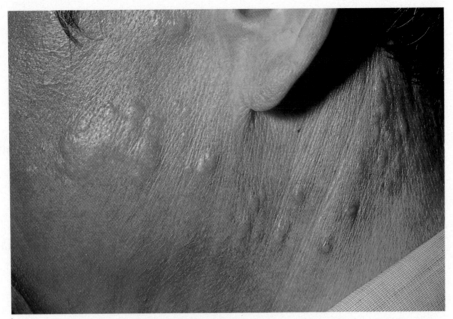

Plaque-type polymorphous light eruption on typical site of side of face and neck.

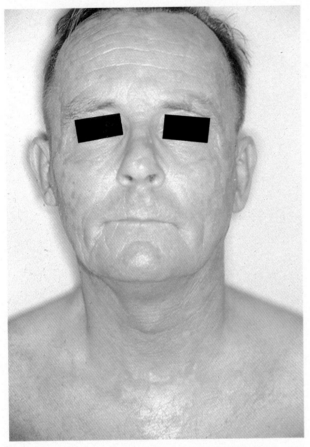

Inflamed and scarred lesions of discoid lupus erythematosus on sun-exposed sites. Note lesion in V of neck.

Photodermatitis

Treatment

- History and physical examination to detect drugs or internal disease. Treat accordingly.
- Reduce sun exposure.
  - ▲ avoid potent 10am to 2pm sun
  - ▲ brimmed hats, long sleeves, gloves
  - ▲ sun-blocking agents (p.316). Use those with broad-spectrum protection.
- Topical corticosteroids (moderately potent) to reduce redness and symptoms.
- Antimalarials (chloroquin, primaquin) help polymorphous light eruption and the rash of lupus erythematosus. **Caution: Antimalarials in high doses are hepatotoxic to patients with porphyria.**
- Phlebotomy or cautious, low doses of antimalarials for porphyria cutanea tarda.
- Refer puzzling and chronic cases to a dermatologist for photo-testing and therapy.

Tinea Facei

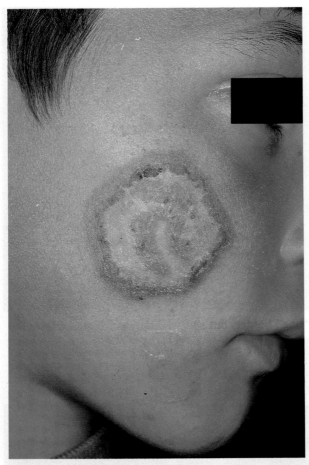

Classic ring type "ringworm" on face.

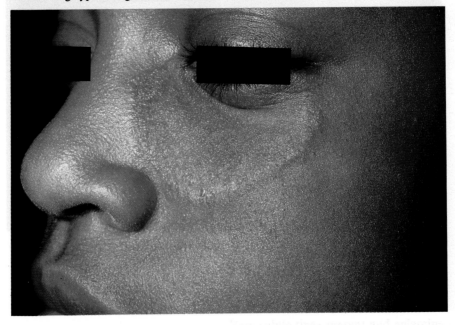

Tinea Facei

Clinical

- In many patients this is typical 'ringworm' (expanding red scaly border).
- May be an amorphous, asymptomatic reddish patch, which **may be photosensitive.**
  - ▲ scaling slight or absent because of oiliness and frequent washing
  - ▲ may be mistaken for polymorphous light eruption, lupus erythematosus, contact dermatitis, and others
  - ▲ topical corticosteroids decrease redness but lesions do not resolve and may enlarge
  - ▲ when an amorphous facial eruption does not respond to conventional therapy, perform a potassium hydroxide (KOH) examination to rule out tinea facei. **If KOH is negative, repeat in two days after patient ceases washing** (to allow scale build-up).

Treatment

- Use topical antifungal agents (p.309) unless hair is involved. Apply an antifungal cream or lotion twice a day for 2-3 weeks, or at least several days past complete clearing of lesion.
- Use *griseofulvin* for the following
  - ▲ recurrent lesions
  - ▲ hairline involvement
  - ▲ extensive ear or eyelid involvement, where adequate topical therapy is difficult
- Alternative oral antifungal is ketoconazole (p.308). It is known to be effective against dermatophytes, but at the time of writing is approved in the US only for generalized candidiasis.
  See Treatment of Fungal Infections, page 307.

Acne

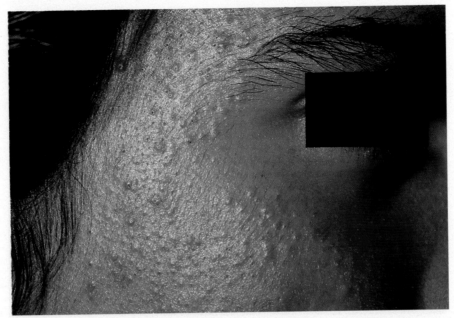

Almost pure open-comedo (blackhead) acne, with only a few inflamed papules.

Close comedones, or whiteheads. They are deep and tenaceous.

Acne

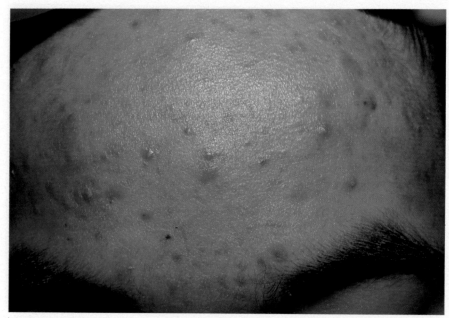

Typical papulo-pustular acne. No comedones are evident.

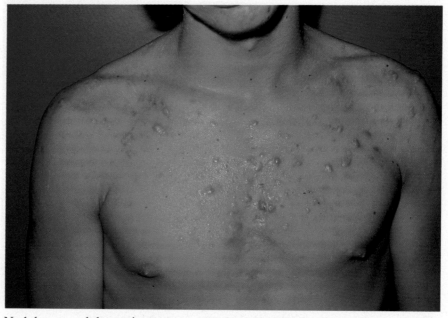

Nodular or nodulo-cystic acne.

Acne

Clinical
- Lesions may be one or more of
  - ▲ comedos – open or closed
  - ▲ superficial papules and pustules
  - ▲ deep papules
  - ▲ nodules and cysts
- Lesions occur in
  - ▲ nearly all teenagers, at least to a slight degree
  - ▲ young men, when severe (nodular)
  - ▲ women in the 20-35 year age group as chronic papules of the lower face, especially the chin
- Occurrence and severity are related to
  - ▲ inheritance (predominantly)
  - ▲ sex hormones
    - ■ more frequent and worse in males
    - ■ better during pregnancy and high-estrogen oral contraceptive use
  - ▲ chronic use of cosmetics, moisturizers, pomades
    - ■ certain ingredients are 'comedogenic'
    - ■ not necessarily related to thickness or oiliness of cosmetic base
  - ▲ stress – in some individuals
  - ▲ sunlight
    - ■ improves acne in many individuals
    - ■ has no effect in some individuals, but masks by tanning
    - ■ aggravates acne in a few (especially the very fair-skinned)
- Exacerbations **not** related to
  - ▲ diet, junk foods, chocolate, vitamins, minerals
  - ▲ sexual activity
  - ▲ cleanliness
- Scarring
  - ▲ is the natural result of healing of dermal inflammation
  - ▲ is related to picking and squeezing only if that manipulation aggravates a specific lesion

Acne

Treatment

■ Patient education is paramount (See Patient Guide, p.275). Critical points that the patient must realize are:
■ The occurrence of acne in them is preordained, and is **not** due to something they did or did not do.
■ Accordingly, they cannot control the disease by manipulating their diet, behavior, or environment.
■ Therapy usually helps, **however,** with the exception of intralesional or systemic corticosteroids it prevents new lesions but does not accelerate healing of old ones, so it should be applied every day to the entire acne-prone area, **not just to individual pimples.**
■ Often no improvement is seen for 3-6 weeks, so be patient.

● Washing with strong soap (including granulated soaps)
  ▲ has only minimal impact on superficial pustules
  ▲ does not prevent or remove comedos
  ▲ often irritates the skin so that burning results from applying effective topical agents (see below) limiting or preventing their use.
  ▲ Encourage a normal frequency of washing with a mild soap (p.149)
● General rules regarding the use of effective topical agents.
  ▲ they should be applied thinly, to the entire acne-prone area
  ▲ they are less likely to be irritating if
    ■ washing is done infrequently, with a mild soap
    ■ they are applied to dry skin more than 15 minutes after washing

Acne

Treatment (continued)

● Effective topical agents.

▲ Benzoyl peroxide (p.306)
- ■ is effective against superficial papules and pustules
- ■ works by killing bacteria, possibly prevents pore-plugging, and possibly suppresses oil production
- ■ water-based gels are less drying and irritating than alcohol or acetone-based products
- ■ concentrations of 2.5% and 5% are sufficiently potent
- ■ may bleach colored fabrics
- ■ occasionally cause allergic contact dermatitis
- ■ should be applied twice daily, if tolerated

▲ Tretinoin (retinoic acid) (p.306).
- ■ effective against comedos and, eventually, papules and pustules
- ■ works by loosening keratin pore plugs, and preventing their development
- ■ may take 6-12 weeks to affect comedos
- ■ lower concentrations (0.01% gel, 0.05% cream) are less irritating, but if they prove ineffective after 8 weeks more potent ones must be tried
- ■ should be applied thinly once daily (usually at night)
- ■ may cause irritation or pimple-like red papules around plugged pores for the first few weeks
- ■ may photoirritate, so limit its use in the summer or during winter vacations
- ■ under certain conditions is a photocarcinogen in the hairless mouse, but relevance to humans is unknown

▲ Topical antibiotics (p.306)
- ■ clindamycin, erythromycin, meclocycline and tetracycline in penetrating alcohol vehicles kill bacteria in follicles, and are effective against papulopustular lesions
- ■ effect is probably equivalent to that of benzoyl peroxides, but without effect on comedos or sebum production
- ■ are usually less irritating than benzoyl peroxides, but alcohol vehicle may be drying (meclosan is available in cream form)
- ■ bacterial resistance frequently develops after months of use, making the treatment ineffective

Acne

Treatment (continued)

- ▲ Combination topical treatment
  - ■ the use of tretinoin and benzoyl peroxide or topical antibiotic by the same individual is better than one drug alone in most papulopustular acne
  - ■ because of chemical incompatibility, drugs must not be applied at the same time – usually, tretinoin is applied at bedtime, and benzoyl peroxide in the morning and at dinner time
  - ■ irritation is common, so use only mild soap and add lubricant or a mild topical corticosteroid if necessary
  - ■ Patient Guide (p.275) encourages correct usage
- ● Systemic Agents.
  - ▲ Antibiotics
    - ■ tetracycline or erythromycin in doses of up to 1g daily usually improves superficial and deep inflammatory acne after 3-4 weeks – dosages of up to 2g daily may be needed for nodular acne
    - ■ minocycline, clindamycin, and trimethoprim/ sulfamethoxazole are alternatives, possibly effective in resistant cases, but with more potential side effects
    - ■ dapsone is antibiotic and anti-inflammatory and may be effective in severe and resistant cases, but has a multitude of potential side effects (refer patients in these cases to a dermatologist)
  - ▲ Isotretinoin (13-cis-retinoic acid)
    - ■ a derivative of vitamin A, it reduces oil gland output by up to 90%
    - ■ it is taken by mouth for 3-5 months. Side effects occur early, improvement lags behind and may continue to increase after stopping treatment for 1-2 months. Side effects resolve in 1-2 months.

> - ■ unlike any other acne therapy, the benefit is prolonged long after the drug is stopped (months or even years)

- ■ side effects and their incidences are: cheilitis (90%), dry, chapped skin (90%), dry nose and/or eyes (80%), hair shedding (10%), peeling of palms and soles (5%), arthralgias and/or myalgias (15%), elevated liver transaminases (15%) and elevated serum triglycerides (25%). The serum abnormalities may return to normal during treatment.
- ■ serum testing is advised before therapy and at 2 to 4 week intervals, or until the results are normal

Acne

Treatment (continued)

> ■ isotretinoin is a potent teratogen. Female patients must use reliable birth control measures, and should have at least one normal menstrual cycle after stopping treatment before becoming pregnant

■ no supplemental vitamin A should be taken during treatment, as that may increase side effects

■ skin dryness can be treated with moisturizers (p.150). Ointments or lip balms may be used on the lips. Methylcellulose 'artificial tears' may be used for dry eyes.

■ dose is 1 to 2mg/kg. Give the lower dose for purely facial acne, the higher one for extensive truncal acne. Severe truncal acne may require a repeat 4-month course, after a 2-month rest period

■ cost is very high.

> ■ because of extensive known side effects and continuing investigation of additional side effects, the US Food and Drug Administration recommends the use of isotretinoin only for severe cystic or nodular acne unresponsive to other medications

■ see page 277 for Patient Guide on isotretinoin.

▲ Oral zinc
  ■ effectiveness is controversial
  ■ up to 20% of patients suffer gastrointestinal upset or diarrhea with a dose of zinc sulfate 220mg three times a day

● Corticosteroids
  ▲ systemic corticosteroids are used occasionally in severe, painful flares of nodular acne, for 1-2 weeks

> ■ intralesional injection of depot corticosteroids is an invaluable tool for individual nodules and large papules – see page 313 for technique. Physicians treating acne should acquire skill in administering this therapy

▲ Estrogens
  ■ low-estrogen pills may have no effect on, and may even worsen, acne
  ■ in the form of high-estrogen oral contraceptives (p.325) often improve acne in women, but benefits and risks must be considered and the patient monitored for side effects – benefit may not be seen for three months
  ■ for the greatest benefit, estrogens should be given with replacement-dose corticosteroid (e.g. prednisone 5mg daily) to suppress adrenal androgens.

Acne

Treatment (continued)

- Office treatments.
  - ▲ mild peeling induced by ultraviolet light, CO_2 slush, liquid nitrogen or mild acid (trichloracetic 20%-30%)
    - ■ may cause mild improvement in superficial comedos and pustules
    - ■ are used less often as self-administered topical agents have become more effective
  - ▲ intralesional corticosteroids (see above)
  - ▲ liquid nitrogen cryotherapy to individual papules and nodules possibly enhances resolution
  - ▲ 'acne surgery'
    - ■ the removal of comedos, and possibly drainage of pustules, with a comedo extractor
    - ■ probably speeds resolution of pustules and prevents development of new ones
    - ■ made easier by the chronic use of tretinoin, which softens comedos
- Treatment of scars.

> **Patients should be referred to a dermatologist or plastic surgeon for these specialized procedures**

  - ▲ dermabrasion, or deep chemical peel
    - ■ destroys superficial dermis and epidermis
    - ■ **causes** scarring, but hopefully it is flat, not pitted and lumpy
    - ■ certain types of scars and certain areas of face respond best
    - ■ residual erythema, keloids, and permanent pigment changes are possible complications
    - ■ often needs to be repeated for best results
  - ▲ excision of elevated or depressed scars
    - ■ effective if only a few obvious scars are causing most cosmetic impact
    - ■ may be combined with dermabrasion to eliminate deepest pits
    - ■ infection and scarring are possible complications
  - ▲ injection of fibrin or processed collagen below depressed scars is another possible method with preliminary studies in progress but it is not in widespread use
    - ■ adequately elevates large depressed areas and some furrows
    - ■ may make 'ice-pick' pits more prominent
    - ■ possible hypersensitivity reaction

Acne

Practical treatment of acne

● For all patients.
  ▲ patient hand-out, destroy myths, relieve guilt (p.275)
  ▲ discontinue excessive washing, abrasives, and irritants
● Comedonal acne.
  ▲ topical tretinoin
  ▲ 'acne surgery'
● Superficial papulopustular acne.
  ▲ benzoyl peroxide alone
  ▲ topical antibiotic alone
  ▲ addition of tretinoin often helpful
  ▲ systemic antibiotic in widespread or resistant cases
● Moderately deep papular acne.
  ▲ topical antibiotic
  ▲ benzoyl peroxide (possible irritant in women in their twenties)
  ▲ systemic antibiotic often required
● Nodular acne.

  Referral to a dermatologist for the complex long-term care
  required is recommended

  ▲ topical agents for superficial component
  ▲ high-dose systemic antibiotic
  ▲ intralesional corticosteroids
  ▲ possibly a brief dose of oral corticosteroids for flares
  ▲ oral contraceptives and replacement corticosteroid in women
  ▲ dapsone
  ▲ isotretinoin

Rosacea

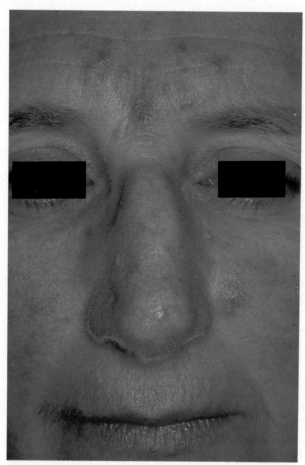

Almost exclusively papulo-pustular acne rosacea.

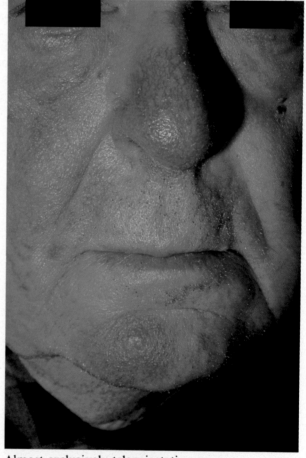

Almost exclusively telangiectatic rosacea.

Rosacea

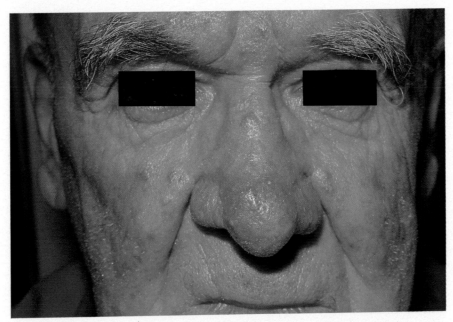

Rosacea with early thickening of the skin on the nose (rhinophyma).

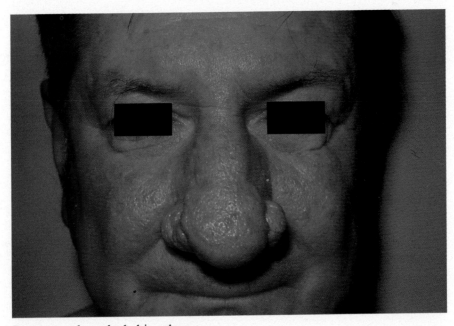

Rosacea and marked rhinophyma.

Rosacea

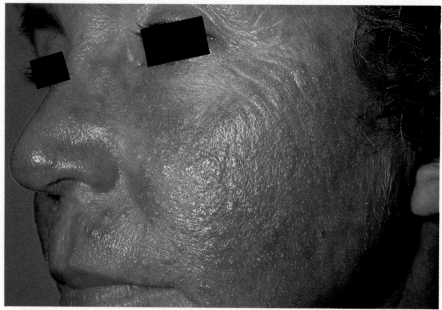

"Steroid rosacea". Marked vascular blush and pustulation from prolonged use of topical potent corticosteroid.

Clinical
● Either or both clinical features of
  ▲ 'blushing erythema', 'ruddy' complexion, and/or telangiectatic matting
  ▲ angry, red pimple-like papules and pustules
● Possible sebaceous gland enlargement with enlargement of nose (rhinophyma) and coarsening of facial skin.
● Location.
  ▲ central forehead
  ▲ nose, 'butterfly' of cheeks
  ▲ central chin
● Occurs in
  ▲ males more frequently than females
  ▲ middle aged people
  ▲ the fair-skinned (especially those of Celtic racial background)
● Idiopathic.
  ▲ worsened by heat, hot or spicy foods, alcohol
  ▲ caused or worsened by *potent* topical corticosteroids

Rosacea

Treatment

- General.
  - ▲ often moderately to poorly responsive to therapy
  - ▲ usually combination of topical and/or oral treatments required
  - ▲ slow to respond (several weeks), and may need treatment for weeks to months – may relapse
  - ▲ avoid heat, spicy and hot food, potent topical corticosteroids.
- Topical therapy.
  - ▲ mild topical corticosteroid creams (hydrocortisone 1%) twice daily for the erythematous component.
  - ▲ benzoyl peroxide gel (water-based) 2.5%-5%, or topical antibiotic solution (see acne therapy, p.306) once or twice daily for the papulopustular component.
- Oral tetracycline 250mg once or twice daily for the papulopustular component, but also helps erythema.
- Oral metronidazole has been reported to be effective in rosacea, but is mutagenic to bacteria; its future use is uncertain.
- For rhinophyma, cold steel shave, or electro- or chemical cautery.
- For resistant cases use the oral vitamin A derivative, isotretinoin, which may induce a prolonged remission. See page 38 for instructions on its use and the extensive side effects it often causes.

Pseudofolliculitis Barbae ('Beard Bumps')

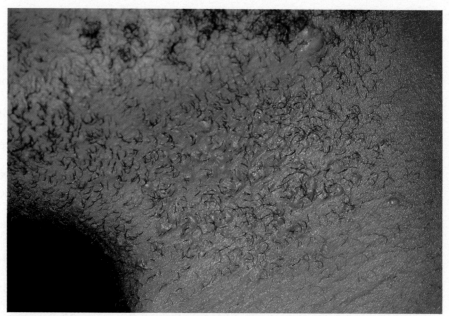

Slightly inflamed papules of pseudofolliculitis barbae confined to the area of beard growth.

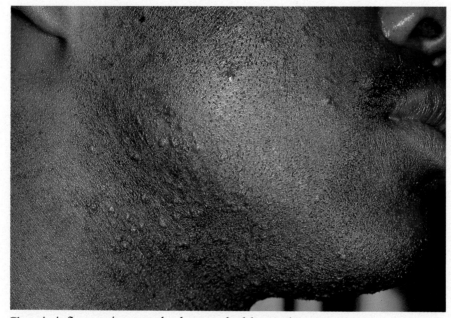

Chronic inflammation may lead to marked hyperpigmentation.

Pseudofolliculitis Barbae ('Beard Bumps')

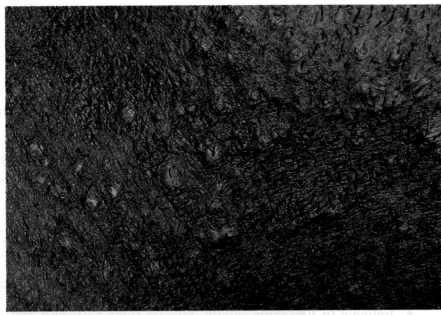

Close inspection shows hairs trapped in papules and pustules.

Clinical
● Ingrowing of tightly coiled beard hairs with resultant inflammation.
  ▲ occurs mainly in Blacks because of characteristically tightly coiled hair
  ▲ after shaving beard hairs close to the skin, the pointed tips then catch on the edge of the pore and pierce the skin
  ▲ inflammation is due to foreign body reaction and presence of skin flora in dermis, as in acne

Herpes Simplex

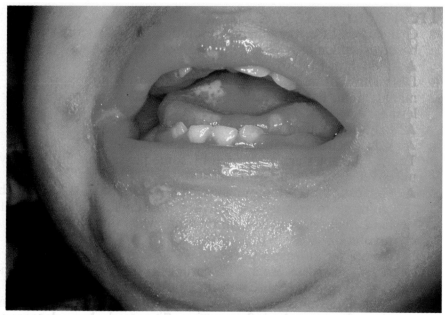

Primary herpes simplex infection of face and mouth in child.

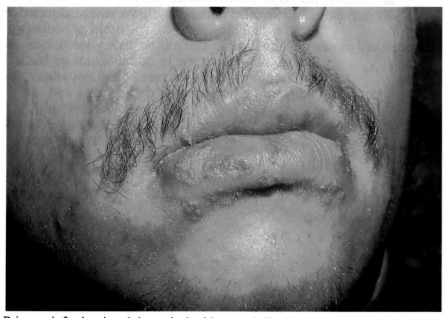

Primary infection in adult, typical widespread distribution around mouth.

Herpes Simplex

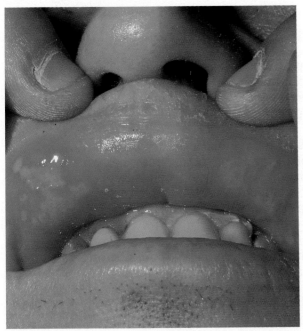

Typical clusters of punctate vesicles and erosions in primary infection.

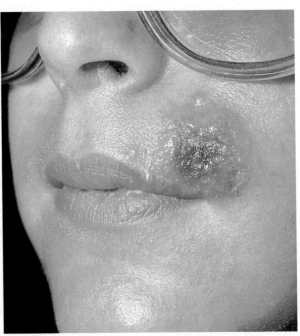

Primary infections are sometimes localized, but severe.

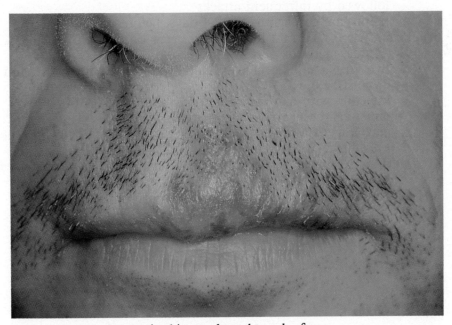

Typical recurrent herpes, in this case brought on by fever.

Herpes Simplex

Clinical

- **Primary** herpes (first attack), usually in a child or young adult, may present as
  - ▲ severe stomatitis, upper respiratory infection, lip and facial eruption, with fever and local adenopathy lasting 7-10 days
  - ▲ very mild stomatitis or upper respiratory infection
  - ▲ frequently completely asymptomatic
- **Secondary** (recurrent) lesions.
  - ▲ less than 30% of individuals who have had primary attack will have recurrent attacks although the latent period may be years
  - ▲ on lips, occasionally on chin, cheek, forehead, eyelids, but always recurring in same or contiguous sites
  - ▲ 'fever blister', 'cold sore' – a few small vesicles or pustules on an erythematous base. In 2-4 days these form crusts, and heal in 5-7 days
  - ▲ may have prodrome of burning at site for a few hours before eruption. Lesion may burn and/or itch for 2-5 days
  - ▲ pain, duration, number and size of vesicles and degree of crusting can vary considerably from attack to attack
  - ▲ recurrences may be provoked by illness, fever, trauma, sunburn, or may be random
  - ▲ an individual may have only a few recurrences in his or her lifetime, or many each year. Cannot predict this early in the course. Often there may be frequent attacks for a few years, followed by infrequent attacks
  - ▲ lesions are contagious for 2-4 days, before dry crusts form
- Primary and recurrent lesions may occur on the genitals (p.65), sacral area, or hands and fingers.
  - ▲ two virus strains occur, usually Type I above the waist, and Type II below
  - ▲ infection with one may not confer immunity to the other
- Conjunctival, corneal and ocular globe infections.
  - ▲ encourage patients with oral or genital lesions not to rub their eyes during an attack, to avoid inoculation
  - ▲ if an eye infection is suspected, refer to an ophthalmologist for complete examination
- Severe or chronic eruptions may occur in immunosuppressed patients.

Herpes Simplex

Treatment
● General

> A reservoir of viruses exists in nerve ganglia. No topical or systemic agent destroys this reservoir, and it is unlikely that any topical agent will ever be developed which will affect it.

   ▲ patient education is paramount (see Patient Guide, p.278)
   ▲ avoid sunburn to face and lips
      ■ hats
      ■ sunscreens, especially to lips (p.316)
● Probably slightly accelerating the healing of a skin eruption are
   ▲ drying agents: camphor, alcohol, ether

> **Caution:** We recommend that ether **not** be used. It will evaporate from any container and is highly flammable. It has caused explosions in confined spaces (especially refrigerators).

   ▲ epinephrine solution 1:100
   ▲ vital dyes (proflavine, neutral red) and visible light
   ▲ idoxuridine solution
   ▲ soaking with tap water or astringent (p.318)
● Chronic oral administration of the amino acid L-lysine, 1g-1.5g daily in divided doses, has been recently reported to suppress viral replication and decrease frequency of attacks. Attacks resume when administration is discontinued. There are no known side effects. Further study is needed.
● Specific herpes simplex vaccines have failed in double-blind studies.

> *Vaccinia vaccinations* are contraindicated
> ● failed in double-blind studies
> ● cause serious side effects in at least 1 in 50 000 patients

Erysipelas

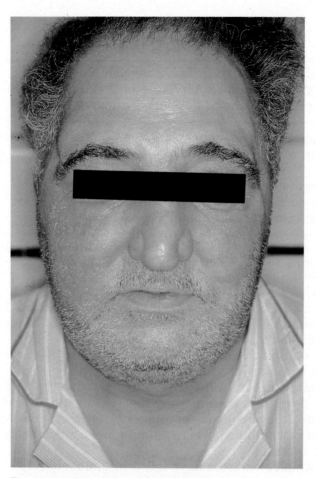

Front and side views of face shows sharply
demarcated bright erythema and swelling on nose
and both cheeks.

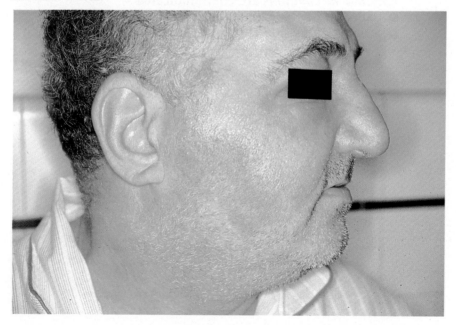

Erysipelas

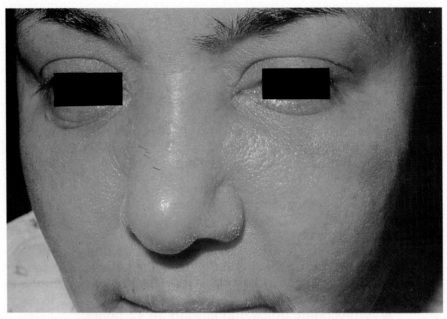

Similar classic facial erythema with involvement of eyelids as well.
Temperature was 39.8°C.

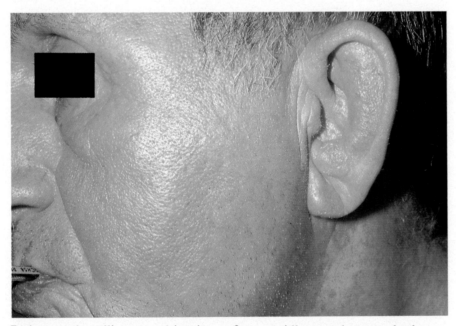

Redness and swelling started in pinna of ear, rapidly spread across cheek.

Erysipelas

Clinical
- Superficial streptococcal cellulitis.
- Typically
  - ▲ sudden onset, painful, rapidly spreading vivid red macule on face
  - ▲ chills, fever, malaise
  - ▲ older adults
- Before the advent of antibiotics erysipelas was often fatal
  - ▲ sometimes a wound, fissure, or nasal folliculitis is the portal of entry, but usually none is evident

Treatment
- **This is an emergency**
  - ▲ if erysipelas is suspected, immediately initiate systemic antibiotic therapy (penicillin, unless the patient is allergic to it)
  - ▲ admit the patient to hospital overnight to insure compliance and monitor response
    - ■ temperature drops dramatically in 12 hours.
  - ▲ cultures grown from wound, fissure, or nasal antrum are only occasionally positive

Melasma (Chloasma)

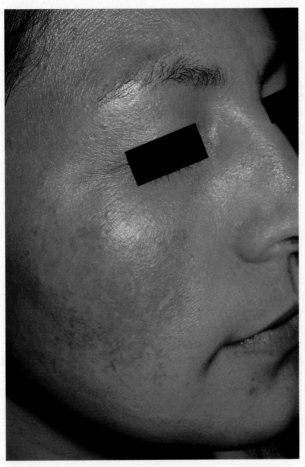

Melasma: splotchy hyperpigmentation with irregular
borders, usually seen on forehead, cheeks, and
upper lip.

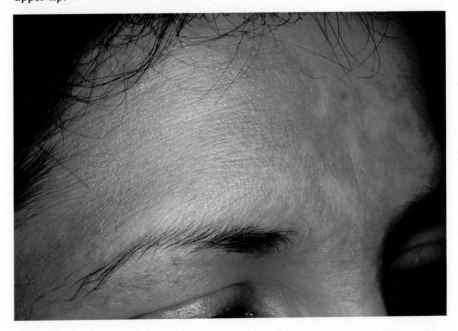

Melasma (Chloasma)

Clinical
● Macular hyperpigmentation, sharply defined but with irregular borders.
● Forehead, malar eminences, upper lip.
● Becomes evident or darkens dramatically with sun exposure.
● Commonly occurs during pregnancy or during use of oral contraceptives or estrogens, but may occur at other times, and occasionally occurs in men. Often improves in months or years.
● Idiopathic. Represents increased melanocyte activity. Pigment is solely in epidermis.

Treatment
● Discontinue estrogens. It may then slowly resolve, or persist.
● Avoid sun exposure
  ▲ shading with a hat is best
  ▲ broad-spectrum sunscreens (p.316)
● Hydroquinone (bleach)
  ▲ topical hydroquinone suppresses melanocyte activity
  ▲ will lighten pigment if epidermal (will not affect post-inflammatory hyperpigmentation, which is dermal)
  ▲ sun must be avoided and broad-spectrum sun-screen must be used during treatment
  ▲ may completely clear melasma in persons with fair skin, but there may be a relapse. Only occasionally clears melasma completely in darker-skinned individuals, and relapse is common

Melasma (Chloasma)

Treatment (continued)

▲ available over-the-counter in 1% concentration though this is
rarely effective. By prescription it is used in 2%-4%
concentrations in creams or lotions (p.317)–these may be
irritating, and occasionally cause a contact allergy.
- apply thinly twice daily to dark areas
- if effective this treatment usually bleaches melasma without
  much effect on surrounding normal skin
- if melasma clears use the bleach only as needed for
  recurrences
- effect seen in weeks in the fair-skinned, but may require
  months of use in the dark-skinned

- more effective and reliable (better penetration) if used
  with tretinoin cream or gel (p.306). This makes irritation
  more likely, so topical corticosteroid is often added, to
  reduce irritation; and it enhances the bleaching action
- These materials may be applied sequentially, usually
  using tretinoin only once a day, hydroquinone twice
  daily, and corticosteroid as necessary. The materials can
  be combined for easy application, and the resulting
  mixture is probably stable for at least two months.

Sample prescription

Tretinoin cream 0.05%	20g
Triamcinolone cream 0.1%	20g
Hydroquinone powder	1g-2g
Ascorbic acid (stabilizer)	100mg-200mg

Apply thinly to dark areas of skin once or twice daily, as
tolerated.

Neurodermatitis (Lichen Simplex Chronicus)

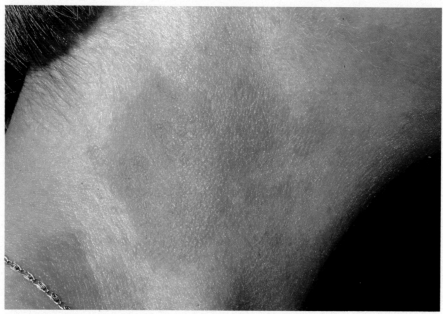

Early (3 weeks) patchy dermatitis on the side of neck. Patient rubs more when tense.

Clinical

● Large (5cm-20cm) fairly well-circumscribed patch of lichenification (skin thickened, scaly, hyperpigmented with accentuation of normal skin marking lines).
● Location
  ▲ rare on the face, but it is common on nape and sides of neck in women
  ▲ in men, it is common on ankles (p.130)
  ▲ perineum in both sexes (p.94)
● Atopic history common.
● Often develops or worsens during stress, but becomes a chronic habit.

Treatment

● Instruct patient that
  ▲ it is not dangerous, contagious or likely to spread
  ▲ it may have been caused by insect bite, contact or other skin problem, but now has become a habit and tension-releasing mechanism (like biting fingernails)
● Treatment of choice is external or intralesional corticosteroids.
  ▲ very potent corticosteroid ointment (because lesion is usually dry) or cream

Neurodermatitis (Lichen Simplex Chronicus)

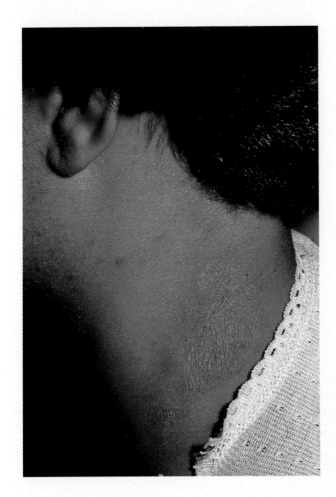

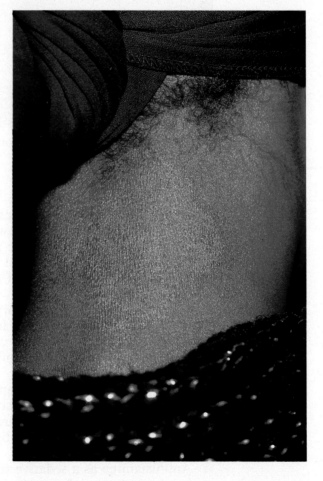

Typical well-circumscribed lichenified patches of lichen simplex chronicus, on the neck in women.

Neurodermatitis (Lichen Simplex Chronicus)

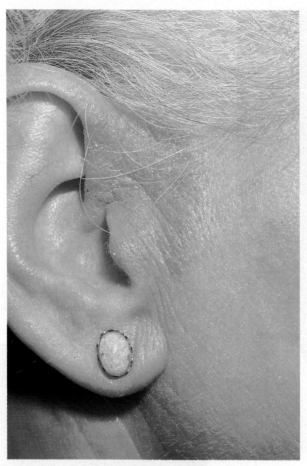

The sides of the face is a less common site.

Treatment (continued)

- ■ apply as often as necessary for itching *instead of scratching* for a few days, then twice or three times a day
- ■ occlusion with plastic film or steroid-impregnated tape (p.311) is very helpful if the above fails because it greatly enhances the effect of the corticosteroid, and blocks scratching
- ■ discontinue potent corticosteroid when lesion is flat. Use milder preparation if itching continues.
- ▲ intralesional injection of corticosteroid (see technique, p.313) is temporarily painful but often helpful, especially if topical therapy fails
  - ■ I sometimes tell patients that they must not rub now that medication is in the skin.
- ● Alternative or concomitant treatment with topical coal tar preparations (p.323), especially in chronic cases. Beware of irritant folliculitis at nape of neck.
- ● Antihistamine as a sedative (p.321), or a mild tranquilizer, may be helpful in tense individuals, but *is not a substitute for topical medication.*

Genitals, Groin and Axillae

Herpes Simplex

He

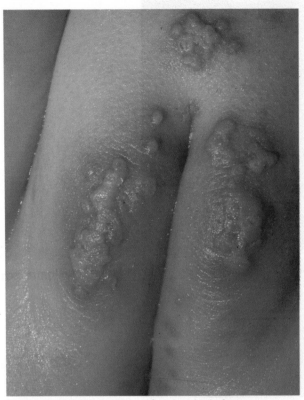

Primary herpes simplex of vulva in infant.
Organism probably from parent's hand during
diaper change.

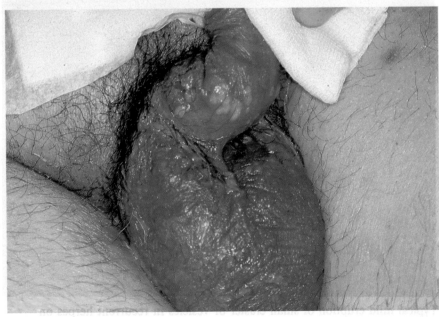

Widespread primary herpes genitalis in adult.

Herpes Simplex

Clinical

- **Primary** attack usually occurs in young adults (as opposed to oral herpes, which often first occurs in children). It presumably is sexually transmitted. It may present as
  - ▲ severe balanitis, vulvitis, or vaginitis with vesicles, edema, pain, and adenopathy – rare. Lasts 7-10 days
  - ▲ localized herpetic vesicular eruption
  - ▲ frequently completely asymptomatic
- **Secondary** (recurrent) lesions
  - ▲ around 50% of individuals who have a primary attack will have a recurrent attack – latent period may be years
  - ▲ in men the lesion occurs on penis, usually distal
  - ▲ in women the lesion may be vulvar or cervicovaginal – the latter may be completely asymptomatic
  - ▲ 'fever blister', 'cold sore' – a few small vesicles or pustules on an erythematous base. In 2-4 days these form crusts, and heal in 5-7 days
  - ▲ may have prodrome of burning at site for a few hours before eruption. Lesion may burn and/or itch for 2-5 days.
  - ▲ pain, duration, number and size of vesicles and degree of crusting can vary considerably from attack to attack
  - ▲ recurrences are often provoked by intercourse but may occur with fever or illness, or be random
  - ▲ an individual may have only a few recurrences in his or her lifetime, or many each year. This cannot be predicted early in the course. Often, there are frequent attacks for a few years, followed by infrequent attacks
  - ▲ lesions are contagious for 2-4 days, before dry crusts form
- Primary and recurrent lesions may occur on the face (p.54), sacral area, or hands and fingers
  - ▲ two virus strains occur, usually Type I above the waist, and Type II below
  - ▲ infection with one may not confer immunity to the other
- Severe or chronic eruptions may occur in immunosuppressed patients.
- If eruption is present during childbirth, newborn may acquire infection during delivery. Infection is often mild but can become systemic and be fatal. Female patients should be told to notify their obstetrician of any history of herpes. The obstetrician will monitor the patient's condition in late pregnancy (with Pap smears), and deliver by cesarean section if genital lesions are present during labor.
- There is a statistical association between the presence of herpes antibodies in women and the occurrence of cervical carcinoma. The causal implications of this finding are unknown.

Herpes Simplex

Treatment
● General

> Since the viral reservoir is *in* spinal ganglia, topical treatments cannot be expected to prevent recurrences. No systemic therapy is available which eradicates the reservoir, so 'cure' is not possible. Only patient immunity will ultimately control the infection.

  ▲ patient education is paramount (see Patient Guide, p.278)
  ▲ condoms, spermicidal jellies and foams probably prevent transmissions of the virus
● Probably slightly accelerating the healing of a skin eruption are
  ▲ drying agents: camphor, alcohol, ether

> **Caution:** we recommend that ether **not** be used. It will evaporate from any container and is highly flammable. It has caused explosions in confined spaces (especially refrigerators).

  ▲ epinephrine solution 1:100
  ▲ vital dyes (proflavine, neutral red) and visible light
  ▲ idoxuridine solution
  ▲ soaking with tap water or astringent (p.318)
● Chronic oral administration of the amino acid L-lysine, 1g-1.5g daily in divided doses, has been recently reported to suppress viral replication and decrease frequency of attacks. Attacks resume when administration is discontinued. There are no known side effects. Further study is needed.
● Specific herpes simplex vaccines have failed in double-blind studies.

> *Vaccinia vaccinations* are contraindicated
> ● failed in double-blind studies
> ● cause serious side effects in at least 1 in 50 000 patients

  ▲ **Note:** See discussion of oral-facial herpes, p.54.

Warts

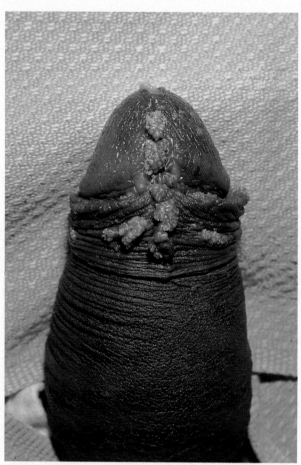

Exuberant growth of penile warts.

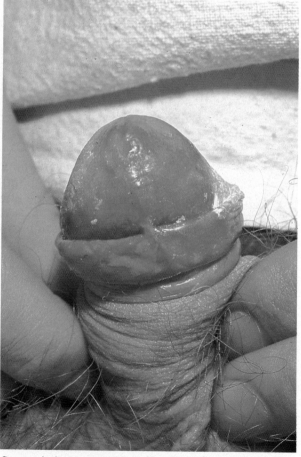

Severe irritant contact dermatitis from podophyllin left on 48 hours.

Warts

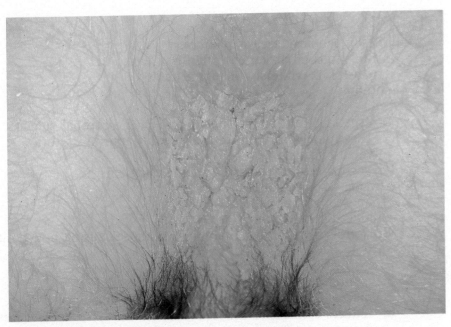

Profuse growth of perianal warts.

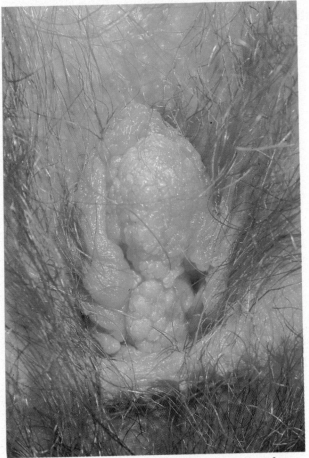

Perianal warts can become so bulky as to interfere with defecation.

Warts

Clinical

- Soft, fleshy papules, tags, or plaques.
  - ▲ in this moist environment often not keratotic
  - ▲ may be pink, whiteish, or pigmented
- Found on
  - ▲ penis
    - especially under the foreskin and in the coronal sulcus
    - occasionally around urethral meatus, and in urethra
  - ▲ vulva and vagina
    - vaginal examination of all female patients
  - ▲ perianal skin, and anus
    - anoscopy of all patients
- Viral-induced benign tumor
  - ▲ virus probably slightly different from those causing non-genital warts
  - ▲ passed by sexual contact
  - ▲ incubation period of several months
    - makes determination of source of infection uncertain
    - reduces confidence in 'cure' because newly seeded viruses may not produce lesion for months
  - ▲ resolves spontaneously in months or years when immunity develops
  - ▲ associated with the development of laryngeal polyps in infants when vaginal warts were present in the mother at childbirth

dylomata Lata

Al-Harmozi, MBBCh, MSc, Doha, Qatar
dul Gaffoor, BSc, MBBS, DV, DDV, FAMS, Doha, Qatar

case of perianal condylomata lata, one of a
of skin lesions manifested in secondary syphi-
esented.

philis, the great imitator, can present with different
manifestations affecting any part of the body. Secon-
ary syphilis can manifest as macular, papular, papu-
ous, or (rarely) pustular skin lesions, which usually
tch. Condylomata lata are moist, hypertrophic,
atous, flat-topped, fleshy-looking papules, which
ed with *Treponema pallidum* and are highly infec-

Report

ar-old married, heterosexual man presented seeking
nt for fleshy growths around the anus that had been
for six weeks. The patient's history included extra-
sexual intercourse two and a half months previously
male partner. He was unaware of any previous geni-
her lesion.

Examination of the patient showed hypertrophic,
lat-topped growths, 1 to 2 cm in diameter around the
gure 1). No macules or papules were seen on other
the body. The blood rapid plasma reagin test's results
active (1:64), as were results of the fluorescent trepo-
ntibody absorption test. The white blood cell count
200/mm³ and erythrocyte sedimentation rate was 15
hour.

Examination of a biopsy specimen from the lesion
2) showed an edematous and hyperplastic epidermis
ng numerous neutrophils. Plasma cell infiltration
dermal blood vessels was visible.

The patient was treated with injected procaine penicil-
,000 units intramuscularly daily for ten days. The size
esions decreased within four days after treatment was
All the lesions cleared during the course of treatment.
s of follow-up serologic tests showed lowering of the
titer.

Comments

Syphilis is acquired by sexual contact. Secondary syphilitic lesions are due to widespread hematogenous or lymphatic dis-
semination of *T. pallidum*. Moist papules are usually poorly
outlined and may be covered by thick, mucoid secretions.[1]
Usually, they are fleshy looking and brown or pink-gray. Individual papular lesions coalesce, resulting in condylomata lata.

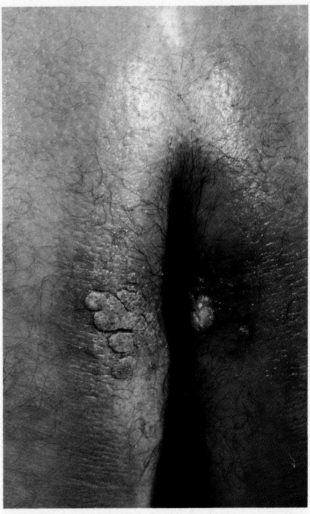

**FIGURE 1. Hypertrophic, fleshy, flat-topped growths
around the anus.**

he Department of Dermatology, Hamad General Hospital,
Qatar.
NT REQUESTS to Dermatology Department, Hamad Gen-
ospital, PO Box 3050, Doha, Qatar (Dr. Gaffoor).

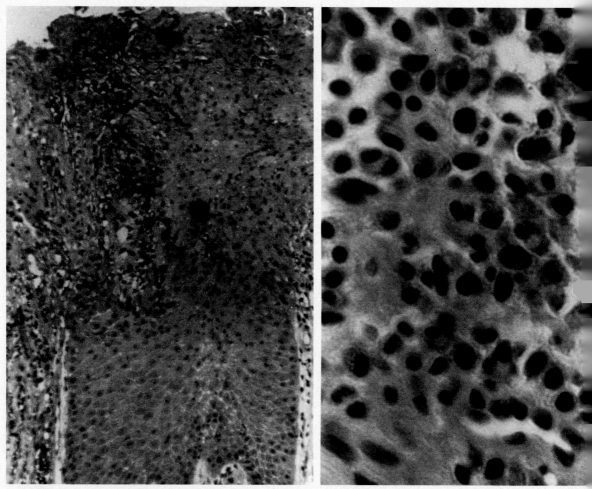

FIGURE 2. A. Hyperplastic epidermis containing numerous neutrophils. Plasma cell infiltration seen aroun mal blood vessels. B. Close-up view of plasma cell infiltration around dermal blood vessels.

Extensive condyloma lata of the neck, axilla, inguinal folds, and inner thighs have been reported.[2] Condylomata lata can occur beneath pendulous breasts, on the umbilicus, and in the webs of toes. Sometimes condylomata acuminata and condylomata lata can occur at the same site. Another similar condition is the condyloma and papilloma of secondary yaws, which also occurs around the anus.

REFERENCES

1. Knox JM, Rudolf AH: Acquired infectious syphilis. In, Sexually mitted Diseases (Holmes KK, Mardh PA, Sparling PF, et al, eds New York, McGraw-Hill, 1984.
2. Shrivastava SN, Gurumohan S: Extensive condyloma lata. *Br Dis* 53: 23-25, 1977.

Warts

Treatment
- Cytotoxic – podophyllin 20%-25% in benzoin.
  - ▲ in office apply to warts with cotton swab
    - ■ dispense only to trustworthy patients in 1ml-2ml amount
  - ▲ may wish to protect surrounding skin with zinc oxide or petrolatum – necessity and effectiveness questionable
  - ▲ wash area with soap and water after certain length of time – from 30 minutes on vulva to six hours on shaft of penis
    - ■ effectiveness in reducing irritation unknown
    - ■ prolonged application (12-24 hours) often causes irritation
  - ▲ repeat applications at weekly intervals
    - ■ increase time left on before washing, if tolerated
    - ■ lesions shrink if responsive
    - ■ three or four applications often required for complete disappearance
  - ▲ light cryotherapy plus podophyllin application may be effective in resistant cases

---

Cautions in using podophyllin
- Severe local irritation can occur from sloppy application, prolonged application, and large lesion application.
- Systemic absorption and cytotoxicity can occur if large area is painted. The fetus is particularly at risk so the use of more than tiny amounts in pregnancy is contraindicated.
- If the warts are numerous or large, treat only part of the lesions on each visit.

- Destruction of wart tissue, if podophyllin fails or the patient cannot return weekly.
  - ▲ liquid nitrogen cryotherapy
    - ■ mildly to severely painful
    - ■ effective
    - ■ follow-up in two weeks to check for regrowth or new lesions
  - ▲ electrocautery
    - ■ painful local anesthesia required
    - ■ often leaves mild scar
    - ■ sometimes the therapy of last resort in huge perianal warts. Close follow-up and repeat treatments are necessary

---

- Keratolytics (salicylic and lactic acid)
- Though safe when used elsewhere, these agents are often highly irritating to genital and perineal skin
- Not effective

- Check for other sexually-transmitted diseases.
  - ▲ serologic test for syphilis

Syphilis

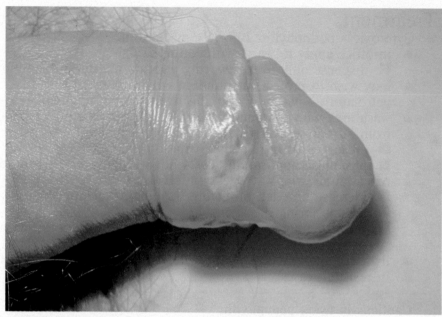

Typical single punched-out ulcer of primary syphilis.

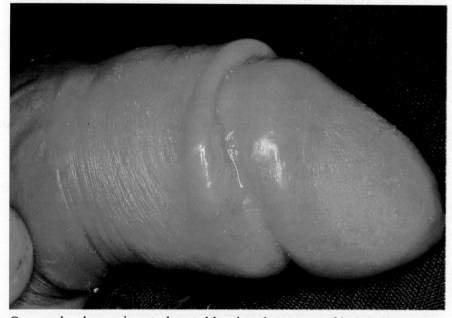

Commonly, chancre is not ulcerated but is only an area of induration.

Syphilis

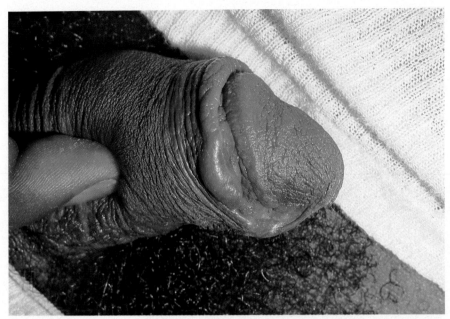

Lesions of primary syphilis may be multiple. Location is commonly in coronal sulcus.

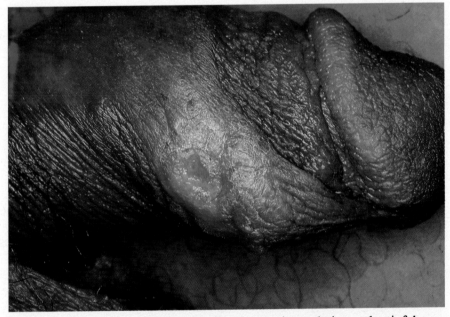

Chancre may become secondarily infected, then is exudative and painful.

Syphilis

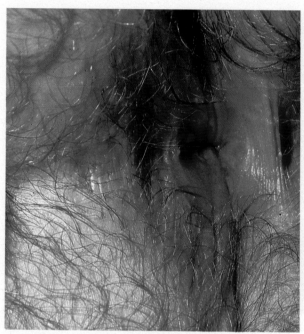

Perianal erosion due to chancre, usually goes
unnoticed by patient and physician.

Clinical

● The primary chancre is typically a single, firm, painless, button-like
  induration with an eroded, oozing surface.
  ▲ infrequently noticed on female genitalia
  ▲ may be multiple
  ▲ may be painful, especially when secondarily infected
  ▲ may be deeply ulcerated
  ▲ usually accompanied by painless, unilateral, rubbery node
    ('bubo')
    ■ may be tender
    ■ may be bilateral
● Secondary syphilis of the genitals may occur in two forms.
  ▲ the rash of secondary syphilis (p.193) usually involves the penis
    and scrotum
  ▲ *condyloma lata* are soft, whiteish, flat-topped velvety plaques in
    genital or perianal creases

> **Note:** In both forms the lesions, teeming with organisms, are
> highly contagious, including to the examiner. Gloves should
> be worn.

What Does the Skin Show?

Answer to quiz on page 12.

1. The man has Kaposi's sarcoma. 2. Of the choices offered, he is least likely to have E) Pneumocystis carinii pneumonia.

The patient pictured has Kaposi's sarcoma, a malignancy believed to be of endothelial cell origin. In its classic form it presents as bluish-red macules or nodules on the lower extremities that gradually spread and become confluent. It is seen primarily in elderly men of eastern European or Mediterranean ancestry. Histology shows a proliferation of atypical endothelial cells in the dermis, which may form vascular slits. Prognosis is usually good and remissions achieved with radiation therapy. Hepatomegaly indicates visceral involvement and may occur after many years.

A more aggressive form of Kaposi's sarcoma occurs in younger patients with the acquired immune deficiency syndrome (AIDS). The skin lesions may be widespread and atypical in appearance. Pneumocystis carinii pneumonia and other opportunistic infections are associated with this form of Kaposi's sarcoma.

Answer to quiz on page 14.

Of the choices given, the least likely diagnosis is B) Dermatofibroma.

A biopsy of the lesion showed islands of basaloid cells originating from the epidermis. This is characteristic of basal cell carcinoma. A large amount of melanin pigment was present in the malignant cells. About 10% of basal cell carcinomas are pigmented clinically and 40% have microscopic pigmentation. Pigmented basal cell carcinomas may look very similar clinically to seborrheic keratoses or malignant melanomas. A biopsy is essential to establish the diagnosis, as the treatment for each of these lesions is different.

Dermatofibromas may be pigmented but they have a dome-shaped configuration and are usually located on the lower extremities.

Answer to quiz on page 17.

The correct answer is C) Syringoma.

Syringomas are benign cutaneous tumors derived from sweat glands. They occur most commonly on the lower eyelids and upper cheeks, but may also present on the neck and trunk. Syringomas are more commonly noted in women in the second or third decade of life. Familial occurrence of syringomas is noted in about one-third of cases.

Xanthomatas usually have a yellowish-to-orange coloration and are most commonly noted bilaterally. Melanocytic nevi may appear to be of normal coloration; however, the development of multiple small nevi in this particular location would be unusual.

Basal cell carcinomas tend to be solitary, pearly-colored, with numerous telangiectasias. They would also be unusual in this young an individual.

Molluscum may appear flesh-colored, but typically have a pearly-colored appearance and develop an umbilicated center.

Answer to quiz on page 50.

The correct answer is D) Hypercholesteremia. This patient presents with tuberous xanthomata, which usually consists of hard nodules over the extensor surfaces of the extremities. The most common biochemical abnormality associated with this eruption is the elevation of the hyperbetalipoproteins. Vascular involvement is frequently associated with this type of xanthoma, particularly coronary and peripheral vascular insufficiency.

Hypertriglyceridema is more likely associated with eruptive xanthomas or xanthelasmas, although it may also occasionally result in tuberous xanthomas. The absence of ceramide trihexosidase is associated with Fabry's syndrome. Cryoglobulinemia may result in painful vasculitic lesions on the extremities.

Answer to quiz on page 59.

The correct answer is B) Angiofibromas.

These papules are termed pearly penile papules and are found in approximately 25% of the male population. They typically develop in the late teenage years and are frequently confused clinically with warts. They commonly develop near or within the coronal sulcus and have a histology similar to angiofibromas. No treatment is required. On occasion, these lesions will spontaneously regress.

What Does the Skin Show?

JONATHAN GOLDFARB, MD
Southern Illinois University
School of Medicine

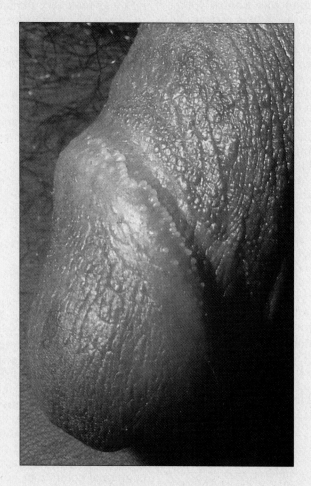

The patient is a 22-year-old black man who presents with a five-year history of white papules occurring on his penis. Histologically, these papules are consistent with:
A) Warts
B) Angiofibromas
C) Angiomas
D) Sebaceous hyperplasia
E) Granulomas

Answer — and a full discussion — appear on page 60.

Syphilis

Clinical (continued)

● Serologic tests – non-specific, and fluorescent treponemal antibody (FTA).
  ▲ in *primary* syphilis may or may not be positive
    ■ FTA often becomes positive before the non-specific serologic test for syphilis (STS) does
    ■ positivity more likely the longer the lesion has been present
    ■ non-specific test often of low titer (up to 1:16)
  ▲ in *secondary* syphilis, both tests should be positive
    ■ titer is high (over 1:8) in non-specific test

> ■ if non-specific test is negative this may be due to the *prozone* phenomenon: the titer is so high that it will not precipitate in test plates at the low dilutions utilized in the screening tests. If secondary syphilis is strongly suspected, send another blood sample and ask for a 'prozone test' or examination of higher dilutions

● Darkfield examination is positive for primary and secondary lesions
  ▲ **training and skill are required for successful examination**
    ■ squeeze fluid from lesions with firm pressure, even using the jaws of a hemostat
    ■ keep the organisms motile in a saline drop on the microscope slide – do not allow to dry out
    ■ examine immediately under a well-calibrated darkfield microscope
● Caution the patient to abstain from intimate contacts until 24 hours after treatment.
● Report to public health authorities.

Syphilis

Treatment

- Be aware of updated national and local treatment recommendations. Current US Public Health Service recommendations for *primary* and *secondary* syphilis are
  - ▲ benzathine penicillin 2.4 million units intramuscularly once.
  - ▲ procaine penicillin 600 000 units intramuscularly daily for 10 days
  - ▲ if the patient is unable to take penicillin then give tetracycline or erythromycin 500mg four times a day for 15 days
- Local soaks or compresses (p.318) may be applied for a few days if ulcer is painful, infected, or oozing copiously.
- Follow-up serologic testing.
  - ▲ FTA remains positive indefinitely – do not retest
  - ▲ non-specific STS
    - ■ check titers every six months for two years
    - ■ usually becomes negative in 6-12 months after treatment for primary syphilis, 12-18 months after treatment for secondary syphilis
    - ■ may fall to low titer (e.g. 1:2) and remain so indefinitely. This is a 'persistent reactor', or 'serofast', and does not require treatment
    - ■ if titers rise, assume new infection and treat again

Pubic Lice (Crabs)
Phthirus

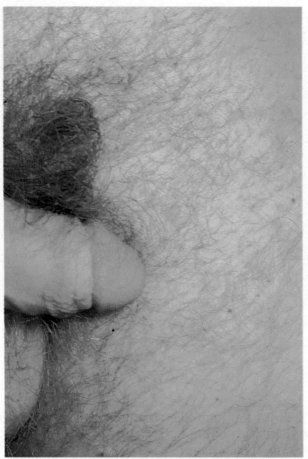

Pubic lice infestation is usually very itchy and on casual inspection shows only scattered excoriations.

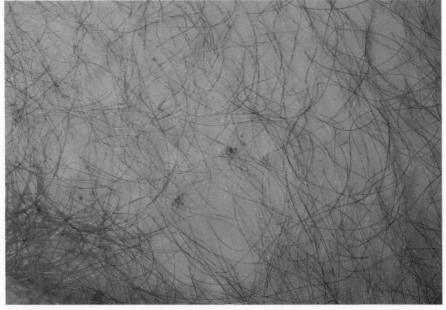

Closer inspection shows some blood-colored "scabs" to be flat, flake-like organisms.

Pubic Lice (Crabs)
Phthirus

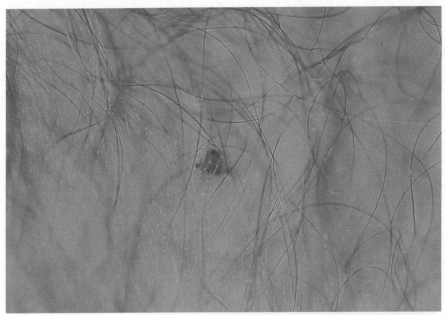

Slight magnification reveals the crab-like organism; in this case headed downward.

Clinical
- *Phthirus pubis* is a 2mm flat crab-like creature which holds onto the base of a hair shaft with one pincer, periodically bites its host, and attaches eggs (nits) to the hairs.
  - ▲ passed by skin contact, usually during intercourse
  - ▲ survives for 1-2 days off the host
- Physical examination.
  - ▲ organism is grey, flake-like, slow-moving and may be difficult to see
  - ▲ grey, oval 1mm nits on scattered hairs
  - ▲ mild to severe itching
    - ■ pubis, lower abdomen, upper thighs
    - ■ axilla, occasionally chest
    - ■ rarely eyelashes

Pubic Lice (Crabs)
Phthirus

Treatment

- Patient instruction (p.279) is important to destroy myths, ensure adequate treatment and discourage overtreatment.
- Pthirocides.
  - ▲ kill adults and eggs, but dead nits remain attached to hairs
  - ▲ apply lotion or cream from waist to knees (or other affected area **except eyes**).
    - ■ lindane–leave on overnight (p.309)
    - ■ pyrethrins–leave on 10 minutes (p.309)
  - ▲ shampoo with gamma benzene hexachloride (lindane) from waist to knees, leave on five minutes, rinse
  - ▲ treat bedmates simultaneously
- For lash infestation.
  - ▲ apply physostigmine ophthalmologic solution or ointment twice daily, with cotton-tipped applicator
  - ▲ apply yellow oxide of mercury or other thick ointment or paste – to smother organisms – twice daily for one week
  - ▲ remove organisms, gently, with fine-toothed tweezers
- Environmental treatment.
  - ▲ wash clothes, bed-linen, and pajamas from previous day
  - ▲ don clean clothes after treatment
  - ▲ not necessary to clean entire wardrobe, bed and rooms because of short life span and relative inertia of organism

Erythrasma

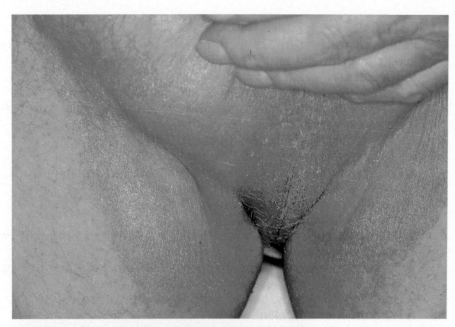

In light-skinned individuals, erythrasma is beefy red.

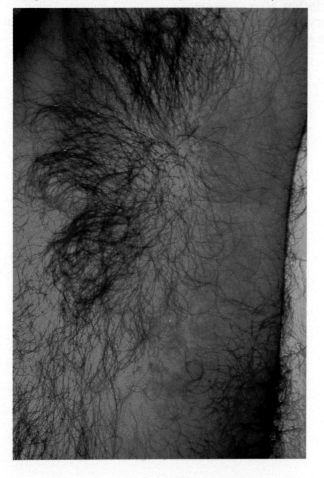

Erythrasma

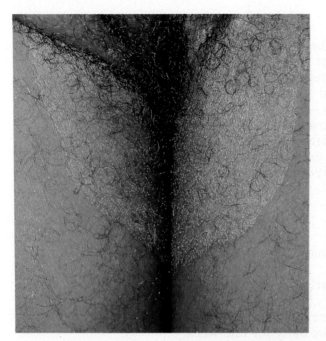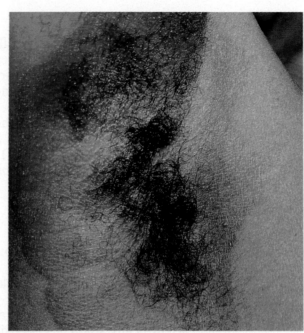

In dark-skinned people, the slightly scaly, circumscribed patches are pigmented.

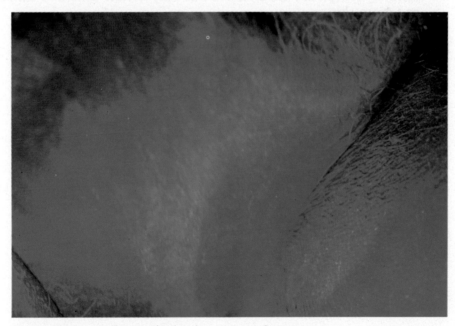

Wood's light reveals the diagnostic coral-red fluorescence.

Erythrasma

Clinical
- Pink-tan to browny-red confluent maculae in axilla or groin folds, radiating down thighs or chest wall.
  - ▲ sharply-marginated but irregular border
  - ▲ mildly scaling or tight and shiny surface
  - ▲ asymptomatic
- Wood's light examination shows coral-red fluorescence.
  - ▲ negative for a few hours after bathing
- Potassium hydroxide (KOH) examination negative.
  - ▲ causative organism is *Corynebacterium minutissimum*

Treatment
- Since erythrasma is asymptomatic, it is not necessary to treat it at all.
- Antibacterial soap used regularly for several weeks will clear most cases.
- Topical antimicrobial drugs are effective, but few have been scientifically studied. Use twice daily for one week.
  - ▲ miconazole cream (p.309) is effective and easy to use
  - ▲ erythromycin cream is effective but not widely available
  - ▲ tolnaftate is not very effective
- Keratolytics (p.323) are effective but may irritate sensitive axillary and groin skin.
  - ▲ Whitfield's ointment (p.323)
  - ▲ sulfur and salicylic acid cream or lotion 3%-6%
  - ▲ salicylic acid 6% in propylene glycol gel
- Systemic antibiotics are effective.
  - ▲ erythromycin 250mg four times a day for two weeks

Tinea Cruris (Jock Itch)

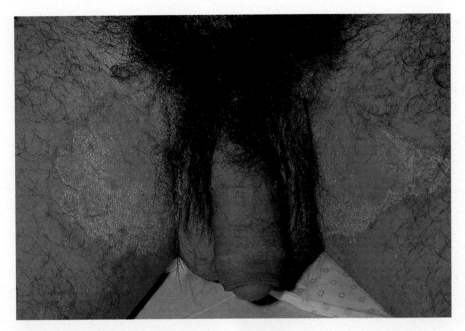

The inner thigh is the typical location for tinea cruris, or "jock itch". The border is pronounced and scaly.

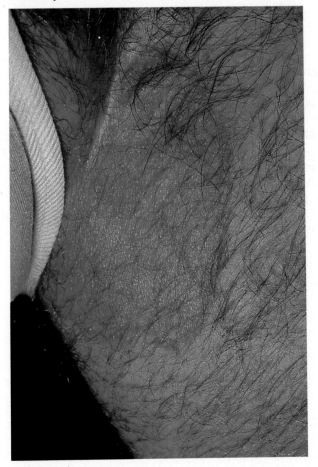

Tinea Cruris (Jock Itch)

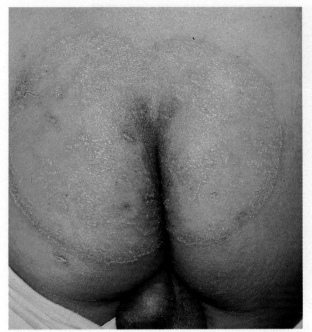

Tinea may thrive in the moist environment of the intergluteal fold.

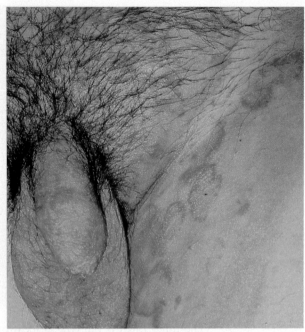

Topical corticosteroid applications activated tinea colonies in this chronic indolent infection.

Clinical

- Brick-red rash enlarging from inguinal folds down inner thighs and into pubic area.
  - ▲ advancing red, scaly border, clearing in center – sharply demarcated
  - ▲ commonly, the penis and scrotum appear uninvolved but close examination and potassium hydroxide (KOH) preparation may reveal subclinical infection
  - ▲ itching absent, or mild to severe
- Often occurs in people who perspire freely, or who are obese.
- Positive potassium hydroxide (KOH) examination (p.293) result is usually easy to obtain.

Tinea Cruris (Jock Itch)

Treatment
● General measures.
  ▲ loose, cool clothing
  ▲ reduce physical activity, to reduce sweating and chafing
  ▲ talcum powder to reduce wetness and chafing
● Topical antifungal agents (p.309) may be applied thinly to the rash and to normal skin a few centimeters beyond borders, twice daily for 2-3 weeks, or for several days past complete clearing.
  ▲ alcohol/propylene glycol solutions are usually superior to creams, but may burn
    ■ penetrate through hair
    ■ drying to the skin
    ■ leave little unpleasant residue
  ▲ medicated powders are poor in the delivery of the active ingredient to the skin.
● Griseofulvin (p.307) 250mg twice daily for 2-4 weeks may be administered if the rash is
  ▲ widespread
  ▲ resistant to topical therapy
    ■ a problem in hairy areas where the fungus might grow down into follicles
    ■ An alternative oral antifungal is ketoconazole 200mg daily (p.308). It is effective against dermatophytes but at the time of writing is approved in the US only for widespread candidiasis.
● Topical corticosteroids.
  ▲ relieve itching quickly
    ■ an antifungal alone may take many days to reduce inflammation and itching
  ▲ a mild preparation (hydrocortisone) is adequate
    ■ good penetration in thin, moist skin
    ■ atrophy and striae may occur after just a few weeks' use of *potent* corticosteroid
  ▲ the lotion or solution vehicle is most pleasant to use
  ▲ a combination of corticosteroid and antifungal
    ■ iodochlorhydroxyquin (vioform-hydrocortisone) is moderately effective against dermatophytes
      ▪ slight yellow staining of underclothes
      ▪ may rarely cause allergic contact dermatitis

■ 'Mycolog'
  ▪ **is not effective against dermatophytes**
  ▪ see page 310 for caveats

Candidiasis

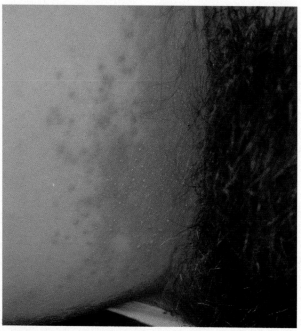

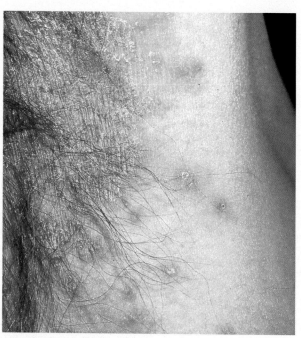

Bright erythema and satellite papules or pustules typify an acute intertriginous *Candida* infection.

Epidermal shedding and satellite lesions are characteristic.

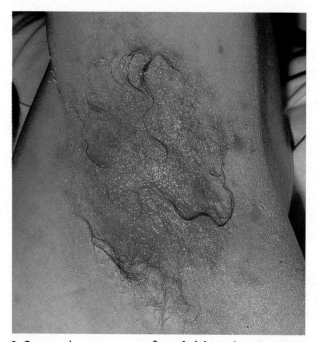

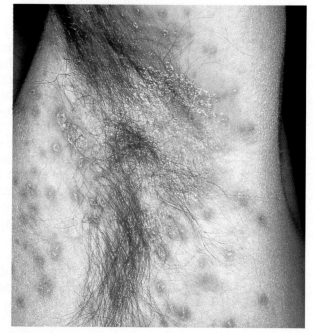

Inflammation may range from bright red and eroded, to dull and scaly.

Candidiasis

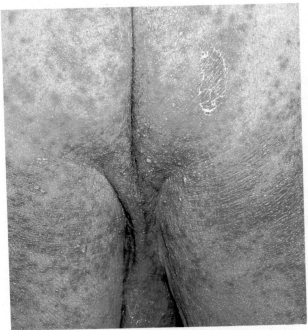 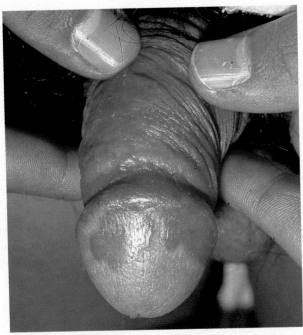

Particularly severe, angry, and widespread yeast infections may be seen in diabetics. Mild incontinence kept the area moist.

Typical bright red patch of *Candida* balanitis.

Clinical
- Bright pink eruption.
  - ▲ distribution
    - ■ groin
    - ■ genitals (including penis and scrotum)
    - ■ intergluteal fold
    - ■ buttocks
  - ▲ surface
    - ■ macerated, desquamating (like wet tissue paper), eroded
    - ■ fine white pustules stippling central area and in satellite lesions
  - ▲ spreading rash with irregular borders and satellite lesions
  - ▲ severe burning and itching
- More common in
  - ▲ persons who perspire copiously, or who are incontinent
  - ▲ the obese
  - ▲ diabetics

Candidiasis

Treatment

- General measures.
  - ▲ loose, cool clothing
  - ▲ reduce physical activity
  - ▲ talcum powder to reduce wetness and chafing

> **Note:** do not powder with corn starch as it may *enhance* the growth of yeast

- Drying agents.
  - ▲ effect
    - ■ dry up pustules and macerated epidermis
    - ■ prepare skin for topical antifungal agents
    - ■ may cure the infection by creating a dry environment hostile to the organism
  - ▲ baths, soaks or compresses, with careful drying afterward, are a mainstay of therapy
    - ■ tap water
    - ■ saline
    - ■ astringent (p.318)
  - ▲ paints (p.306)
    - ■ drying
    - ■ contain ingredients which kill yeast
      - ■ gentian violet
      - ■ Castellani's paint
- Topical anti-yeast medications (p.309).
  - ▲ use after lesions have been dried by baths or soaks
  - ▲ apply thinly twice daily for 1-3 weeks
  - ▲ alcohol/propylene glycol solutions are superior, but may sting. They are drying agents in these moist areas and leave little residue
  - ▲ medicated powders are poor vehicles for the delivery of active ingredients to the skin
- Topical corticosteroids, used *with* topical anti-yeast medications.
  - ▲ relieve itching quickly
    - ■ anti-yeast medications used alone may take days to reduce inflammation and itching
  - ▲ a mild preparation (hydrocortisone) is usually adequate
    - ■ good penetration in thin, moist skin
    - ■ atrophy and striae may occur after just a few weeks' use of *potent* corticosteroid
  - ▲ the lotion or solution vehicle is most pleasant to use
  - ▲ steroid/anti-yeast combinations
    - ■ 'Mycolog' ('Kenacomb') is effective, but see p.310 for caveats
      - ■ use ointment form to minimize occurrence of allergic contact dermatitis
    - ■ iodochlorhydroxyquin (Vioform-hydrocortisone) is usually effective, but
      - ■ slight yellow stain noticeable on white underclothes
      - ■ vioform may rarely cause allergic contact dermatitis

Diaper Dermatitis (Nappy Rash)

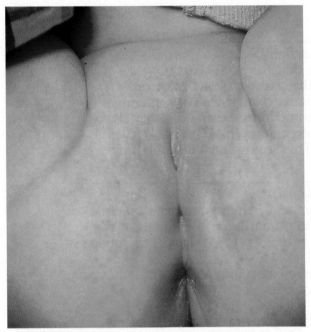

Mild irritation of the perineal skin from wet diapers.

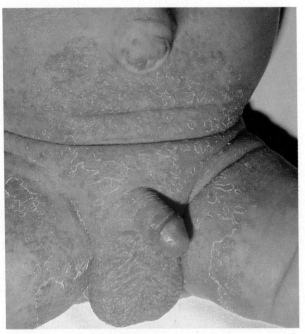

Extensive pustular and erosive yeast diaper dermatitis. Infant also had oral thrush.

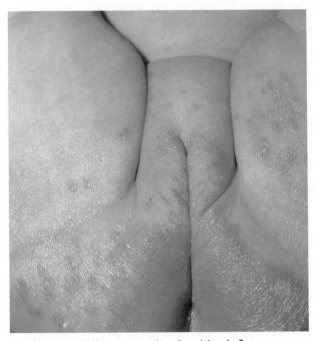

Typical yeast diaper eruption in older infant.

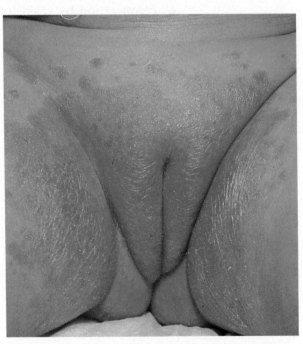

Severe, angry yeast infection and irritation. Note satellite lesions which typify *Candida* involvement.

Diaper Dermatitis (Nappy Rash)

Clinical

> The diaper area of infants is constantly exposed to moisture
> and irritants, so it is surprising that the skin is usually
> completely normal. However, the skin occasionally becomes
> irritated, and sometimes it becomes overgrown with micro-
> organisms. The diaper area is sometimes the site of other skin
> conditions, such as seborrheic dermatitis (p.1), psoriasis (p.161),
> and atopic dermatitis (p.137). This section includes only the
> common local eruptions.

- Irritant contact dermatitis ('chafing').
  - ▲ chronic exposure to moisture and irritants produces a faint,
    poorly-demarcated erythema, primarily on the domes of the
    skin folds of the abdomen, perineum, and thighs. The surface is
    tight and glazed.
  - ▲ may be noticed at one diaper change and absent at the next, or
    may persist for a few days at a low level of activity
- *Candida* dermatitis.
  - ▲ in contrast to irritant dermatitis, this rash is a brighter red,
    consists of sharply-demarcated patches with satellite lesions, and
    usually involves and radiates from the skin folds. The surface is
    tense and shiny, and may be desquamating or even pustular
  - ▲ *Candida* dermatitis is persistent and uncomfortable
  - ▲ colonization by yeast from the bowel, as well as by bacteria

Diaper Dermatitis (Nappy Rash)

Treatment

● Irritant dermatitis.
- ▲ tends to resolve spontaneously with frequent diaper changes, or after leaving diapers off for a few hours
- ▲ various mild lubricants may be protective and accelerate resolution. This tendency to spontaneous healing and response to various preparations has given rise to numerous 'successful' old family remedies for this condition.

● *Candida* dermatitis.
- ▲ if a diaper rash persists after the preceding measures, it may be super-colonized with yeast and bacteria
- ▲ this rash usually responds well to topical mild corticosteroid and antibiotic, combined. Apply thinly twice daily for 1-2 weeks
  - ■ hydrocortisone 1% cream or lotion, followed by topical anti-yeast agent (p.309)
  - ■ hydrocortisone 1% and iodochlorhydroxyquin 3% cream or lotion (may leave slight yellow stain on diaper)
  - ■ 'Mycolog' ('Kenacomb') cream or ointment–see p.310 for caveats

> The more potent corticosteroid in this preparation could cause temporary skin atrophy or permanent striae if used for more than a few weeks. Advise the parents to use it for not more than two weeks without specific permission.

● If rash persists, relapses repeatedly, or spreads, refer to a dermatologist for evaluation.

> **About diapers:** There is no more or less irritation from the use of disposable paper diapers or correctly-laundered cloth diapers. Only inadequate washing or rinsing of a cloth diaper could make it irritating.

Neurodermatitis

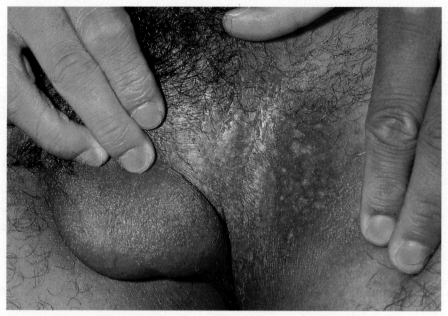

Six months of rubbing has produced this leathery, thickened skin.

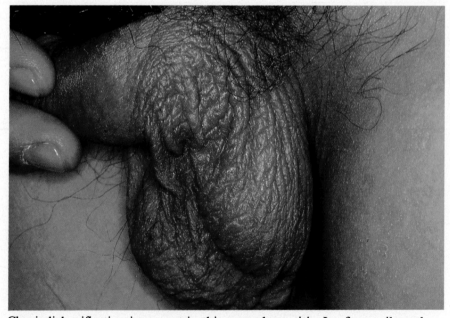

Classic lichenification is present in this neurodermatitis. Is often unilateral.

Neurodermatitis

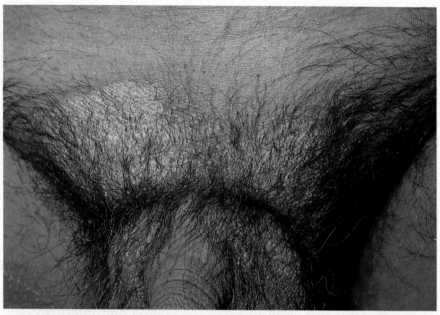

Over three years of rubbing, scratching, and pinching produced these lesions.

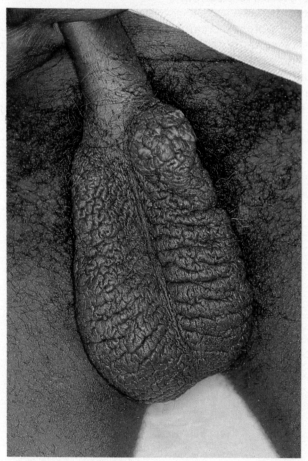

Marked lichenification is seen in this psychotic who
constantly rubbed his genitals. A fibrotic nodule
results from repeated pinching.

Neurodermatitis

Clinical

- A diagnosis of exclusion. Persistent unexplained itching and rash in absence of contactant, intertrigo, fungus, or other cause.
- There will be a lichenified patch or plaque.
  - ▲ elephantiasis–thickening of entire genital skin in severe cases
- The condition may worsen in times of stress.
  - ▲ if mutilating, may represent severe psychopathology
- The condition may result from unfounded concern about genital or perianal hygiene. Some neurodermatitis is at least partially a 'dishpan groin' from overzealous washing or use of antiseptics or cleansers.

Treatment

- General.
  - ▲ explain role of rubbing to patients so that they may bring it to a conscious level and control it
  - ▲ routine hygiene during normal bathing
    - ■ keep area clean to avoid maceration and intertrigo
    - ■ discourage excessive cleaning
- Topical corticosteroids.
  - ▲ mild to moderate potency creams twice daily
  - ▲ potent creams twice daily if the rash remains resistant, but only for a few days or weeks
    - ■ thin genital skin is particularly subject to atrophy from potent corticosteroids
    - ■ switch to mild potency (hydrocortisone 1%) when itching is improved or lichenification is reduced

Extremities

Hand Dermatitis

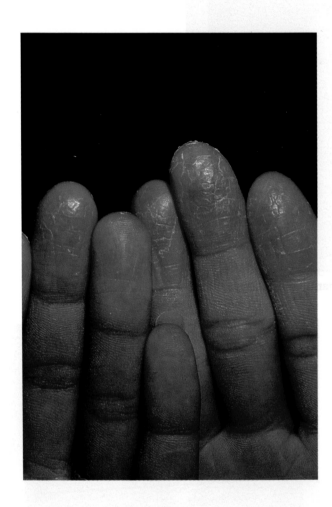

Typical "dishpan hands". Low-grade irritant dermatitis from water and cleansers. Skin is dry, tight, glazed, and cracked.

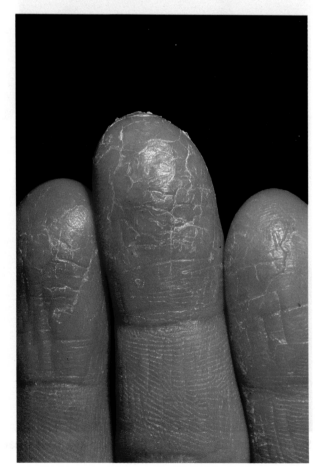

Hand Dermatitis

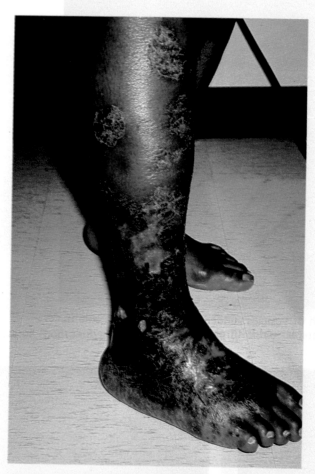

A fractured ankle led to a stasis dermatitis, then palmar "id" eruption.

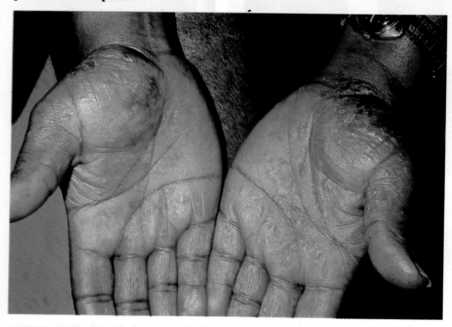

Hand Dermatitis

Clinical (continued)

● Psoriasis.
  ▲ psoriasis may present as a chronic hand and/or foot rash, in
    one of two forms
    ■ well circumscribed area of redness, scaling and/or deep
      desquamation on palm
    ■ chronic or recurrent 1mm-3mm vesicopustules with
      desquamation
  ▲ look for typical nail changes (p.164) and rash elsewhere

> **Note:** when examining a patient with a hand dermatitis,
> always take a complete history for water exposure and past
> or present dermatologic disease, and do a complete
> examination for evidence of atopic dermatitis, psoriasis, and
> rashes of the ankles and feet.

Treatment
● General measures.
  ▲ stop all lotions, vitamin creams, moisturizers and so on as they
    often contain irritants
  ▲ decrease exposure to water, cleansers and irritants

> ■ protective gloves induce sweating (which macerates the
>   skin), accumulate moisture, soap, and dirt, and may
>   themselves be allergic sensitizers (if rubber). They should
>   be used when handling strong irritants (oven cleaner,
>   silver polish). Vinyl gloves are the least irritating
>   protection if worn over a thin cotton glove which can be
>   changed periodically as it becomes soaked with sweat,
>   but this is so awkward and inconvenient as to be
>   impractical for many uses

Hand Dermatitis

Treatment (continued)

- ▲ treat inflammatory disease of the ankles, feet, and legs to control the 'id' eruption.
- ● Acute vesicular eruption (pompholyx, 'id', pustular psoriasis).
  - ▲ tap water or mild astringent soaks (p.318) thrice daily for 10-15 minutes, followed by potent topical corticosteroids
  - ▲ individual tense vesicles and bullae should be punctured if there is significant discomfort. A hypodermic needle or pointed scalpel blade is ideal and patients can do it, carefully, themselves. Follow with soak, and topical corticosteroid
  - ▲ systemic corticosteroid in a fairly high dose (e.g. prednisone 50mg) tapering over a 10-day period, should be administered in severe cases
  - ▲ antihistamine should be given as a sedative (p.321) especially at bedtime, or if pompholyx attack is related to stress
- ● Chronic inflammation, cracking, and desquamation.
  - ▲ topical corticosteroids are the mainstay of therapy
    - ■ potent forms (p.315) are needed initially, and often chronically. Use less potent ones when possible
    - ■ ointment form often indicated to lubricate dry, cracked skin
    - ■ apply twice or thrice daily, but may also use plain lubricant several times a day
    - ■ vinyl glove occlusion (p.311) can be worn over corticosteroid for a few hours a day, or overnight, in stubborn cases. Monitor closely for signs of skin atrophy, then reduce potency of corticosteroid, or discontinue occlusion

---

Tip: if only palm involved, cut off glove fingers for comfort.

Hand Dermatitis

Treatment (continued)

▲ lubrication
- ■ stress that the patient cease using cosmetic lubricants, as they may contain irritants or allergens
- ■ if topical corticosteroids are not required (because of absence of inflammation and itching) stress frequent use of a thick, bland lubricant. Lotions are too thin (mostly water) and may be drying. Use lanolin-free cream or ointment (e.g. wood alcohol [Eucerin], hydrated petrolatum)
- ■ vinyl glove occlusion worn over the emollient enhances lubrication. After occlusion, rinse hands and immediately reapply lubricant to prevent drying

▲ in recalcitrant chronic cases may need to use
- ■ coal tar or tar derivative cream or gel mixed with corticosteroid, which occasionally enhances effect. **Do not occlude tars**
- ■ coal tar/ultraviolet light (Goeckerman treatment, p.170) or psoralen/ultraviolet photochemotherapy (p.170)
- ■ chronic systemic corticosteroids as daily low-dose, alternate-day, or occasional long-acting parenteral repository injection

> **Note:** for chronic cases patients may need to make permanent changes in their habits, and constantly or periodically use lubricants or corticosteroids. Use the Patient Guide (p.281) and repeatedly urge compliance.

Tinea Pedis

Tinea pedis can occur in anyone but may be more frequent or more severe in people with moist feet (excessive sweating, occlusive shoes), especially after friction and trauma (athletes). There are three clinical forms.

Chronic Plantar Scaling

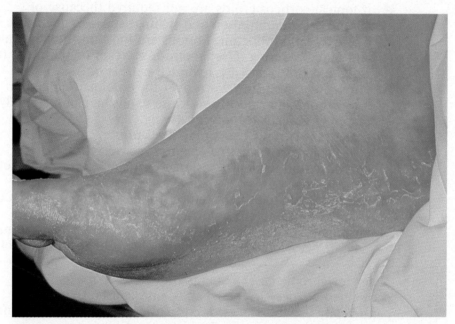

Moderately severe chronic tinea pedis with redness and scaling in "moccasin" distribution.

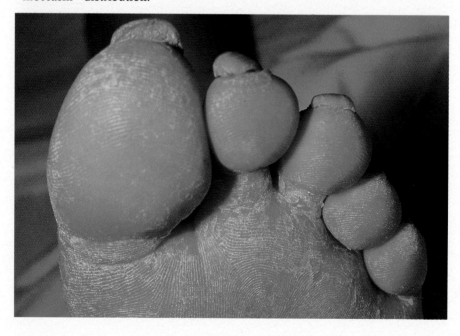

Tinea Pedis

Chronic Plantar Scaling

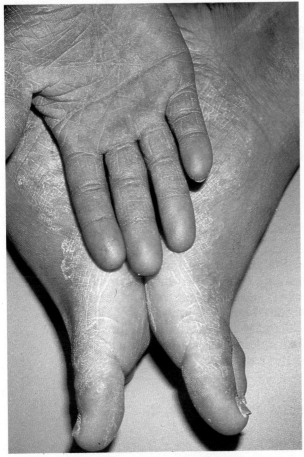

Typical "two-foot-one-hand" pattern in chronic
tinea manuum. Other palm was unaffected.

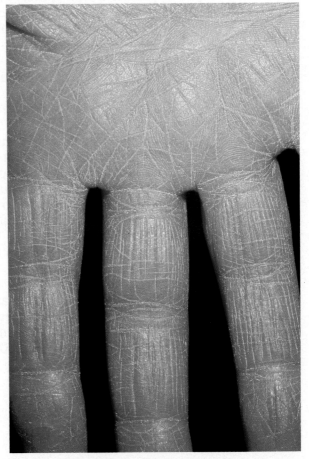

Chronic tinea of palm sometimes described as
"painter's palm" with white scale building up in
skin creases, like paint after cleaning painting hand.

Tinea Pedis
Chronic Plantar Scaling

Clinical

- 'Moccasin' distribution, on plantar surface and around sides of feet.
  - ▲ generally absent to mild redness
  - ▲ mild to profuse scaling
    - ■ often accentuated in normal fold lines as a white powder
    - ■ may build up as hyperkeratosis on weight-bearing surfaces, especially around the edges of the heel
- One or more toenails often involved (p.113).
- Generally absent itching.
- Difficult to find organism on potassium hydroxide (KOH) examination (p.293).

Treatment

> Ten to twenty per cent of people are constitutionally incapable of mounting an immune response to the organism *Trichophyton rubrum*, so it exists peaceably on the foot, and usually recurs (from environmental contamination, or persistent skin spores) after adequate treatment. Therefore, treatment is not recommended unless symptomatic or cosmetically objectionable to the patient.

- Keratolytics (p.323).
  - ▲ chronic application minimizes or abolishes scale, thus reducing organism population
  - ▲ useful adjunct to topical antifungal agents
  - ▲ rarely curative
  - ▲ apply ointment or gel thinly once or twice daily or as necessary
    - ■ Whitfield's ointment (p.323)
    - ■ salicylic acid 6% in propylene glycol gel
  - ▲ may be irritating, especially on non-plantar skin
- Topical antifungal agents (p.309).
  - ▲ chronic applications minimize or suppress eruption
  - ▲ sometimes curative
  - ▲ apply cream or solution twice daily, powder form not very active
  - ▲ occasional development of resistance
- Systemic antifungal agents are suppressive but rarely curative. Possible side effects rarely justify use.
  - ▲ griseofulvin (p.307) 250mg (micronized) twice daily for 6 weeks
  - ▲ ketoconazole (p.308) 200mg daily

Tinea Pedis

Acute Vesicular Tinea Pedis

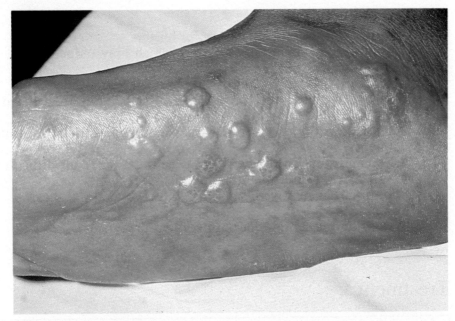

Acute vesicular tinea pedis. Close inspection of vesicles shows that they are multiloculated, unlike uniloculated friction blisters.

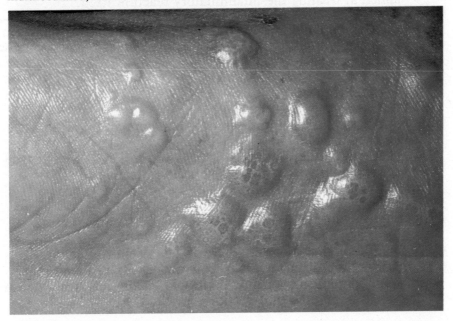

Tinea Pedis

Acute Vesicular Tinea Pedis

Clinical

- Sudden eruption of pruritic or painful blisters.
  - ▲ often as sudden event in teenagers, which may induce immunity from further infections
  - ▲ sometimes on background of chronic scaling tinea
  - ▲ small, individual vesicles, or, characteristically, multiloculated bullae
  - ▲ often follows, by one or two days, sweating and friction to soles (athletics)
- Positive potassium hydroxide (KOH) examination result difficult to obtain (p.293) because inflammation kills organisms.
  - ▲ roof of blister removed, soaked in KOH several minutes, examined
  - ▲ blister fluid is serum, does not contain organisms

Treatment

> Acute tissue reaction (blisters) kills fungi, so treatment is aimed at treating the inflammatory reaction itself.

- Decrease sweating by minimizing occlusive footwear and friction.
- Soaks or baths should be used two or three times a day for a few days to dry up blisters.
  - ▲ tap water
  - ▲ astringents (p.318)
  - ▲ dry thoroughly after soaks
- If tense blisters are painful, carefully puncture and drain blisters with a clean needle.
  - ▲ blister top settles onto eroded base and serves as dressing—**do not remove blister tops** as they prolong healing
  - ▲ continue soaks until blisters are dry, to reduce chance of secondary infection
- Astringent paint (p.306) should be applied to denuded areas.
  - ▲ Castellani's paint twice daily after soaks
- A potent topical corticosteroid cream helps relieve itching.
- Specific antifungal therapy is usually not necessary because inflammation kills organisms. If chronic scaling remains, treat as described in the preceding section.

Tinea Pedis

Interdigital Tinea Pedis

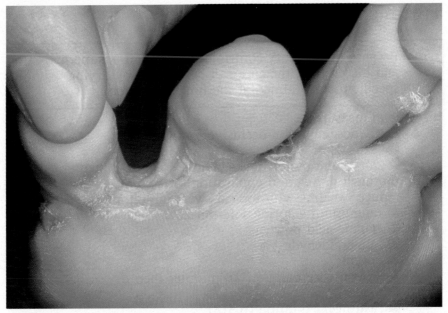

Itchy, eroded, and malodorous interdigital tinea.

Clinical
- ● Erosion, scaling and fissuring in toe webs.
  - ▲ fourth web most common
- ● This is usually itchy, burning, or painful.
- ● It is more common in people with sweaty feet or occlusive footwear.
  - ▲ marked malodor often noticeable
- ● It represents maceration with colonization by fungi and Gram-negative bacteria.
  - ▲ often occurs in absence of tinea of sole
  - ▲ potassium hydroxide (KOH) examination often negative (p.293)
  - ▲ Gram-negative bacteria may cause burning and offensive odor

Tinea Pedis

Interdigital Tinea Pedis

Treatment

> Because the primary contributing problem is superhydration and maceration, the cure can be effected by drying, without specific therapy aimed at the fungi or bacteria.

- General measures.
  - ▲ light, loose and non-occlusive footwear
    - ■ sandals
    - ■ absorbent cotton socks (white, colored, or patterned)
  - ▲ thorough drying and application of talcum powder after bathing
  - ▲ reduce sweating with topical sweat-inhibitors
    - ■ aluminum chloride solution 20%
    - ■ tannic acid powder
    - ■ glutaraldehyde 5%
- Drying agents.
  - ▲ soak feet twice daily for 10 minutes then dry well
    - ■ water
    - ■ astringent solution (p.318)
  - ▲ drying paints may be applied twice daily with cotton-tipped applicator (p.306)
    - ■ Castellani's paint
    - ■ aluminum chloride 6%-20%
- Antimicrobial agents.
  - ▲ antifungal solution (p.309) (drying vehicle) applied twice daily
  - ▲ combined antifungal and antibacterial therapy
    - ■ antifungal agent with neomycin or bacitracin
  - ▲ griseofulvin does not work

Onychomycosis (Tinea Unguium)

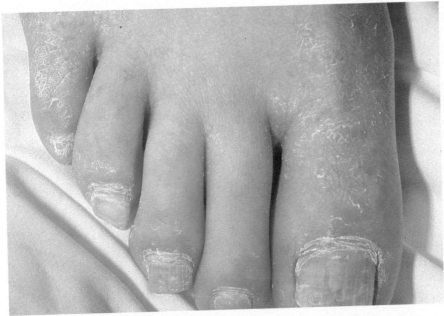

Nails of patient shown on page 106 are thickened, and have accumulated crumbly sub-ungual debris.

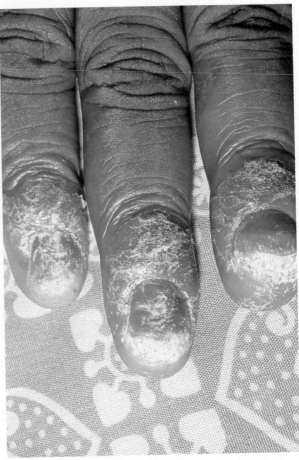

This diabetic had particularly marked nail and skin involvement with dermatophytes.

Onychomycosis (Tinea Unguium)

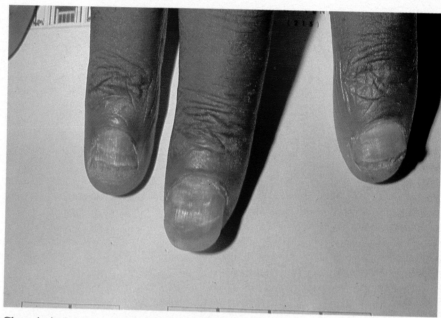

Chronic indolent onychomycosis caused only slight
thickening and longitudinal striation of these
fingernails.

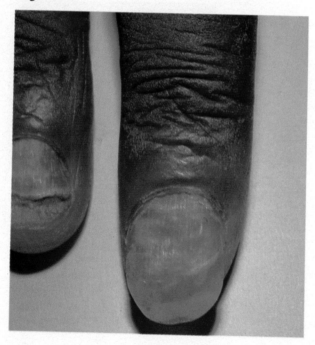

Onychomycosis (Tinea Unguium)

Clinical
● Infection of the nail and/or the nail bed with dermatophyte (ringworm) fungi.
  ▲ many species can cause infection
  ▲ secondary colonization with non-pathogenic fungi is common
  ▲ potassium hydroxide (KOH) examination and fungal cultures are often negative, even with excellent technique (p.293)
    ■ diagnosis is predominantly clinical
● Clinical characteristics.
  ▲ distal nail edge onycholysis (separation of nail plate from nail bed) with yellowish thickening of nail plate and accumulation of tan crumbly debris beneath separated portion of nail
    ■ distal edge of nail may split and crumble and eventually shorten considerably through 'erosion'
    ■ nail may thicken, become elevated and grossly distorted, and be painful from pressure of shoes
    ■ black or greenish sub-ungual color may occur from secondary colonization by non-pathogenic fungi (e.g. *Aspergillus*)
  ▲ often seen in association with tinea pedis or tinea manum
  ▲ toenail involvement is much more common than fingernail
    ■ may occur in single nail (often great toenail) or in multiple nails
    ■ if isolated and skin unaffected, may be secondary to traumatic damage to nail, which is a portal for infection
  ▲ usually lasts a lifetime, rarely heals spontaneously
    ■ more nails may become involved with passage of time, especially if skin of soles and palms is affected

Treatment
● General.
  ▲ continuous treatment of chronic palm or sole tinea (p.106) probably decreases the likelihood of nail infection
  ▲ well-established onychomycosis is difficult to cure and it is best to warn the patient of the poor prognosis and the possibility of relapse
  ▲ after discussion, the patient might decide to forgo treatment
    ■ keep the nail neatly clipped and buffed flat (with file or pumice stone) for cosmetic appearance and to prevent painful pressure by shoes

Onychomycosis (Tinea Unguium)

Treatment (continued)

- ● Topical therapy.
  - ▲ rarely curative unless only a small part of the distal nail edge is involved, and then treatment is usually only palliative
  - ▲ trim free edge of nail as far as possible and gently scrape out sub-ungual debris
  - ▲ apply antifungal solution (p.309) twice daily under free edge of nail
    - ■ clotrimazole
    - ■ miconazole
    - ■ haloprogin
    - ■ tolnaftate
- ● Systemic antifungal agents.
  - ▲ often, 'normal' nails will grow in while the patient is taking an oral antifungal agent
    - ■ some nails do not respond
  - ▲ the patient must take the medication until the 'normal' nail grows in completely
    - ■ this may take up to six months for fingernails
    - ■ this may take up to 18 months for toenails
  - ▲ unfortunately, the relapse rate for patients with affected toenails is very high (90%) a few months after therapy is stopped
    - ■ relapse rate is less than 50% for patients with affected fingernails
  - ▲ because of the long duration of therapy, possible side effects, and high relapse rate, oral agents are *used rarely for onychomycosis of toenails, but are worth a try for onychomycosis of fingernails*
    - ■ griseofulvin (p.307) 250mg-500mg twice daily
    - ■ ketoconazole 200mg daily (p.308)
- ● Nail avulsion. Removal of a single involved nail sometimes allows a normal nail to grow again.
  - ▲ the relapse rate is high, especially if more than one nail is involved or if the sole is involved and not treated
  - ▲ treat with topical antifungal solution or oral antifungal agent during regrowth
  - ▲ surgical avulsion is standard, but should be performed only by a trained practitioner
    - ■ to do this, use ring block anesthesia (without epinephrine), apply a tourniquet, use a periosteal elevator to separate the entire nail plate from the nail bed and cuticle, pull the nail out of the matrix with hemostat or pliers, then gently curette the bed to remove infected debris. Lightly cauterize bleeding points, but do not curette or cauterize matrix as that may permanently prevent nail growth). Remove tourniquet, and have the patient soak the digit twice or thrice daily in warm water or astringent for 2-4 days (until oozing stops)
  - ▲ **Note:** see page 117 for *Candida* paronychia, which may be confused with onychomycosis.

Paronychia

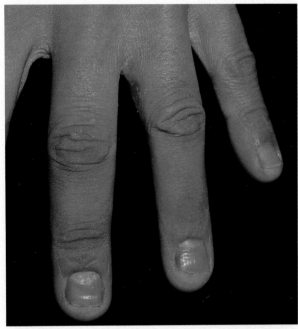

Mild puffiness of paronychial tissues. Note that nail dystrophy occurs only distal to where cuticle is absent.

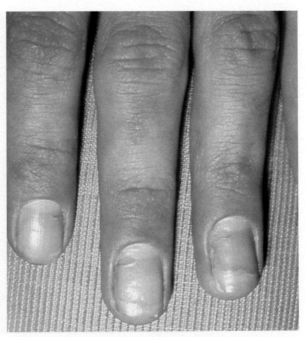

Slightly more inflamed peri-ungual folds in bartender, who also has onycholysis (separation of distal part of nail plate from nail bed).

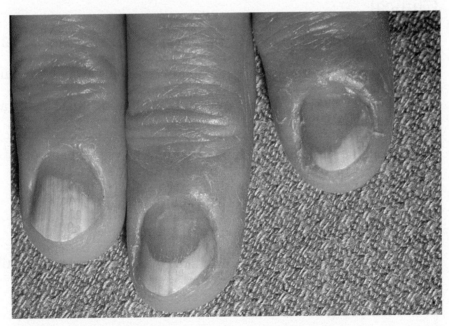

Marked paronychia and onycholysis in professional hairwasher.

Paronychia

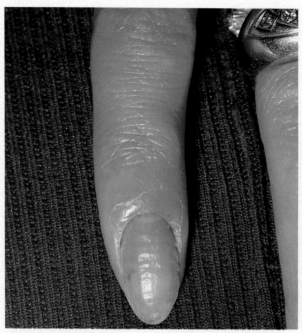

Marked nail dystrophy in this chronic *Candida*
paronychia, which also has an area of acute
bacterial paronychia.

Clinical
● Appears as
  ▲ mild to moderate redness and edema of posterior and lateral
    nail folds
  ▲ absence of cuticle with retraction of nail folds away from nail
    plate
  ▲ mild to severe nail plate dystrophy, with horizontal ridging and
    discoloration.

> **Note:** a related condition is distal onycholysis (separation of
> nail plate from nail bed). This may appear as opaque
> whiteness, or as a yellowish or green stain (from secondary
> fungal or *Pseudomonas* colonization).

● Caused by the following sequence of events.
  ▲ excessive water exposure (as with a housewife, bartender or
    beautician) softens the cuticle and it pulls away from the nail.

> **Note:** vigorous manicuring of cuticles greatly contributes to
> this process.

  ▲ continued water exposure prevents reformation of cuticles and
    encourages the colonization of *Candida* and bacteria under the
    posterior or lateral nail fold
  ▲ the presence of yeast and bacteria prevents reformation of
    cuticle
● The condition is usually only mildly tender, but painful acute
  bacterial paronychia occasionally develops which drains pus and
  resolves, leaving the chronic process unchanged.

Plantar Warts

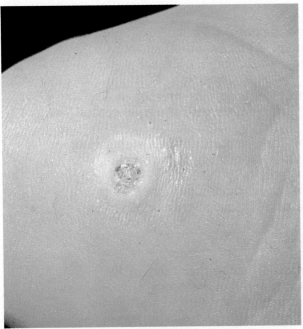

Typical isolated plantar wart surrounded by callus.

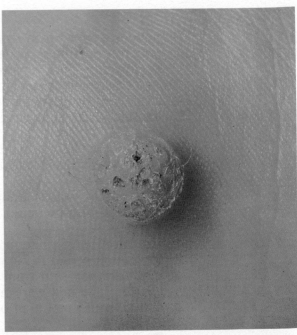

This protuberant plantar wart was painful during walking. Pressure caused irritation of surrounding skin.

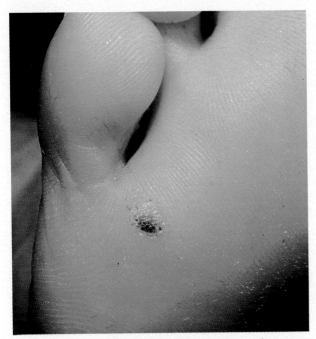

Sometimes the capillaries in the wart clot, often heralding spontaneous resolution.

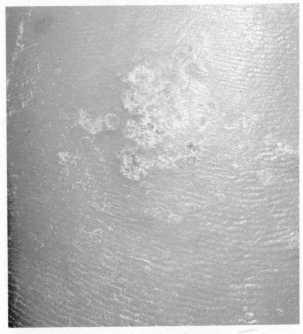

Mosaic plantar wart is cluster of perhaps single verrucae.

Plantar Warts

Clinical
● Discrete or grouped firm keratotic masses on the sole.
  ▲ center of wart mass has granular, crumbly, pitted surface
    ■ tiny dark dots, representing clotted capillaries, are occasionally present
  ▲ a callus of surrounding normal skin is usually present
  ▲ 'mosaic' wart is one covering a large area with multiple central cores
  ▲ wart may be asymptomatic or may be painful when standing or walking (as space-occupying mass), especially if on weight-bearing area
    ■ typically, wart is tender to lateral pinching (as well as to direct, firm pressure), and corn is tender only on direct pressure
● A viral infection of epidermal cells.
  ▲ incubation period is 2-4 months
  ▲ new warts can seed from the initial one, either early in the course of the first wart or after months of existence
  ▲ spontaneous involution occurs when immunity to wart virus develops
    ■ occurs after months or years
    ■ duration generally shorter in children than in adults
    ■ development of immunity is variable–some individuals have only one wart briefly, others are plagued with various warts for years.

Plantar Warts

Treatment
- No effective antiwart-virus medications exist (except for genital warts, p.70). Therapy, therefore, is either palliative or destructive. Destructive therapy may yield a cure of one or two isolated warts. Mosaic warts nearly always recur after such treatments so only palliative therapy is recommended.
- Palliative. Keeps warts asymptomatic until spontaneous resolution occurs. There is a risk that new warts may seed from the original during this time.
  - ▲ no treatment if asymptomatic
  - ▲ apply a keratolytic agent (keratin-softening) (p.323) overnight every few days, so that the keratin becomes soft and can be easily scraped off
    - ■ salicylic acid 40% plaster
    - ■ salicylic acid 16% and lactic acid 16% in flexible collodion
  - ▲ the patient can pare the wart with a knife or scalpel, or grind it down with a nail file or pumice stone
  - ▲ many physicians favor alternating this keratolytic therapy with drying by formalin soak or compress on subsequent nights, claiming that this speeds removal of keratin and even shortens the duration of the wart
- Destruction of wart tissue.

> **Note:** If only wart or epidermis is damaged then healing will occur without a scar. *If the dermis is damaged then a scar will result. A scar on the sole, especially on the weight-bearing area, can be painful permanently. This rare outcome is particularly tragic since the wart will heal eventually without treatment.* Only considerable discomfort justifies this risk and the patient should be fully informed of the possible consequences.

  - ▲ cryotherapy is rarely successful with just one treatment, because of the depth of the wart, although repeated treatments may be successful, or treatment after keratolytic treatments (above)
    - ■ considerable pain is a major drawback for several days, especially when walking
    - ■ scarring is rare unless treatment is too deep
  - ▲ repeated parings (every week or two in the office) or several weeks of keratolytic treatment may thin the wart to the point where acid (trichloracetic 60%) repeatedly applied by pointed wooden applicator may eradicate it
    - ■ recurrences are common
    - ■ skill is required to avoid dermal injury
  - ▲ curettage and chemical cautery (trichloracetic acid or phenol 88%) or *light* electrocautery after local anesthesia is successful about 80% of time for isolated (single) warts
    - ■ local anesthesia of sole is painful
    - ■ postoperative tenderness may be considerable for a few days, and healing may take 2-3 weeks.

> **Excessive curettage or cautery could result in painful scar.**

- Patient Guide on warts see page 292

Stasis Dermatitis

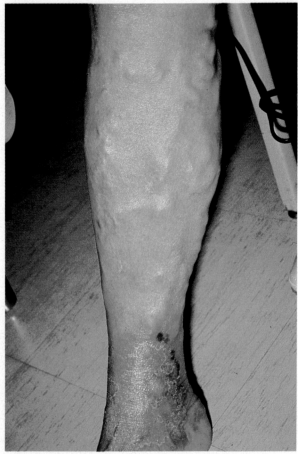

Obvious varicose veins, and chronic stasis dermatitis of ankle.

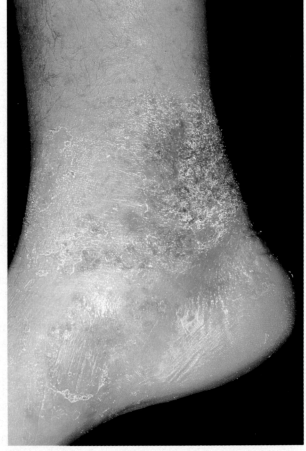

Early (5 days) acute stasis dermatitis over most distal perforator vein connecting the deep and superficial systems.

Stasis Dermatitis

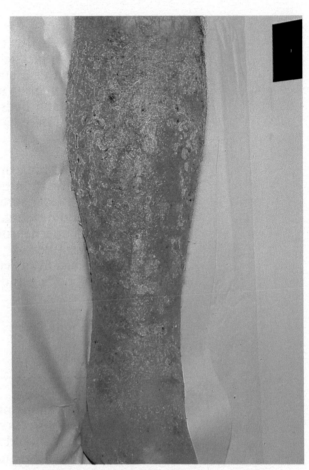

Very widespread acute stasis dermatitis rapidly enlarging from original site on ankle.

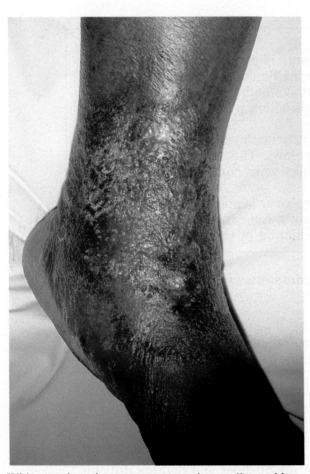

Widespread stasis eczema on a quite swollen ankle.

Stasis Dermatitis

Clinical
- Caused by increased hydrostatic venous pressure.
  - ▲ more common in people who stand for prolonged periods
  - ▲ there is usually a rash and/or ulcer on the medial side of ankle where the most inferior perforator connects deep and superficial venous systems and hydrostatic pressure is greatest
  - ▲ veins and valves may have been damaged by clots, infection, or injury
- Eruption.
  - ▲ ranges from mild pink or pigmented to raging angry red; oozing necrosis and ulceration may occur
  - ▲ there may be a local spread on the leg or distant 'id' (autosensitization) dermatitis, especially on hands (p.102)
  - ▲ lichenification and neurodermatitis may supervene after stasis element has remitted
  - ▲ secondary infection (usually staphylococcal) may occur
    - ■ increasing oozing and crusting
    - ■ pain

Treatment

- ■ General.
  - ■ Reduction of venous pressure is paramount. Educate the patient to avoid stress on malfunctioning veins.
    - ■ The patient should avoid standing still (walking is not harmful because muscle action pumps blood through veins).
    - ■ Recommend that the patient elevates feet when sitting, using an ottoman or pillows. This lowers gradient back to the heart, and unkinks veins compressed when the knee is bent.
    - ■ If standing is necessary, wear support hose, surgical support stockings, or custom-measured elasticized stocking to minimize dilation of veins.

- To treat dermatitis.
  - ▲ if oozing – soaks, baths or compresses (p.318) thrice daily for 15 minutes
    - ■ discontinue when dry
  - ▲ topical corticosteroids
    - ■ mild to potent, depending on degree of inflammation
    - ■ do not use potent preparations longer than necessary, to avoid atrophy
    - ■ ointment form is more lubricating and contains fewer sensitizers
  - ▲ zinc oxide (Unna) boot
    - ■ do not use if oozing is copious
    - ■ mildly soothing
    - ■ cumbersome, makes wearing of shoes and bathing difficult
    - ■ may apply over topical corticosteroid
    - ■ change every two to seven days

Stasis Dermatitis

Treatment (continued)

● To treat ulcers.

> This is one of the most diverse areas of treatment in
> medicine. Treatments include oral zinc, topical zinc oxide,
> gold leaf, benzoyl peroxide, hyperbaric oxygen, and many
> others. Mild ulcers respond to elevation, soaks, and time.
> Severe, chronic ulcers may respond to repeated application
> of an Unna boot.

● Modalities shown to hasten healing of ulcers are
  ▲ grafting
    ■ 'pinch' or 'postage stamp' grafts to base of ulcer
    ■ excision and split-thickness graft
  ▲ macromolecular dextran beads
  ▲ repeated application of specially-prepared, banked porcine skin
    grafts

> Specific instructions for the use of these modalities are
> beyond the scope of this book and should be sought
> elsewhere.

● Treatment of secondary bacterial infection.
  ▲ prevention and cure of superficial infections may be achieved
    by
    ■ soaks and baths (p.318)
    ■ benzoyl peroxide (p.306)
    ■ topical antibiotics (p.307)

> **Caution:** topical antibiotics containing *neomycin* are
> frequent sensitizers in this setting

  ▲ deeper or stubborn infections require systemic antibiotics

Neurodermatitis (Lichen Simplex Chronicus)

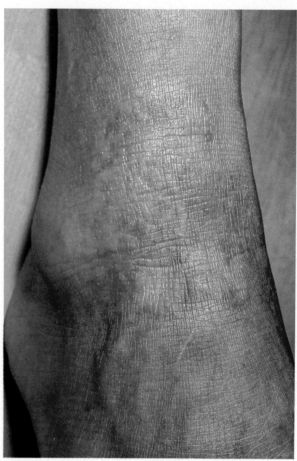

Lichen simplex chronicus of ankle which patient
has been rubbing, especially when tense, for 10
years.

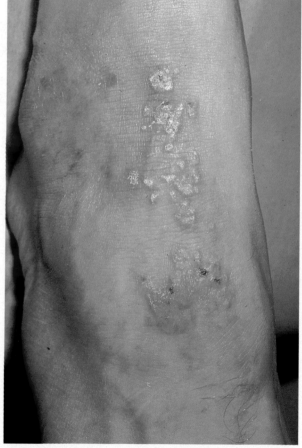

This anterior surface of the ankle has been rubbed
for months, producing this hobnail type of
lichenification.

Neurodermatitis (Lichen Simplex Chronicus)

Massive lichenification verging on self-mutilation in a psychotic.

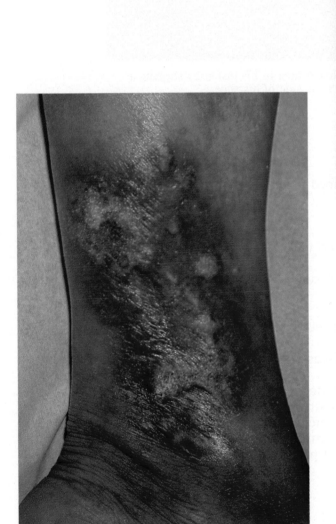

Years of vigorous rubbing and scratching produced a leathery, scarred dermatitis.

Neurodermatitis (Lichen Simplex Chronicus)

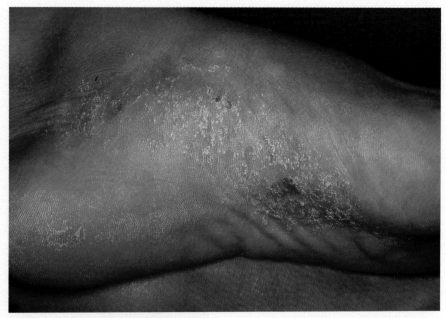

For two years this man rubbed this linear area in his instep by slipping a finger along the side of his foot under the side of his shoe.

Clinical

- Thick, lined, well-circumscribed lichenified patch.
  - ▲ often hyperpigmented
  - ▲ usually solitary
  - ▲ location
    - ■ lateral and medial sides of ankle
    - ■ lower shin
    - ■ occasionally on the dorsum or instep of the foot
- Seen more commonly in
  - ▲ older men
  - ▲ in women is usually on neck (p.62) or arms
  - ▲ rare in children
  - ▲ adults who had atopic diseases as children
  - ▲ Asians
- The result of an unexplained itch-scratch cycle.
  - ▲ often worsens in times of stress
  - ▲ often, the rubbing and scratching is unconscious
- One plaque of psoriasis may mimic lichen simplex chronicus.
  - ▲ look elsewhere for signs of psoriasis

Neurodermatitis (Lichen Simplex Chronicus)

Treatment
- General.
  - ▲ even though the disease may be tied to stress, it is impractical to treat only by reducing stress because the lichenified skin itself itches
  - ▲ making the patient aware of the role of rubbing in maintaining the disease may bring the rubbing to a conscious level
- External corticosteroids.
  - ▲ reduce itching and reverse inflammation and lichenification
  - ▲ creams and ointments
    - ■ potent ones usually necessary
    - ■ at the beginning the patient should apply every time there is itching, to convert the rubbing habit to a medication habit
    - ■ usually apply twice daily
    - ■ slow improvement over several weeks
    - ■ use a milder preparation as lesion thins to normal thickness, to prevent atrophy
  - ▲ occlusion over topical steroid
    - ■ greatly enhances effectiveness of drug
    - ■ prevents rubbing
    - ■ corticoid-impregnated tape (Cordran) a convenient system for small lesions
  - ▲ intralesional injection of corticosteroid (p.313)
    - ■ usually effective in resistant cases
    - ■ may need to repeat at monthly intervals
- Tars (p.323).
  - ▲ may be applied alone or with corticosteroid
  - ▲ mild anti-inflammatory effect
- Systemic agents.
  - ▲ corticosteroids *not* indicated
  - ▲ antihistamines or tranquilizers
    - ■ drowsiness often makes them impractical for daytime use
    - ■ useful at bedtime if the patients scratch in their sleep

Nummular Eczema

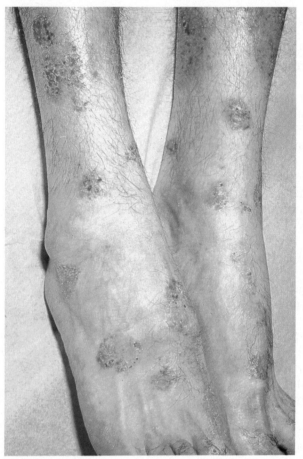

Typical scattered coin-like lesions of indolent dermatitis in nummular eczema.

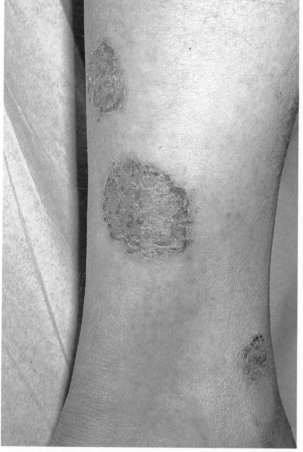

Inflammation and dryness may lead to fissuring of lesions.

Nummular Eczema

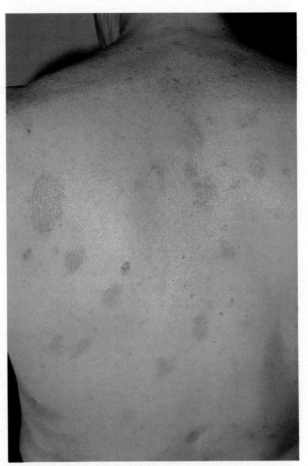

Patients with nummular eczema of the trunk usually have similar lesions, which appeared earlier, on the legs or arms.

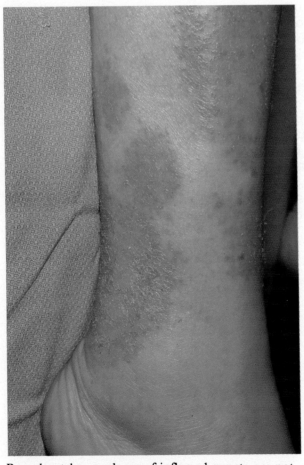

Round patches made up of inflamed puncta are not unusual.

Nummular Eczema

Clinical
● Coin-shaped ('nummular') moderately well-demarcated patches of subacute dermatitis.
  ▲ predominantly on legs, but may occur on arms and trunk
  ▲ occasionally patches enlarge and become confluent
  ▲ usually very itchy
  ▲ typically in middle-aged men
  ▲ often associated with dry skin
    ■ increases in dry weather
    ■ worsens with excessive bathing
● Idiopathic.
  ▲ may be a form of, or eventuate into, psoriasis

Treatment
● In nummular eczema there is often a paradox of clinical appearance and response to therapy; the mild-appearing dermatitis requires potent treatment.
● Corticosteroids.
  ▲ potent topical corticosteroids are often necessary
    ■ use milder ones for maintenance
  ▲ ointments provide better potency and lubrication
  ▲ occlusion should be used for resistant cases
  ▲ systemic corticosteroids, briefly, for stubborn cases.
● Tars (p.323).
  ▲ usually should be used with corticosteroids, to enhance effect in stubborn cases
  ▲ should be used alone for mild cases or maintenance
  ▲ usually work well, but a cumbersome method, with daily ultraviolet light therapy (p.169), as for psoriasis
  ▲ may cause tar folliculitis on legs
    ■ **do not occlude tars**
● Prevention and treatment of dry skin (p.149).
  ▲ probably prevents or minimizes nummular eczema

Trunk and Generalized

Atopic Dermatitis

Note: Many patients and physicians use the word 'eczema' for atopic dermatitis, but eczema is merely a synonym for 'dermatitis' and should have a qualifier preceding it (e.g. stasis or contact).

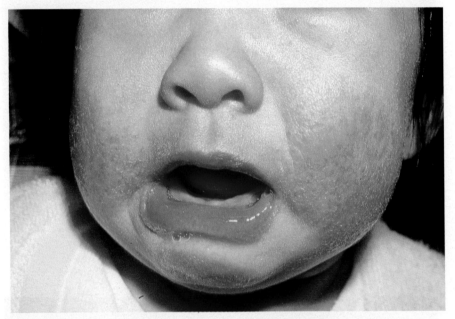

Early acute atopic dermatitis as typical "chapped cheeks" in infant.

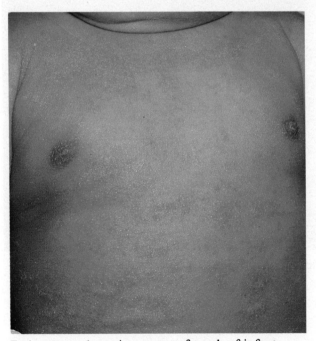

Early scattered atopic eczema of trunk of infant.

Atopic Dermatitis

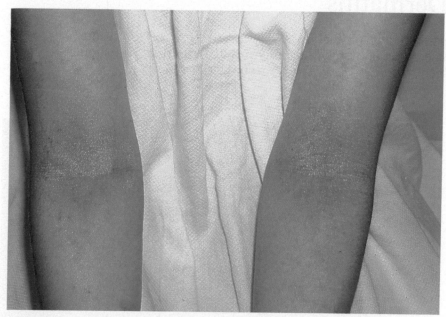

Acute flare of atopic dermatitis in 10 year old.

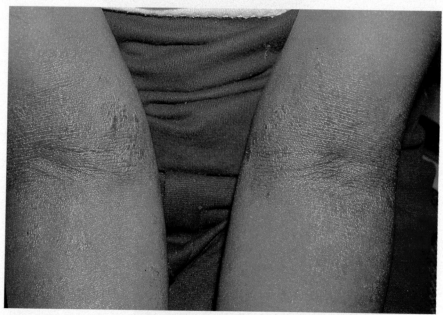

Chronic lichenified atopic dermatitis in 10 year old child.

Atopic Dermatitis

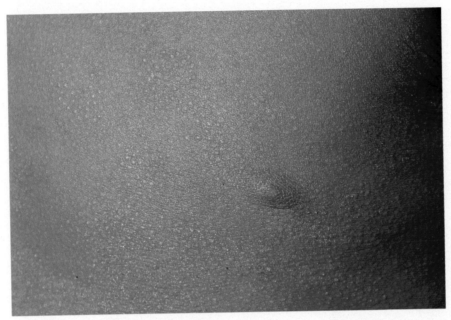

Mild papular eczema in Black child.

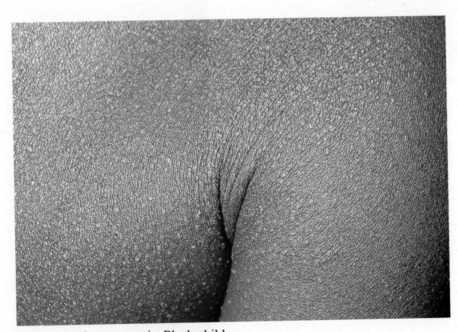

Severe papular eczema in Black child.

Atopic Dermatitis

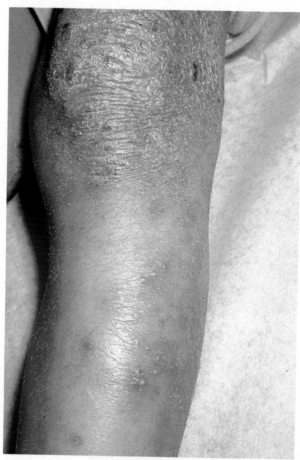

Infected eczema of knee with *Staph.* pustules on skin.

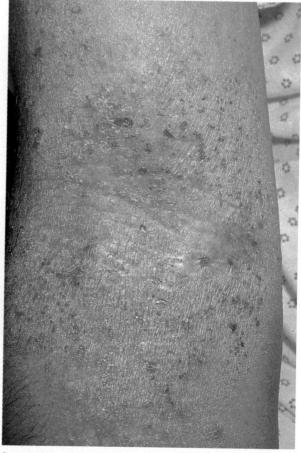

Severely infected flexural atopic dermatitis.

Atopic Dermatitis

Clinical

● Atopic dermatitis is a complicated inherited condition the appearance of which varies greatly and which can change with age and environment. The rash can be bright red, edematous, and oozing; it can be chronic, lichenified, and hyperpigmented; or it can be a mixture of both. Typical clinical patterns are

  ▲ *infantile* atopic dermatitis is subacute (red and oozing) and appears on the scalp, face, trunk, and extensor sides of the extremities, with onset from two to six months of age. Itching may make the infant irritable and hyperkinetic

  ▲ *juvenile* atopic dermatitis follows the infantile stage or occurs *de novo* after one year of age. It is typically chronic and lichenified, occurs in flexural sites (antecubital, popliteal, neck), very itchy and characterized by flares and remissions

  ▲ *adult* atopic dermatitis may be persisting juvenile atopic dermatitis, or a chronic dermatitis appearing years after juvenile dermatitis has cleared. It may be flexural or may appear particularly on the face and hands

● Stigmata associated with atopic dermatitis.

  ▲ family history and/or personal history of other atopic diseases (rhinitis, asthma)

  ▲ dry, flaky, easily irritated skin

  ▲ hyperlinear palms

  ▲ increased propensity to developing heat rash (miliaria, p.190)

  ▲ peripheral vascular dysfunctions, such as white dermographia

Atopic Dermatitis

Clinical (continued)

● Etiology and mechanisms.
  ▲ Atopic dermatitis is familial (there is a 70% chance of a patient developing it if both parents had it)–functionally it is best to regard it as a condition in which the skin has
    ■ a low threshold to itching (a symptom provoked by dryness, rough clothing, solvents, and so on which do not cause itching in non-atopic patients)
    ■ an ability to develop dermatitis when scratched or rubbed (most or all of the rash of atopic dermatitis is produced by scratching)

■ **Note:** itching and scratching can occur during sleep, aggravating the dermatitis and causing restless sleep.

  ▲ the relationship of atopic dermatitis to allergy is controversial
    ■ favoring immunological mechanism are: occurrence in persons with true allergic disease (asthma, hay fever); usually increased serum levels of immunoglobulin E (IgE); transiently depressed immunoglobulin A (IgA) serum levels in infancy; decreased sensitization to *Rhus* antigen; frequent positive results for intradermal skin tests. There is some evidence that breast-fed infants have less severe atopic dermatitis than do bottle-fed babies
    ■ against an allergic mechanism are: occurrence in persons with normal or absent serum levels of IgE; no correlation of skin test results with provoking agents; no benefit from withdrawal of suspected allergens or hyposensitization therapy. Diet manipulation may be of some relief to children and adults
  ▲ anxiety and tension often contribute to increased itching and scratching, which aggravates the dermatitis

Atopic Dermatitis

Clinical (continued)

● Infections of the skin by bacteria and viruses are more common or widespread in individuals with atopic dermatitis. This susceptibility is probably due to the multitudes of breaks in the physical barrier of the skin, but atopic patients also suffer transient dysfunctions of neutrophils and lymphocytes (while the dermatitis is flared) which may contribute to susceptibility.

▲ secondary bacterial pyodermas (p.209) are common in atopic dermatitis, with 95% of eczema patients carrying *Staphylococcus aureus* on their skin. True infection may be manifested as

■ increased itching and resistance of the dermatitis to previously effective therapy

■ scattered tiny erosions in the dermatitic sites; itching is more intense and mild tenderness is present

■ obvious pyoderma with redness, pain, oozing and yellow crust formation

▲ viral infections of the skin can become widespread and even systemic and life-threatening

■ vaccinia and herpes simplex can quickly spread from their small localized sites to involve wide areas of skin, usually resolving in one to two weeks, but viremia, pneumonia, and meningitis can occur

■ molluscum contagiosum may multiply to hundreds of lesions, but will resolve in three to six months

Atopic Dermatitis

Treatment

● General.

  ▲ it is important to educate the patient and the family (see Patient Guide, p.283) about the constitutional nature of the condition; that the skin will itch when subject to various physical stimuli, and that scratching will provoke the rash. Point out that you will instruct and treat to prevent itching and then the patients will be comfortable and have little or no rash. Telling patients that 'allergens' do not influence the rash will relieve feelings of guilt and prevent repeated and frustrating attempts to find the 'cause' of the rash. Guilt is also relieved by mentioning to patients that the rash may flare with anxiety and tension, but that is true for most diseases, and that 'nerves' do not 'cause' atopic dermatitis

● Prevent irritation of the skin.

  ▲ dry skin itching is common in atopic patients, especially in dry climates, or in cold climates in heated buildings (where relative humidity is very low). Prevention and care of dry skin is important and consists of

   ■ adequate but not excessive bathing. Baths and showers should be short and not extremely hot. Mild superfatted soaps should be used instead of detergent and deodorant soaps–a light lotion, such as Cetaphil, can be used as a soap substitute

   ■ after bathing replace skin oil with an oil, cream, or ointment; lotions (p.304) are pleasant to use but often contain too little lipid to be adequately lubricating

   ■ as needed, lubricate dry skin with an oil, cream, or ointment (p.304) once or twice daily. For very dry skin, a thick ointment is necessary

  ▲ avoid unlined wool and polyester clothing, as they are physically rough and irritating and cause itching (NOTE: this is not a wool 'allergy'). Cotton and cotton blends are the least irritating.

  ▲ minimize or avoid jobs or hobbies requiring excessive skin contact with grease, dirt, and solvents, or excessive water exposure (photographic developing, ceramics, automobile repairing, hairdressing, dishwashing, and so on). Protective vinyl gloves are of some benefit but provoke sweating which can macerate and irritate the skin

  ▲ avoid hot, humid jobs or climates if heat rash occurs readily, as it does in 10%-20% of atopic patients. Thick ointment may provoke heat rash in these individuals

● Topical treatment of dermatitis.

  ▲ soaks are rarely needed

   ■ the dermatitis is rarely acute and vesicular

   ■ anything drying the skin, such as soaks, may provoke dermatitis

Atopic Dermatitis

Treatment (continued)

> ▲ topical corticosteroids (p.311) are the mainstay of therapy

- ■ do not hesitate to use potent ones for acute, severe, or thickly lichenified dermatitis as they can stop itching after 30 minutes of use, and short-term use is safe
- ■ corticosteroid of mild potency (hydrocortisone 1%) is adequate for mild disease or for maintenance after use of potent corticosteroid
- ■ corticosteroid of moderate potency may be necessary for maintenance in severe cases
- ■ use an adequate lubricating vehicle (ointment or thick cream) in dry dermatitis, where a thin vehicle (lotion or solution) may worsen drying
- ■ use occlusion with caution as it may provoke heat rash and enhance bacterial growth

▲ tars (p.323) are occasionally used alone or in combination with corticosteroids in chronic dermatitis
- ■ only mildly anti-inflammatory
- ■ slight unpleasant odor and may stain clothing

● Systemic treatment.
▲ oral antibiotics are indicated when clinical signs of infection (see above) occur but as culture growths are positive in over 90% of atopic patients, this is not conclusive
▲ oral or intramuscular corticosteroids
- ■ excellent response, but as it is such an easy 'fix' many patients will shop around to continue treatment
- ■ if the patient's condition does not respond to topical treatment, referral to a dermatologist is the next step

▲ antihistamines are not directly antipruritic (p.321) but will deaden perception of itching and promote comfortable sleep
- ■ especially useful in agitated children for first few days of treatment with topical corticosteroids
- ■ useful at bedtime if the patient is sleeping poorly because of itching and scratching

Dry Skin (Xerosis, Asteatosis, Winter Itch)

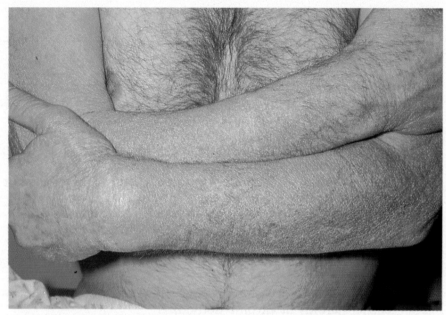

Marked dry skin of arms and trunk.

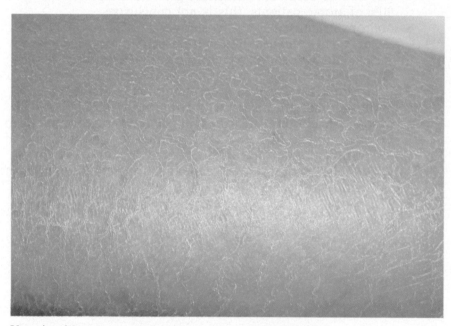

Xerosis with "eczema craquelé", or cracks in keratin layer.

Dry Skin (Xerosis, Asteatosis, Winter Itch)

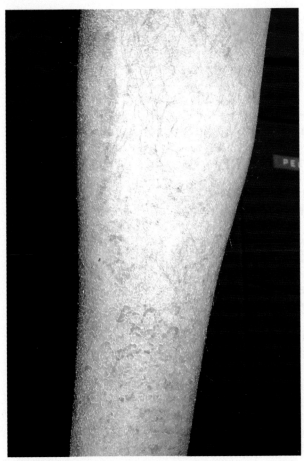

Xerosis with hemorrhage in keratin cracks. Sometimes mistaken for petechiae.

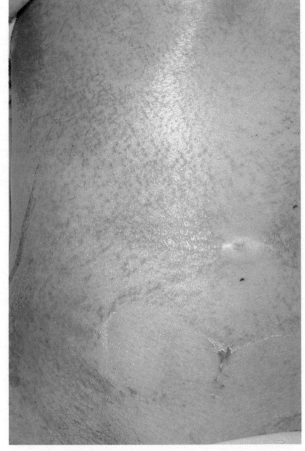

Severe xerosis with cracking and hemorrhage in patient repeatedly washed in hospital. Note sparing where dressing occluded the skin.

Dry Skin (Xerosis, Asteatosis, Winter Itch)

Clinical

- Typically, this condition consists of moderate to severe itching of legs, predominantly with the appearance of dry, scaly skin.
  - ▲ may have marked itching with normal-appearing skin

> By far the most common cause of pruritus 'without rash'.

  - ▲ other common sites are arms and trunk, but spares face and moist, flexural areas
- A tendency to dry skin is inborn, but is often not expressed until middle age or later.
  - ▲ more common in atopic patients (p.137)
  - ▲ unmasked and exacerbated by dry weather, typically in winter when central heating causes extremely low interior humidity
  - ▲ exacerbated by bathing, as water and soap leach oil from the skin and cause 'dishpan body'
- Helpful diagnostic clues are
  - ▲ description of itching as intense, 'boring', or like hundreds of pinpricks or insect bites (sometimes leads to delusions of parasitosis)
  - ▲ itching often flares a few minutes after going to bed
  - ▲ itching is 'all over', but usually absent on face, scalp, and in flexural areas
  - ▲ itching ceases when patient is in the bath or shower for several minutes; the skin becomes hydrated
    - ■ often leads patient to bathe more, causing more drying
  - ▲ itching explodes 15-30 minutes after bathing, as skin dries out
  - ▲ resolution during humid weather or when the patient visits a warm, humid climate
- Xerotic eczema is a condition in which dry skin may be so severe as to crack and fissure, becoming red and inflamed in the fissures (eczema craquelé), or scattered round areas of subacute eczema may develop (nummular eczema, p.134)

Dry Skin (Xerosis, Asteatosis, Winter Itch)

Treatment
● Patient Guide see page 285.
● Environmental manipulations are impractical. Interior humidity can be raised only by the addition of gallons of water to the air in each room each day. A large humidifying unit on a central hot-air heating system may be sufficient in a well-insulated house. The placing of pans of water on radiators is of negligible benefit.
● Practical treatment consists of decreasing washing and of applying lubricants.
● Washing, without subsequent lubrication, causes the skin to become drier and drier. Water alone can cause significant drying (persons who swim regularly may become very dry; they often erroneously attribute the dryness to chlorine in the water).
▲ persons with dry skin should not bathe excessively (less than daily, usually)
▲ some physicians recommend infrequent bathing (e.g. once a week), especially in atopic children. They often suggest cleansing the skin on other occasions with a thin lotion, such as Cetaphil, instead of bathing. This material is applied to the skin and then wiped off with a soft cloth or tissue. Irritation may occur from these lotions, due to their propylene glycol preservatives
▲ of late, more physicians have recommended fairly frequent bathing (e.g. 3-4 times per week) but with emphasis on the application of lubricants (see below) immediately afterwards – this recommendation is generally more acceptable to the patient
▲ mild oilated or superfatted soaps are probably less drying than regular and deodorant bath soaps. Pure soaps efficiently remove oil and are drying. Oilated soaps remove less oil and may deposit some lubricant during bathing, so the user feels less 'squeaky clean' when finished

Dry Skin (Xerosis, Asteatosis, Winter Itch)

Treatment (continued)

● Lubricants (p.304) should be applied immediately after bathing, and perhaps once or twice daily to dry skin areas. Some physicians recommend application to wet skin, then gentle towel drying. However, brisk towelling followed by application of lubricant is probably as effective. Thin applications are sufficient and are more pleasant for the patient, which encourages compliance.
Lubricant selection is important. The ideal lubricant is a thick, *pure grease* (e.g. petrolatum), because of its occlusive properties. However, this is sticky and objectionable to most patients. An *oil* is more acceptable. This is still pure lubricant, but lighter in weight. Mineral oil, bath oils (usually mineral oil with surfactants) or vegetable oils (e.g. olive oil) are convenient and widely available. Also effective and usually acceptable are *water-in-oil thick creams*, such as hydrated petrolatum and aqua-aquaphor (Eucerin, Nivea). Plain, stiff, canned vegetable shortening (e.g. Crisco) is similar in texture and just as effective; however, it is unattractive to most patients! Thinner oil-in-water *vanishing creams* are pleasant to use but leave enough lubricant only for mild dry skin. Even less satisfactory are *lotions,* which contain mostly water and are sometimes drying to the skin.
　▲ other lubricants
　　■ urea cream 10%-20%. Urea is hydroscopic, draws water from the atmosphere and softens keratin. It is probably no better than thick lubricant, but it is thinner – often burns when applied to dry cracked skin
　　■ lactic acid lotion 5%. Lactic acid supposedly softens scale, but the effect is best in thick ointment – then the vehicle alone is adequate for dry skin
● Occlusion.
　▲ severe dry skin may be stubborn and not show improvement with lubricants. To obtain fast results, apply lubricant, then occlude with plastic wrap overnight, if possible. Plastic bags with the bottoms cut out can be used for legs and arms, or use a vinyl exercise suit. In the morning, bathe lightly and reapply lubricant.

> **Note:** This is useful as a diagnostic test and to convince the patient that itching is from dry skin. Cessation of itching when the skin is hydrated rules out metabolic causes (uremia, diabetes, internal malignancy) and scabies.

● Topical corticosteroids, in ointment base, are used if there is xerotic or nummular eczema (p.134).

Contact Dermatitis

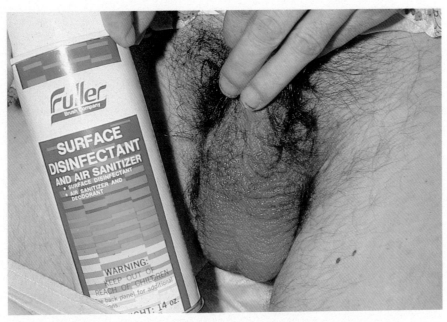

Chemical burn from disinfectant spray designed for use on countertops. Patient used it to treat pubic lice.

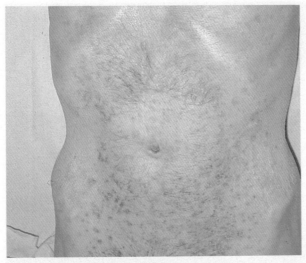

Allergic contact dermatitis from topical antihistamine "anti-itch cream".

Contact Dermatitis

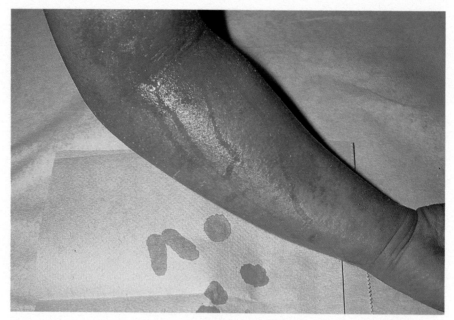

Acute weeping allergic contact dermatitis to topical anesthetic "anti-itch cream".

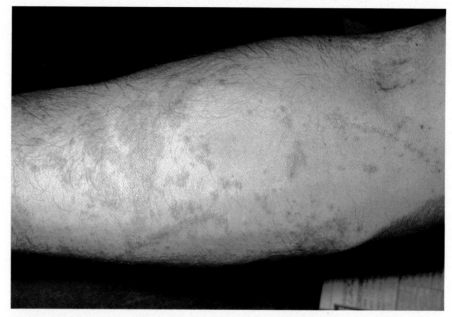

Typical linear allergic dermatitis from *Rhus* plant contact. Lines result from brushing of branches as person walks through underbrush.

Contact Dermatitis

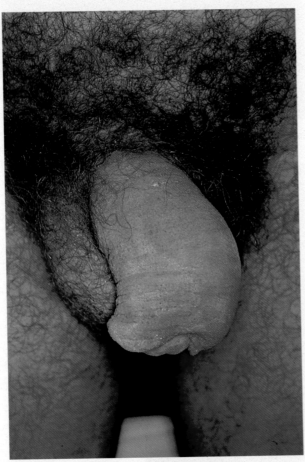

Rhus allergy. Antigen is carried on hands to seemingly protected sites.

Contact Dermatitis

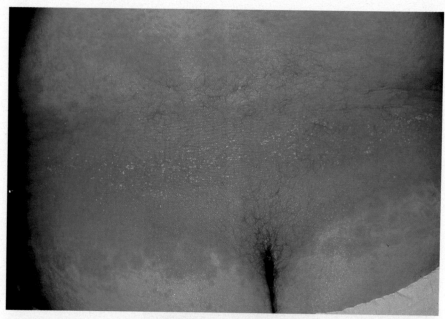

Rubber allergy is manifest as reaction to elastic in underwear and socks in this individual.

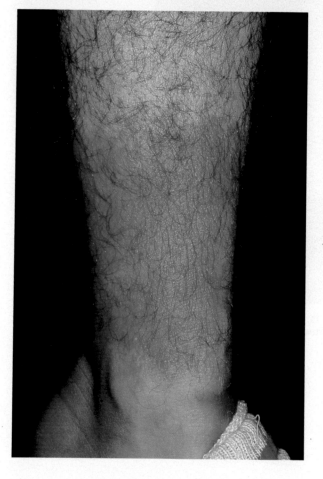

Contact Dermatitis

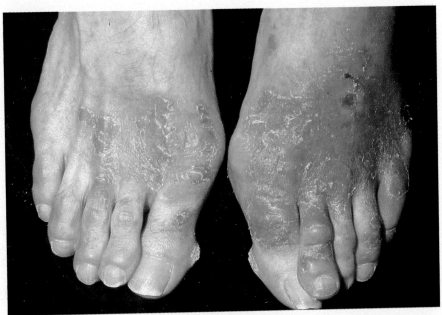

This patient is allergic to leather in his shoes. Earlier had reacted under a leather watchband.

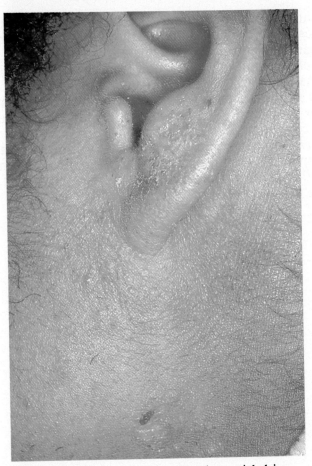

Contact dermatitis in person allergic to nickel in jewelry (earring).

Contact Dermatitis

Clinical

- There are two forms.
  - ▲ irritant
  - ▲ allergic
- Irritant contact dermatitis is the more common.
  - ▲ occasionally occurs acutely, with one exposure, as a chemical burn
  - ▲ more commonly occurs slowly with chronic exposure
    - ■ dryness, scaling, fissuring, mild inflammation
    - ■ may require years of exposure, or just days
    - ■ most common is hand dermatitis (p.97) from water and cleansers, or from lubricants and industrial chemicals
    - ■ also occurs on face, from cosmetics (p.22)
- Allergic contact dermatitis varies with cultures and environments
  - ▲ since sensitization is required it cannot occur on first exposure
    - ■ if exposure is constant patients can develop sensitization and react in as little as 10 days
    - ■ patients may become sensitized on first exposure, or only after many exposures, or never become sensitized, depending on unknown host factors and the potency of the antigen (*Rhus* plants sensitize 60%-80%, rubber sensitizes 0.01%)
  - ▲ for *Rhus* plant antigens (poison oak, poison ivy, mango rind), topical medications, and liquid antigens, reaction is often an acute vesicular dermatitis
  - ▲ for leather, rubber, and nickel, reaction is often a low-grade chronic dermatitis
  - ▲ the *first time* an individual reacts acutely, the rash usually starts 1-4 days after contact, new lesions may occur for 10 days, and the eruption commonly lasts 2-3 weeks
  - ▲ with *subsequent exposures* and reactions, the rash often starts earlier, new spots appear for only a few days, and resolution occurs in 7-10 days. However, the course may be prolonged, similar to the primary reaction

Contact Dermatitis

Clinical (continued)

> **Note:** the daily development of new lesions, especially in primary attacks, has given rise to the myth that scratching or blister fluid 'spreads' the reaction. In reality the antigen becomes fixed to skin proteins in about 15 minutes. Before that time, it can be washed off to prevent or diminish a reaction. After that time, the fixed antigen cannot be removed. Excess antigen can be washed off with water and soap (no special soap is necessary unless the antigen is a chemical or medication in an unusual base). Excess antigen can be spread by rubbing, until it becomes fixed. The new lesions developing days after the rash began just represent areas which were exposed to less antigen initially, or they represent a variable immunological response.

▲ diagnosis of allergic contact dermatitis is by history and by the presence of an eruption in patterns suggestive of the causative agent. Local factors determine the most common culprits. In the US
  ■ *Rhus* plant allergy is by far the most common, and often occurs in linear patterns from the brushing of stems against the skin during gardening or walking in underbrush, or on the face or genitals where hands deposit antigen
  ■ rubber sensitization occurs from shoes and under elastic (underwear)
  ■ leather dermatitis occurs from shoes and watchbands
  ■ nickel dermatitis occurs from jewelry
  ■ topical medicament dermatitis occurs from antibiotics, benzocaine, antihistamines, preservatives, and vitamin E

> **Note:** allergic contact dermatitis rarely occurs before 10 years of age. In children, contact dermatitis is usually irritant: wool and soap 'allergy' in children is always mildly irritant, usually in atopic children with low itch threshold (p.137). Allergic reactivity diminishes in the elderly.

● Patch testing is performed in persistent, puzzling cases. Refer the patient to a physician experienced in this procedure.

Contact Dermatitis

Treatment

- General
  - ▲ determine cause and suggest avoidance
  - ▲ for chronic irritant hand dermatitis, refer to p.97 for complete discussion
  - ▲ if substitution (e.g. leather, rubber) is difficult, refer the patient to an experienced dermatologist, who usually knows of sources of substitutes
  - ▲ in jewelry dermatitis, many patients can tolerate high-grade gold and silver, which is low in nickel. If they cannot, they may coat jewelry with urethane varnish for 'special occasions'. Clear nail polish is sometimes suggested but wears off more easily
- Mild to moderate dermatitis is treated with topical corticosteroids (p.311).
  - ▲ vehicle
    - ■ ointments for dry, scaly, and fissured dermatitis
    - ■ solutions for scalp or moist fold areas
    - ■ creams for most other areas
  - ▲ potency
    - ■ potent corticosteroid for inflamed, itchy, and/or thickened dermatitis
    - ■ mild to moderate potency for mild dermatitis or after the condition has improved with treatment with a potent preparation

Contact Dermatitis

Treatment (continued)

● Acute, vesicular, and/or widespread dermatitis (prototype is *Rhus* plant allergic dermatitis).
  ▲ a small area can be treated with soaks, baths, or compresses thrice daily for 10-20 minutes
    ■ tap water or astringent solutions (p.318)
    ■ follow soaks with potent topical corticosteroid
  ▲ widespread or severe dermatitis (edema of face or hands, difficulty in sleeping) usually responds only to *systemic corticosteroids*

Be sure to establish any history of glaucoma, hypertension, diabetes, and so on and monitor if appropriate. Warn the patient of possible gastric irritation and psychological side effects (depression, euphoria, depersonalization) during short-term use.

  ■ the oral route is as fast as the intramuscular; the benefit starts in 12-16 hours
  ■ for adults, dosage usually starts at 40mg-60mg of prednisone or equivalent taken in the morning. This may be taken with food to minimize gastrointestinal upset
  ■ if there is no benefit in 36-48 hours, increase the dose to 100mg daily for several days
  ■ corticosteroids help edema, redness, and itching, but often do not completely clear the rash **Note:** new, but mild, spots of rash may appear during treatment, especially in the primary attack. Warn patient of this to anticipate disappointment

Contact Dermatitis

Treatment (continued)

- ■ if *primary attack,* administer the initial dose for about five days, then slowly taper off over 2-3 weeks. If the medication is ceased too soon the rash will flare (since immune reaction is not complete)
- ■ if *repeated attack* (patient has had recent eruptions) it may be possible to taper off the treatment over 10-12 days.

> **Note:** if it has been some years (over 10) since the last attack, a new attack is more likely to behave like a primary attack and last three weeks.

- ▲ widespread lesions may also be treated with baths and soaks (p.317), especially if vesicular
- ▲ oral antihistamines or sedatives may be used at bedtime to aid sleep
- ● Desensitization is not effective or practical.
- ▲ in the US, over-the-counter oral *Rhus* preparations exist for supposed desensitization. They do not work and often cause gastrointestinal upset and perianal dermatitis
- ▲ experimental desensitization has been achieved but is difficult and must be continued as long as there is risk of allergen exposure

Psoriasis

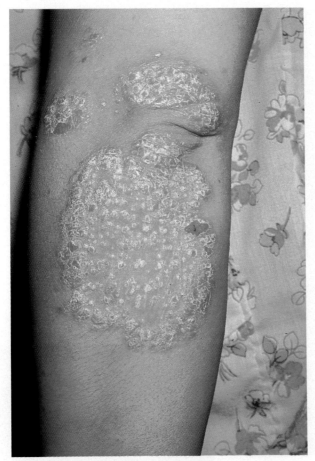

Typical bright red scaly plaque of psoriasis with silvery scale, over a joint.

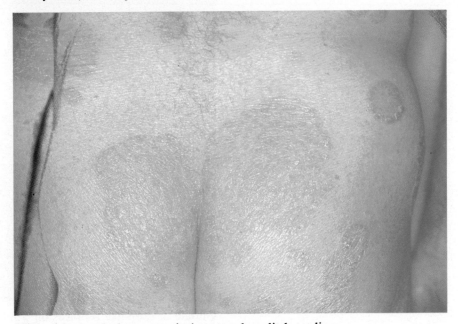

Mild widespread plaque psoriasis, may show little scaling.

Psoriasis

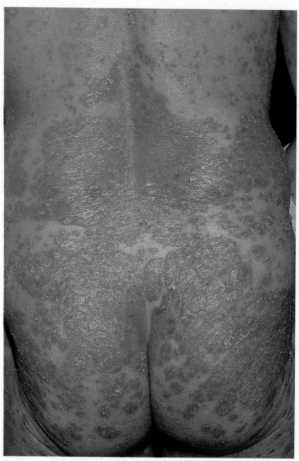

Acute angry flare of psoriasis.

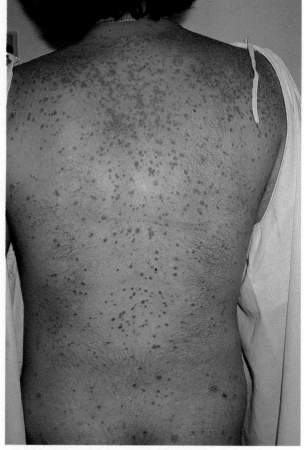

Guttate or drop-like psoriasis on trunk. Eruption
often follows a streptococcal pharyngitis.

Psoriasis

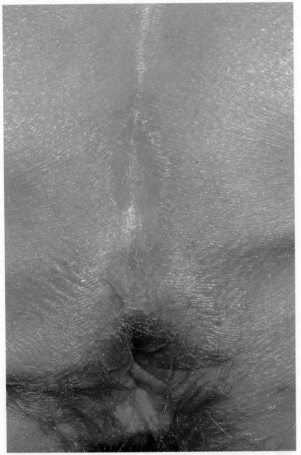

"Intragluteal pinking" is a common stigma of psoriasis.

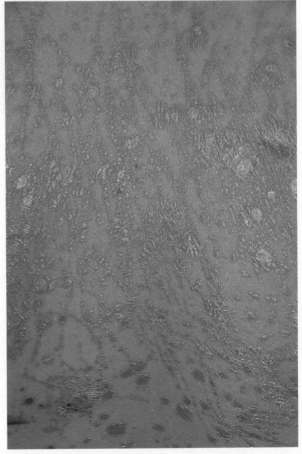

"Koebner phenomenon" or development of psoriasis at sites of trauma, in this case scratching.

Psoriasis

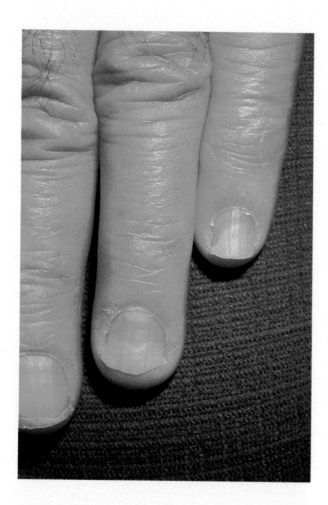

Nail changes in psoriasis may include onycholysis (splitting of distal edge of nail plate from the nail bed), accumulation of sub-ungual debris, and pitting of the nail surface.

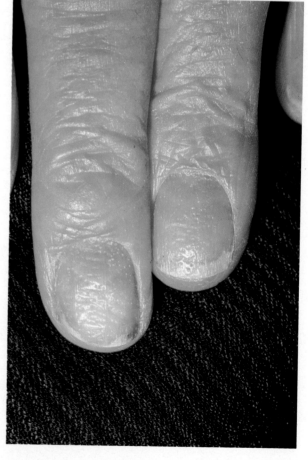

Psoriasis

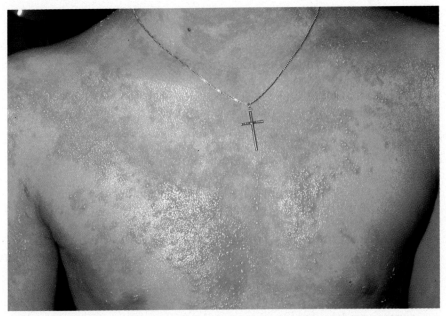

Acute widespread pustular psoriasis. Often the eruption is bright red with bizarre patterns and pustules predominantly at the margins.

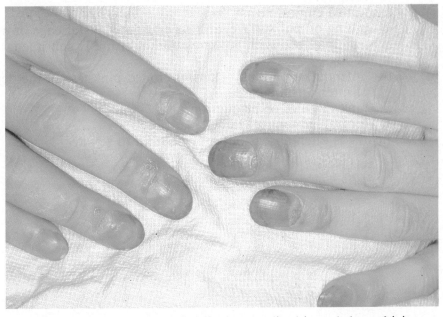

Acute psoriatic arthritis, typically affecting the distal interphalangeal joints. The nearby nails are almost always involved.

Psoriasis

Clinical

- Psoriasis is an inherited constitutional ability of skin to form psoriatic lesions.
  - ▲ onset is usually young adulthood, but range is from infancy to the elderly
  - ▲ usually waxes and wanes over the years
  - ▲ expression of lesions may be influenced by environmental factors
    - ■ sun and humidity suppresses
    - ■ injury to skin can induce lesions at the site of injury ('Koebner reaction')
    - ■ streptococcal pharyngitis may trigger a flare
    - ■ in some patients emotional upset triggers a flare
  - ▲ pathophysiology
    - ■ epidermal cells proliferate too fast and pile up
    - ■ abnormal keratin is produced which forms loosely-adherent scales
    - ■ dermal inflammation occurs
- The condition appears as widespread bright pink plaques surmounted by loose, silvery scale.
  - ▲ location
    - ■ over joints and extensor surfaces of extremities
    - ■ on trunk, especially lower back and buttocks
    - ■ palms and soles (p.102)
    - ■ scalp (p.4)
  - ▲ associated clinical signs
    - ■ pitting of nail surface, and separation of distal edge of nail from nail bed with accumulation of crumbly sub-ungual debris
    - ■ 'intergluteal pinking' – almost eroded pinkness in the depths of intergluteal crease
    - ■ pink macules or plaques on penis
    - ■ geographic tongue (rarely)
  - ▲ itching is often absent but may be mild to severe

Psoriasis

Clinical (continued)

● Uncommon clinical variants.
  ▲ guttate (drop-like)
    ■ many small lesions scattered profusely over trunk and extremities
    ■ scalp and nails often spared
    ■ often follows streptococcal pharyngitis
    ■ quite responsive to therapy and often resolves completely in a few months
  ▲ inverse (flexural)
    ■ occurs in fold areas such as axilla, groin, and under breasts
    ■ because of moist occlusion usually has no scale
  ▲ pustular
    ■ almost eroded bright red areas with scattered superficial pustules
    ■ not infected; pustules are sterile
    ■ painful or burning discomfort
    ■ usually accompanied by fever and malaise; may lead to cachexia and death
    ■ responds poorly to therapy and signals low likelihood of future mild psoriasis
  ▲ erythroderma
    ■ bright erythema of most or all of skin surface
    ■ disturbs temperature regulation (hypothermia), and doubles or triples demand on cardiac output
    ■ responds poorly to therapy and signals low likelihood of future mild psoriasis
● Systemic signs and symptoms.
  ▲ psoriatic arthritis
    ■ destructive arthritis of distal interphalangeal joints, spine, and large joints
    ■ rheumatoid factor negative
    ■ may occur with no, or only subtle, skin signs, but nail changes are usually present
  ▲ in severe widespread psoriasis it is possible to see
    ■ benign lymphadenopathy
    ■ fever, chills and hypothermia
    ■ increased cardiac demand and heart failure
    ■ increased levels of uric acid, decreased serum levels of iron and albumin

Psoriasis

Treatment

Since psoriasis is inborn it can be suppressed but not cured. It may stay in spontaneous or induced remission for weeks, months, or years. Therapies are many and attack the disease in different ways. A summary of the agents and their effects follows.

Agent	Probably kerato-lytic	Suppress epidermal prolifera-tion	Anti-inflamma-tory	Improve arthritis	Remission after therapy
Topical salicylic acid	+				0
Tar	+	+	?		0
Ultraviolet light (UVL)		+	±		++
Tar and UVL	+	++	+		+++
Anthralin (dithranol)	+	+	±		++
Topical corticosteroids		+	+++		0
Topical psoralen & UVL		+	?		++
Oral psoralen and long wave UVL (PUVA)		++	++	?	±
Systemic antimetabolites		++		++	0

● Complete clearing of psoriasis is often not achieved, so the physician and patient must have realistic goal: diminish scale, itching, and cosmetic deficit.
● See p.4 and p.97 for treatment of scalp and palmar psoriasis.
● See Patient Guide page 291

Psoriasis

Treatment (continued)

- Mild to moderate psoriasis.
  - ▲ topical corticosteroids (p.311)
    - ■ potent ones usually necessary
    - ■ mild ones for face and genitals, and for maintenance
    - ■ occlusion (p.311) for stubborn areas (shower cap, plastic bags, vinyl suit, steroid-impregnated tape)
  - ▲ salicylic acid/keratolytics (p.323)
    - ■ ointment base or propylene glycol gel most effective
    - ■ occlusion enhances effect
    - ■ often in combination with corticosteroids
    - ■ use intermittently when scaling resolved, to avoid irritation
  - ▲ tars (p.323)
    - ■ usually as adjunct to corticosteroid
    - ■ judicious exposure to sunlight enhances effect
    - ■ do not occlude. May induce irritant and infectious folliculitis
  - ▲ anthralin (p.324)
    - ■ used alone or in combination with ultraviolet light is fairly effective, however, it is difficult to administer because of irritation. Should be used only by experienced practitioner.
- Severe plaque psoriasis.
  - ▲ the treatments discussed above for milder forms may be effective, especially if occlusion is used. If they are not, then much more complex, expensive, time-consuming, or risky therapy must be attempted – refer to a dermatologist if possible
  - ▲ artificial ultraviolet light (UVL) in sunburn wavelengths (UVB)
    - ■ used in conjunction with tar or methoxalen ointment 0.1%
    - ■ total-body 'light-box' most convenient
    - ■ twice or thrice weekly treatments in office
    - ■ the patient may construct or purchase 'box' for home use
    - ■ maintenance treatment should be performed a few times a month after 2-4 weeks of intensive treatment

Psoriasis

Treatment (continued)

▲ admission to hospital, or a day care center (patient spends eight hours each day at center)
  - ■ hospitalization alone often has great benefit, possibly by reducing tension and assuring compliance
  - ■ 'Goeckerman' treatment of twice daily tar baths, tar ointments, and UVB
  - ■ remission is often achieved in 2-3 weeks and lasts 2-6 months or longer

▲ PUVA – oral psoralen and long-wave UVL (UVA)
  - ■ should be administered only by highly-trained individuals in offices
  - ■ excellent response, but quick relapse if not given 1-4 times a month
  - ■ long-term safety unknown (still under investigation in the US)

▲ antimetabolites
  - ■ use only if other treatments have failed or cannot be used
  - ■ methotrexate is most effective and safest
  - ■ should be administered only by experienced practitioner
  - ■ perform physical examination, routine laboratory screen, and liver biopsy. Give 5mg methotrexate orally or intramuscularly, check white blood cell response in two days. If white cell count remains normal then give 15mg-30mg methotrexate orally or intramuscularly weekly. Psoriasis begins to improve in 2-4 weeks and the maximum benefit is received in 6-10 weeks. Taper off by 2.5mg or 5mg doses to find the lowest effective maintenance dose (often 10mg-15mg). Settle for less than total eradication of lesions. Check white cell count weekly or bi-weekly until maintenance dose is reached, then check monthly for white cell count drop. Every 4-6 months check liver enzyme levels. Liver biopsy should be repeated after total dose of about 2g. Patient should stop alcohol consumption during therapy to minimize risk of cirrhosis. Do not use methotrexate in an alcoholic patient or a person with liver disease
    Note: see official Guidelines of American Academy of Dermatology in the Journal of the American Academy of Dermatology Feb. 1982, p.145

● Pustular psoriasis and erythroderma require immediate referral to a dermatologist. Admission to hospital and intensive topical therapy are usually required.

● Psoriatic arthritis.
  - ▲ standard arthritis therapies often of benefit
  - ▲ if they fail, methotrexate usually effective

Pityriasis Rosea

Two typical cases of pityriasis rosea, with scattered
scaly oval lesions on the trunk. Large lesion is the
"herald patch".

Pityriasis Rosea

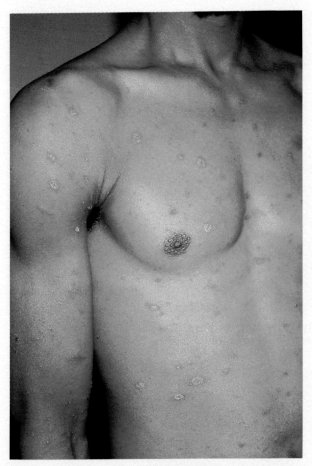

Quite inflamed and scaly lesions. Axis of ovals are
along fold lines radiating from the axilla.

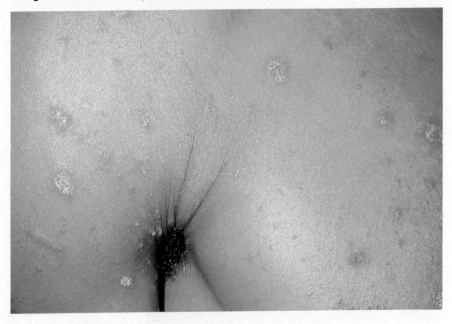

Pityriasis Rosea

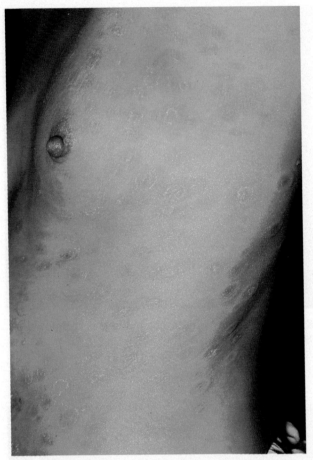

Large annular lesions are somewhat unusual in
pityriasis rosea.

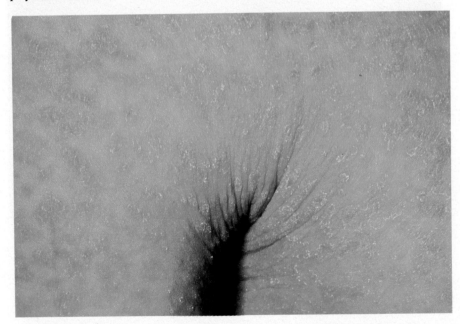

Markedly inflamed and scaly lesions, again showing radiation along fold
lines from axilla.

Pityriasis Rosea

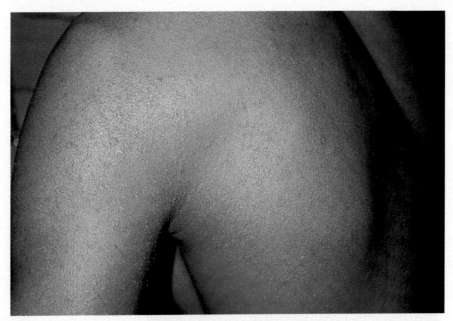

In dark-skinned persons, pityriasis rosea is often not red and is composed of small papules. Patterning along fold lines is still evident.

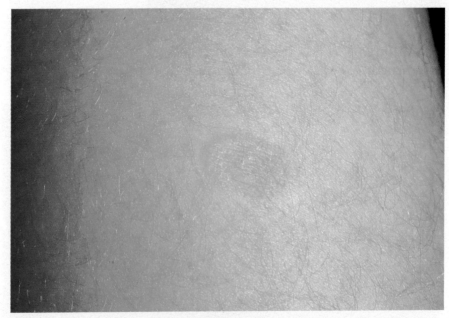

Typical lesion is a faint pink oval with collarette of scale well inside the border. Patient had a total of only three lesions.

Pityriasis Rosea

Clinical

> There is a typical age group, lesion appearance and pattern for this disease, but atypical cases are common. Experience teaches the broad range of possibilities.

● A large (1cm to 10cm) 'herald patch' occurs first in 50% of patients.
● Numerous smaller patches appear over the next few days.
  ▲ lesions
    ■ oval, fawn-colored (pink-tan) with lighter or darker centers
    ■ macular, to slightly elevated, to quite papular (especially in the dark-skinned)

> ■ characteristically, fine collarette of scale inside the pink border–scale is peripherally attached and pointing inward, so to lift scale with fingernail one must scratch from the center of the lesion outward to get under the free edge. This is in contrast to tinea and other annular eruptions where scale is at advancing edge, not behind it, and is randomly attached.

  ▲ location
    ■ usually trunk, proximal parts of extremities
    ■ spares face, hands and feet
    ■ atypical patterns include just flexural (axillae, groin, neck), face, and acral (hands and feet)
  ▲ pattern
    ■ oval patches oriented on lines radiating from flexures and in 'Christmas tree' pattern from spine
  ▲ duration
    ■ typically six weeks, but may last eight to ten weeks, and rarely three months
    ■ eruption spreads and increases markedly the first two or three weeks, and more slowly thereafter
  ▲ itching
    ■ usually mild and intermittent
    ■ occasionally severe, especially in the more papular cases
● Systemic symptoms.
  ▲ mild malaise has been reported as a prodrome of, or accompanying, the rash, but true association is questionable
● Idiopathic.
  ▲ virus suspected because
    ■ characteristic age group (young adults, but seen in children and the middle-aged)
    ■ seasonal and temporal 'epidemics' in large populations
    ■ remits after set course
    ■ rarely recurs
  ▲ against a viral etiology
    ■ virus cannot be recovered
    ■ is not contagious in family, school, and work groups

Pityriasis Rosea

Treatment

● General.
  ▲ there is no 'cure', and disease runs its course
  ▲ patients require education (See Patient Guide, p.286) and reassurance
    ■ it will go away by itself
    ■ the face and arms are usually not affected
    ■ it will not leave scars
    ■ it is not contagious
    ■ internal organs are not affected
    ■ it rarely recurs
● Itching may be treated by
  ▲ antihistamines (p.321)
    ■ at bedtime to allow sleep
    ■ usually too sedative for daytime use
  ▲ cool baths (colloidal oatmeal) or shake lotions may be somewhat soothing
  ▲ topical corticosteroids
    ■ potent ones may relieve itching of individual patches
  ▲ systemic corticosteroids
    ■ a high dose (40mg-60mg of prednisone) may be necessary to control itching for the most symptomatic first two or three weeks
  ▲ ultraviolet light (or sunlight)
    ■ an erythema (peeling) dose often relieves itching for a few days, and may hasten resolution of lesions
    ■ repeated treatments are often required

Lichen Planus

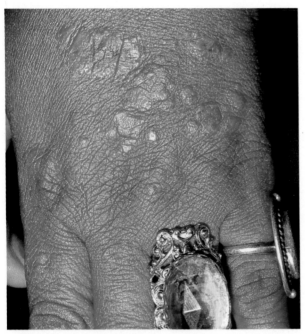

Typical lichen planus lesions: polygonal, scaly, flat-topped, and violaceous.

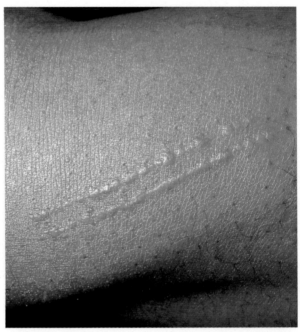

"Koebner phenomenon", or development of lesions in areas of trauma.

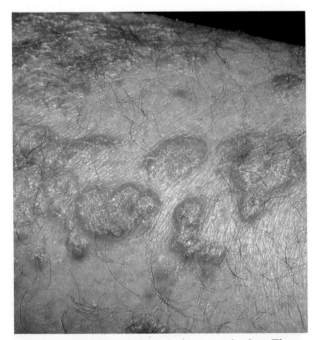

Early hypertrophic or thick lesions on the leg. Fine white etched lines on the surface are Wickham's striae.

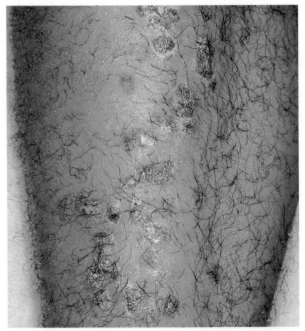

Dry, chronic hypertrophic lesions, present two years.

Lichen Planus

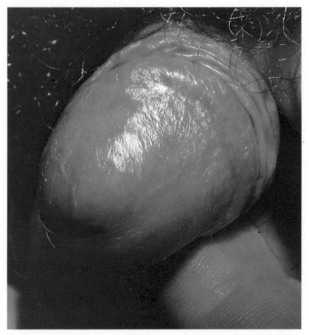 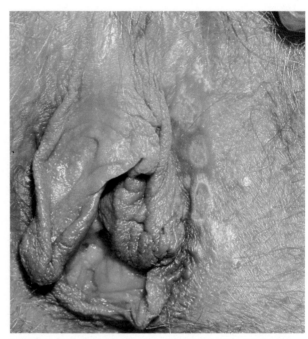

The genitals are a common site for lichen planus. The lesions are usually annular with a light-colored border.

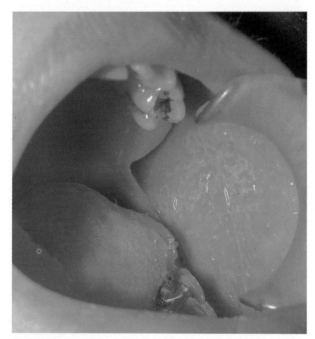 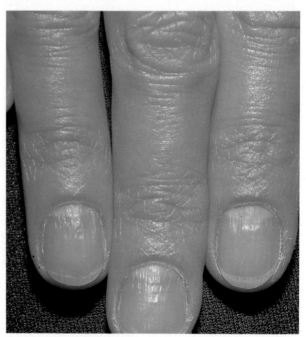

Oral lesions are usually on the buccal mucosa and are lace-like.

Nail involvement is not uncommon. The nail plate is thinned and has longitudinal ltriations.

Lichen Planus

Clinical
● Lichen planus is an uncommon eruption of small, polygonal, flat-topped violet-colored papules.
  ▲ often confined to wrists, ankles, and groin, but may be generalized
    ■ genitals commonly involved
  ▲ papules are 2mm-15mm, usually with shiny surface due to slight scale
    ■ on shins may be hypertrophic, with thick, verrucous scale
    ■ they quickly become hyperpigmented and leave a deep pigment when healed
● Oral involvement is common, and sometimes the only manifestation.
  ▲ lacey white or light grey reticulate pattern on buccal mucosa
  ▲ occasionally persistent, painful erosions
● Idiopathic.
● The condition usually lasts 6-24 months, except hypertrophic and oral lesions, which may last longer.
● Itching ranges in intensity from absent to severe.
  ▲ usually worst during first few weeks when erupting, then milder after stabilized

Treatment
● No treatment shortens the course of the disease; it just relieves itching or improves the cosmetic appearance.
● Topical corticosteroids are the most common treatment.
  ▲ potent ones (p.315) are usually required (except for the genitals)
  ▲ occlusion or intralesional corticosteroids are often needed for hypertrophic lesions
● Systemic corticosteroids may be used for a few weeks.
  ▲ if there is severe itching (interfering with work or sleep) during the eruptive phase
    ■ 30mg-40mg of prednisone once a day for an adult
    ■ intramuscular depot corticosteroid such as triamcinolone acetonide 40mg-60mg may be another treatment
● Oral antihistamines (p.321) may be administered as sedatives and antipruritics at bedtime.
  ▲ usually too sedative for daytime use
● Oral lichen planus.
  ▲ no treatment if asymptomatic
  ▲ corticosteroid in carboxymethylcellulose, gelatin and pectin (Orabase) twice daily
  ▲ intralesional corticosteroid (p.313) if stubborn
  ▲ vitamin A acid (tretinoin) gel 0.01% twice daily recently reported to be effective

Urticaria (Hives)

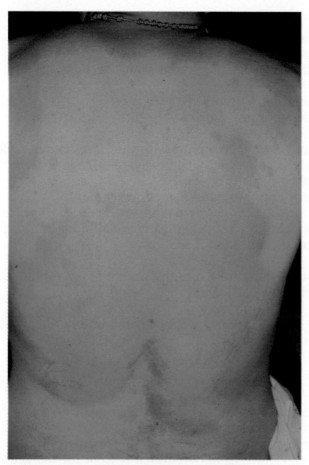

Huge wheals in patient allergic to penicillin.

Small confluent hives in person reacting to unknown illicit drug. Normal skin is the light area.

Urticaria (Hives)

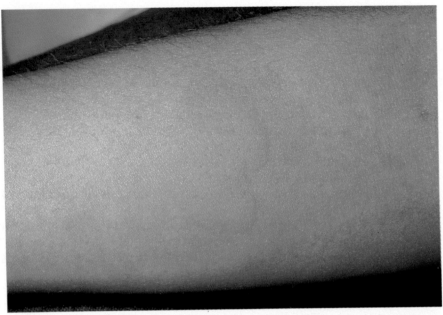

Wheal induced in clinic with artificial ultraviolet light in a person with solar urticaria.

Clinical

- Urticaria consists of pink edematous papules and plaques with normal overlying epidermis.
  - ▲ lesions may have blanched halos, or be so tensely edematous as to be blanched themselves
  - ▲ randomly scattered over body, including the face and scalp
  - ▲ edema of lips, hands, and feet is common
  - ▲ no one lesion lasts over 24 hours, but new ones may occur
- Itching is usually severe, but may be mild or absent. Severe edema of face, hands, or feet may be painful.
- Usually the condition is of abrupt onset.
  - ▲ in *acute* hives reaches peak in 1-3 days, fades in 7-21 days
  - ▲ in *chronic* hives waxes and wanes for months or years
  - ▲ there may be recurrent attacks separated by months or years

Urticaria (Hives)

Clinical (continued)

- Causes.
  - ▲ in *acute* hives cause is found 20%-30% of time, most commonly
    - ■ drugs, inoculations, foods or food additives, intravenous radio-opaque contrast medium, hymenoptera stings
    - ■ internal acute infections (usually bacterial), or inflammations (rheumatoid flare, inflammatory bowel disease, and so on)
    - ■ marked emotional tension may precipitate (cholinergic urticaria) or exacerbate hives
  - ▲ in *chronic* hives (over six weeks) the cause is found in less than 5% of cases
    - ■ drugs (including vitamins, laxatives, mints, toothpaste and other non-medicinal substances)
    - ■ chronic occult bacterial infections (sinusitis, tooth abscess and so on)
  - ▲ food as cause of hives is controversial
    - ■ infants may flush and urticate when introduced to formula and new foods, but this reaction ceases by one year of age, when digestive enzymes mature, and re-exposure later in life does not result in hives
    - ■ strawberries and certain seafood in large quantities can induce hives by a non-immunologic mechanism. Future consumption often does not produce hives
    - ■ true allergy can occur to seafood, nuts, fruits, and other foods
    - ■ much study has been done on reactions to naturally occurring salicylates in food, and salicylate, tartrazine, and benzoate additives, but their real role is undetermined
  - ▲ certain chemicals can degranulate mast cells by non-immunologic means and may worsen hives, so their intake during an attack of hives should be avoided
    - ■ aspirin (definitely), and the chemically related tartrazine food dye (controversial)
    - ■ morphine, codeine
    - ■ reserpine, polymyxin B, alcohol
- Special clinical types of hives.
  - ▲ cholinergic urticaria, mediated by acetylcholine, not histamine, is non-immunologic
    - ■ young adults
    - ■ evanescent papules on the upper trunk
    - ■ triggered by heat, exercise, emotion
  - ▲ physical urticarias, immune reaction triggered by physical exposures – rare, familial or sporadic
    - ■ cold
    - ■ pressure
    - ■ sunlight
  - ▲ dermographia ('skin writing') is the production of hives by light rubbing or trauma – non-immunologic – familial or sporadic, congenital or acquired

Urticaria (Hives)

Treatment

● General. Triggering factors should be identified and removed, but
the patient should be told that such identification is unlikely.
Frustration and dissatisfaction commonly occur and tax the doctor-
patient relationship.

▲ obtain a careful history, particularly of medications, vitamins,
tonics, digestive mints, and other non-prescription cultural
remedies. Ask about stings, inoculations, and radiographic tests.
Inquire about diet fads (e.g. kelp, flavoring agents). Review all
systems with an eye toward occult bacterial infections. Ask
about emotional tension – repeat these inquiries at each visit

▲ laboratory tests are usually unproductive but certain ones are
advocated by various investigators. Those usually recommended
are

■ complete blood count, sedimentation rate
■ urinalysis
■ liver function tests
■ ear, nose and throat examination and sinus X-ray
examination
■ dental examination, including X-ray

▲ as a last resort, a 5-day trial where the patient abstains from
food except water, one type of meat, one vegetable, and one
type of starch will rule out dietary factors. If the hives subside
then add a new food every two days until the rash recurs. Often
the rash continues when the food is again removed, confusing
the issue further

● Acute anaphylactic urticaria.

> The treatment of acute urticaria associated with hypotension,
> shock, and bronchospasm is outside the scope of this book. In
> addition to the following measures one should start an
> intravenous drip, establish an airway, and administer
> subcutaneous or intravenous epinephrine (adrenaline) and
> possibly intravenous antihistamines, corticosteroids, and
> vasoconstrictors. This procedure should be closely monitored
> with blood gas determinations, cardiograms, measurement of
> urine output, and other procedures.

Urticaria (Hives)

Treatment (continued)

- Topical therapy.
  - ▲ cool baths or compresses often give temporary relief and reduce inflammation. Colloidal oatmeal baths are often particularly soothing
  - ▲ calamine or other shake lotions may give temporary relief. The addition of menthol or phenol may give added benefit
- Systemic agents are usually required.
  - ▲ epinephrine (adrenaline) 1:1000, 0.3ml-0.5ml subcutaneously for acute episodes, to give fast relief
  - ▲ antihistamines (p.321)
    - ■ effect starts 45-60 minutes after oral dose; reaches peak in two hours. Response from intramuscular dose is only slightly faster
    - ■ choose one and give the dose which induces no more than mild drowsiness. If ineffective, switch to one from another family and keep trying until a satisfactory one is found
    - ■ give every six hours until hives subside – may give higher dose hourly. Often one morning dose only is adequate, especially if hives occur mostly in the latter part of the day (as commonly occurs)
    - ■ hydroxyzine seems particularly effective in cholinergic urticaria
    - ■ warn patient about risk of operating automobiles or dangerous machinery while taking antihistamines
  - ▲ corticosteroids
    - ■ often have little impact on acute hives but help reduce edema of face, hands, and feet
    - ■ if all else fails in chronic urticaria, corticosteroids may induce remission

Erythema Multiforme

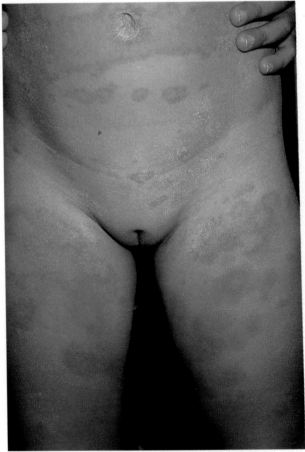

Scattered annular lesions of acute erythema
multiforme in a child with *Mycoplasma* pneumonia.
Target lesions were present on the palms and soles.

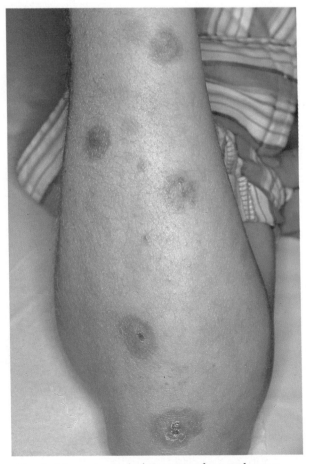

Classic iris or target lesions secondary to herpes
simplex of lips.

Erythema Multiforme

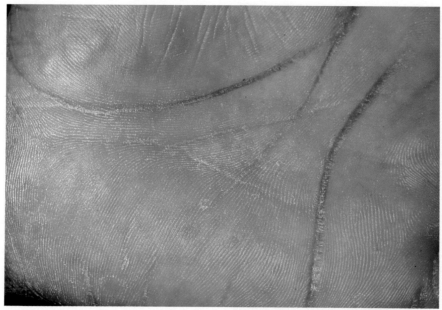

Typical annular lesions secondary to herpes simplex of the genitals.

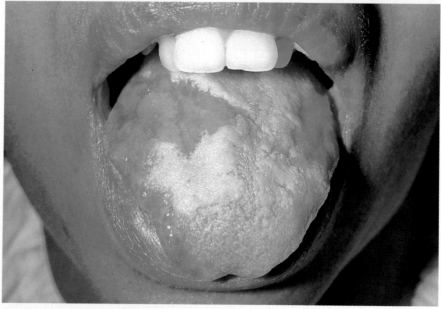

Idiopathic recurrent oral erythema multiforme.

Erythema Multiforme

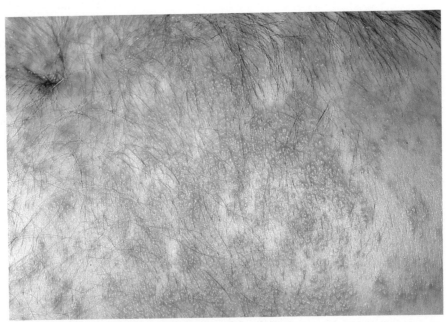

Generalized idiopathic erythema multiforme with tiny vesicles in centers of many lesions. The patient felt well and had no mucous membrane lesions.

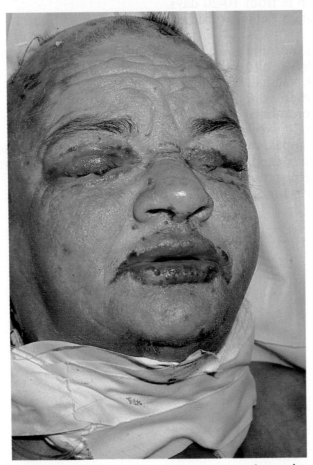

Stevens-Johnson syndrome secondary to phenytoin. This was the patient's second episode caused by the same drug.

Erythema Multiforme

Clinical

- Classically, erythema multiforme consists of 'iris' or 'target' lesions (concentric rings of shades of red) on the palms, soles, genitals, mouth, and extensor surfaces of arms and legs. However, lesions can be of many types ('multiforme'), such as morbilliform, large patches of erythema, or long-lasting wheals (true hives always resolve in less than 24 hours). Occasionally the lesions are vesicular or bullous.
  - ▲ may be localized or widespread
  - ▲ mild to severe itching, or tenderness
- The cause is presumed to be immunologic reaction to various antigens.
  - ▲ commonly (in US up to 80%) viral or mycobacterial
    - ■ most commonly herpes simplex, then may recur with each attack
    - ■ also atypical *(Mycoplasma)* pneumonia, and influenza viruses
  - ▲ occasionally a reaction to drugs. Nearly any type can be the culprit, but often reported to sulfa drugs, thiazides, anticonvulsants, and barbiturates
  - ▲ frequently (up to 30%) idiopathic
- The usual duration is from 10-20 days.
- Oral lesions are often bullous or eroded. May occur without cutaneous lesions.
- Stevens-Johnson syndrome is erythema multiforme with systemic illness (fever, malaise), and significant mucous membrane involvement (oral, vaginal, conjunctival).
  - ▲ rash usually severe, often vesicular, but may be mild
  - ▲ occurs most commonly in children
  - ▲ duration often 3-6 weeks
  - ▲ mortality rate appears to be 10%-20% without therapy, due to widespread skin denudation, fluid loss, infection, and inability to eat (because of oral lesions)
  - ▲ triggered by drugs more often than by infection, but may be idiopathic

Erythema Multiforme

Treatment

- General.
  - ▲ question and examine the patient for herpes, *Mycoplasma* pneumonia, other infections, and drugs (including street drugs)
- Mild to moderate erythema multiforme.
  - ▲ potent topical corticosteroids may relieve mild lesions
  - ▲ the administration of oral corticosteroids (e.g. prednisone 40mg-60mg) for a few days relieves severe itching and discomfort
  - ▲ oral antihistamines (p.321) may be administered at bedtime to aid sleep if itching is severe
- Stevens-Johnson syndrome.

Admission to hospital and supportive measures (see below) are mandatory. A major controversy surrounds the use of systemic corticosteroids. Once standard therapy and life-saving, the use of systemic corticosteroids now has been shown to prolong time in hospital and increase morbidity, while not reducing mortality. Feelings are strong on each side. A high dose for a few days relieves the pain of edema of oral, palm, and sole lesions.

- ▲ admit patient to hospital under care of experienced practitioner
- ▲ establish intravenous infusion and closely monitor fluid and electrolyte levels
- ▲ keep oral and skin lesions clean and monitor for infection by culture. Fevers which accompany the disease make clinical evaluation difficult
- ▲ scrupulous ocular and oral hygiene necessary to prevent infection and residual scarring (microstomia, synechia of eyelids)
- ▲ patient may undergo several febrile relapses over a two to four week course

Miliaria (Heat Rash)

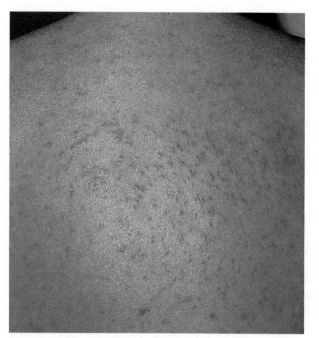

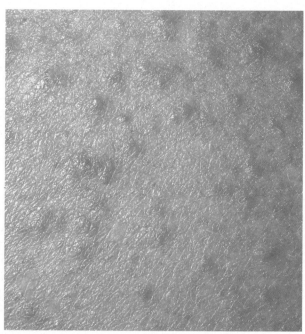

Typical miliaria rubra, or heat rash: scattered discrete edematous bright red papules.

This woman sat in a hairdresser's chair for three hours. The vinyl upholstery prevented the escape of sweat, but her cotton brassiere absorbed it.

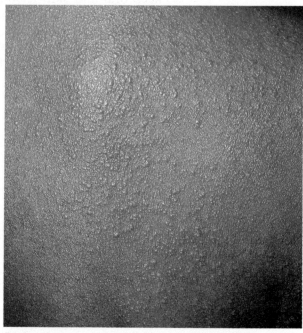

Redness may not be evident in dark-skinned people. Papules are so edematous as to appear almost vesicular.

Miliaria (Heat Rash)

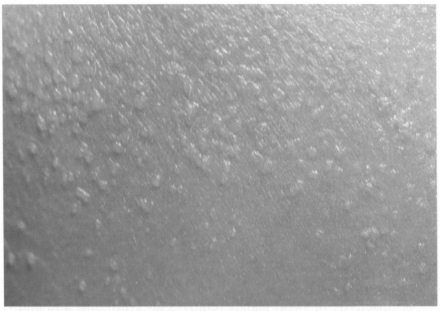

Miliaria crystallina: tiny vesicles just under the keratin layer cause no inflammation or itching.

Clinical

- Miliaria results from the rupture of sweat ducts. Sweating pumps irritating sweat through these defects, inducing lesions and symptoms.
- Miliaria rubra ('prickly heat') consists of bright red punctate macules and papules clustered in susceptible areas.
  - ▲ occasionally papules are so succulent as to appear vesicular or pustular
  - ▲ occurs on areas of occlusion under non-absorbent clothes, under folds of skin, or at points of skin contact with non-absorbent upholstery – common examples are
    - ■ on the faces of infants, when saliva-soaked skin is pressed against plastic mattress covers
    - ■ on domes of buttocks and back in drivers and office workers sitting on plastic-covered seats
    - ■ under plastic bathing suits and non-absorbent tight clothing
  - ▲ more common in humid weather, not just hot weather
    - ■ new residents may acclimatize after several days
  - ▲ in patients where the condition is widespread, sweating may be so disrupted as to produce heat stroke

Miliaria (Heat Rash)

Clinical (continued)

- ▲ itching is often prominent
  - ■ an insistent prickling occurs when sweating is induced, and diminishes as the temperature drops
- ▲ healing occurs in a few days if sweating is minimized, and acclimatization occurs
  - ■ for a few weeks thereafter the affected sites may relapse upon exposure to mild provoking conditions
- ● Miliaria crystallina consists of tiny (1mm) thin-roofed, clear drop-like vesicles.
  - ▲ the vesicles are not inflamed or red
  - ▲ they rupture easily because of the thin roof
  - ▲ they are not symptomatic

Treatment
- ● General.
  - ▲ inactivity of sweat glands removes all symptoms and allows healing
    - ■ only environmental control achieves this
    - ■ no medication stops sweat gland activity (antiperspirants [p.324] work by blocking sweat ducts)
    - ■ absorption or removal of sweat from the surface of the skin is of no benefit
- ● Healing occurs if sweating is avoided for several days.
  - ▲ this is best done in a cool, dry environment
    - ■ eight hours of each 24 hours are often adequate
  - ▲ reduce physical activity
  - ▲ avoid occlusive clothes and furniture
- ● Topical corticosteroids.
  - ▲ may reduce inflammation and itching
  - ▲ use non-occlusive lotion base, not ointment

Secondary Syphilis

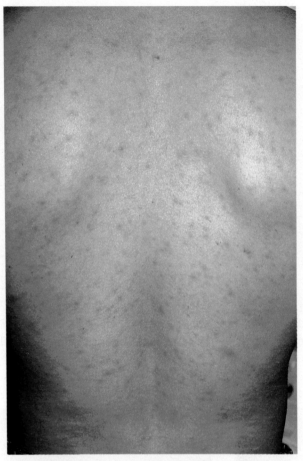

Generalized rash of secondary syphilis. VDRL was
1:512. Often the lesions are fewer, larger, flatter,
and scaly.

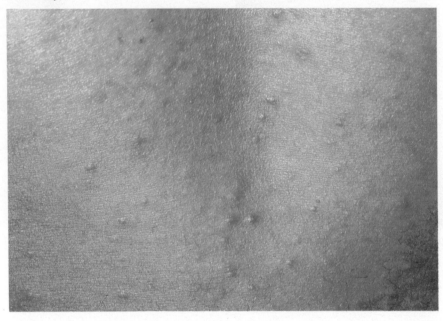

Secondary Syphilis

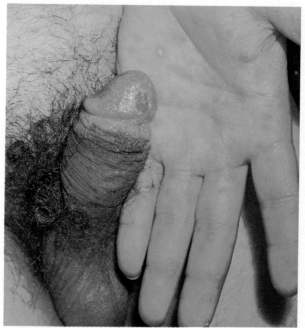

"Ham-colored" macules of the palm. Primary chancre is still present.

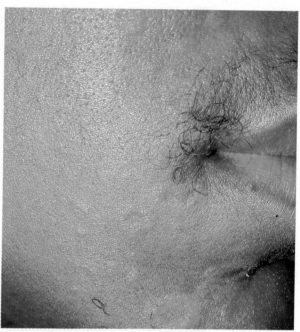

Facial lesions are often round ("nickel and dime lesions") and grouped around orifices.

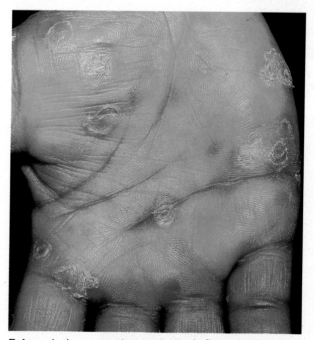

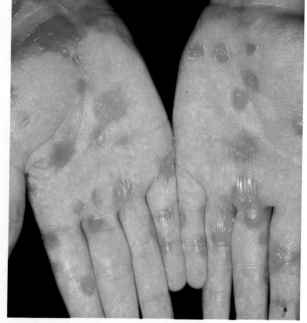

Palmar lesions may be markedly inflamed, but often are dry and keratotic.

Secondary Syphilis

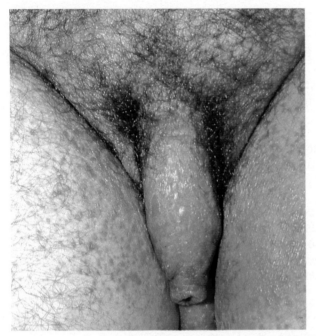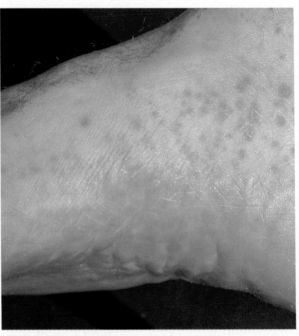

The genitals and fold areas are common sites of secondary syphilis, as in this case in which the soles were also involved. The VDRL was 1:128.

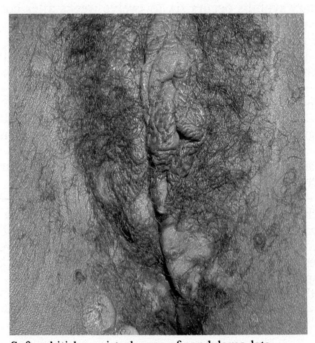

Soft, whitish, moist plaques of condyloma lata.

Secondary Syphilis

Clinical
- Rash.
  - ▲ lesions ranging in quantity from a few to many are most frequently found on
    - ■ palms and soles, often straddling crease lines
    - ■ face, especially at the angle of mouth, eyes, and nose
    - ■ genitals (p.74)
    - ■ trunk
    - ■ mouth ('mucous patches')
  - ▲ the lesions have the following appearance
    - ■ flat or slightly elevated
    - ■ smooth or scaly
    - ■ ham-colored to dusky red, sometimes with darker centers
    - ■ hyperkeratotic, on palms and soles
    - ■ almost never vesicular or oozing
  - ▲ they are usually not pruritic, but may itch severely
  - ▲ there is a patchy 'moth-eaten' alopecia of scalp and beard
- Systemic symptoms.
  - ▲ fever and malaise
  - ▲ sore throat
  - ▲ non-painful (usually) generalized adenopathy
  - ▲ rarely
    - ■ syphilitic hepatitis
    - ■ bone and joint pain
- Secondary syphilis occurs six to twelve weeks after contact.
  - ▲ the primary chancre may still be present
  - ▲ the rash lasts four to six weeks without treatment
    - ■ it may recur two or three times over the next two years
  - ▲ syphilis is highly contagious in the secondary form

Examiner should wear gloves.

- Serologic tests – non-specific and fluorescent treponemal antibody (FTA)
  - ▲ in *secondary* syphilis, the results of both tests should be positive
  - ▲ titer is high (over 1:8) in non-specific test

If the non-specific test result is negative, the cause is the *prozone phenomenon:* the titer is so high that it will not precipitate in test plates at low dilutions, which are the only ones used in screening tests. If secondary syphilis is strongly suspected, send another blood sample and ask for 'prozone test', or examination at higher dilutions.

Secondary Syphilis

Clinical (continued)

● Darkfield examination is positive for primary and secondary
  lesions.
  ▲ **training and skill are required for successful examination**
    ■ squeeze fluid from lesions with firm pressure, even using the
      jaws of a hemostat
    ■ keep the organisms alive in a saline drop on the microscope
      slide – do not allow to dry out
    ■ examine immediately under a well-calibrated darkfield
      microscope
● Caution the patient to abstain from intimate contacts until 24
  hours after treatment.
● Report to public health authorities.

Treatment
● Be aware of updated national and local treatment
  recommendations. Current Public Health Service recommendations
  for *primary* and *secondary* syphilis are:
  ▲ benzathine penicillin 2.4 million units intramuscularly once, or
  ▲ procaine penicillin 600 000 units intramuscularly daily for 10
    days
  ▲ if the patient is unable to take penicillin then give tetracycline
    or erythromycin 500mg four times a day for 15 days
● Local soaks or compresses (p.318) may be applied for a few days if
  ulcer is painful, infected, or oozing copiously.
● Follow-up serologic testing.
  ▲ FTA remains positive indefinitely – do not retest
  ▲ non-specific STS
    ■ check titers every six months for two years
    ■ usually becomes negative in 6-12 months after treatment for
      primary syphilis, 12-18 months after treatment for
      secondary syphilis
    ■ may fall to low titer (e.g. 1:2) and remain so indefinitely.
      This is a 'persistent reactor', or 'serofast', and does not
      require treatment
    ■ if titers rise, assume new infection and treat again

Scabies

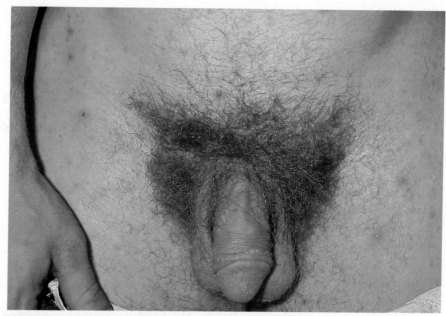

Typical excoriated papular eruption of scabies. Penile papules are very characteristic.

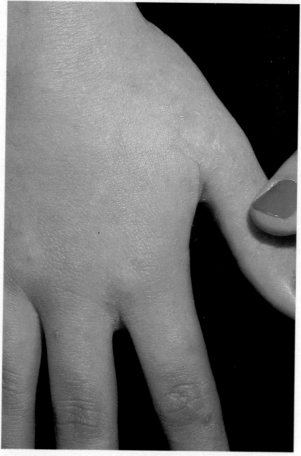

Severe itching but only scattered fine papules typify scabies. Fingerweb involvement is very common.

Scabies

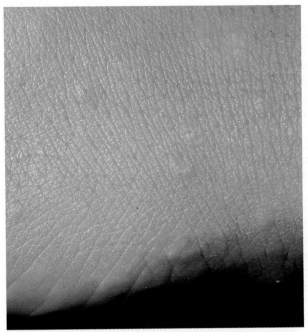

Most of the rash is an allergic reaction. The J-shaped white lesion in the center of the photograph is a burrow which contains an organism.

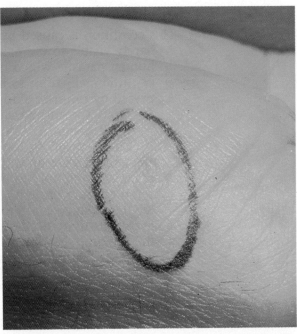

A linear burrow on a typical location, the margin of the palm.

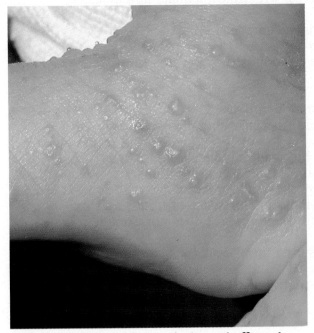

Scabies in infants is often vesicular and affects the palms, soles, and face.

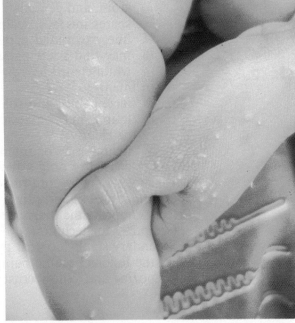

Secondarily infected scabies in a mother and child.

Scabies

Clinical

- This condition is caused by the mite *Sarcoptes scabiei.*
  - ▲ barely visible to the naked eye
  - ▲ human parasite which burrows into keratin layer
    - ■ little inclination to be shed from skin
  - ▲ passed by intimate skin contact
    - ■ rarely spread by casual contact (handshake, or medical examination)
    - ■ rarely spread by fomites
- Itching and rash are an immune reaction.
  - ▲ organisms multiply to dozens in two to three weeks, but no symptoms are present
    - ■ the organisms are most contagious at this time
  - ▲ hypersensitivity occurs in 10-20 days, then the rash appears
  - ▲ the immune reaction kills many organisms, so that only a few are present when the rash occurs
    - ■ most lesions are an immune reaction; few contain organisms
  - ▲ itching persists for days to weeks after successful scabicide therapy
  - ▲ if scabies is acquired again in an immune individual then the rash appears in two to three days
- Rash.
  - ▲ typically in sexually active young adults
    - ■ very itchy, especially at night
    - ■ concentrated in fingerwebs, wrist folds, axillae, umbilicus, groin, and genitals
    - ■ spares the face, scalp, palms and soles
    - ■ fine, excoriated papules
    - ■ may find a few papules surmounted by a 1mm-4mm fine, white etched *burrow*
  - ▲ in infants
    - ■ face, palms, and soles may be involved
    - ■ lesions may be vesicular, especially on palms and soles
  - ▲ in the elderly
    - ■ itching may be intense but rash may be absent, or may consist of only a few papules in atypical locations
- Diagnosis may be confirmed by shave and microscopic examination of appropriate lesions. The presence of mites, eggs or feces confirms the diagnosis, but their absence does not exclude it (see p.297 for technique).
- Secondary staphylococcal pyoderma may occur.
  - ▲ the lesions become painful
  - ▲ oozing and yellow crust formation occurs

Scabies

Treatment
● General.

> Patients should be educated about the characteristics of the disease so that they can understand the possible sources, the contagiousness during the incubation period, and the persistent itching after treatment (see Patient Guide, p.288).

● Scabicides (p.309).
   ▲ a cream or lotion should be applied to the entire body from neck to feet, being sure to treat the genitals, umbilicus, and all body folds – it is left on overnight and washed off in morning
      ■ crotamiton should be applied two or more nights in succession to ensure cure. It is safe to use in children and pregnant women
      ■ gamma benzene hexachloride (lindane) is applied only once and is very effective. It may be toxic to infants, so most physicians use it only in children over four years of age
      ■ benzyl benzoate is applied daily for three days. It is not readily available in the US
   ▲ an alternative scabicide is sulfur 5%-10% in petrolatum
      ■ apply twice daily for three days
      ■ may be irritating
      ■ a topical corticosteroid is often added
   ▲ Note: pyrethrins (p.309) are effective against lice but are *not* effective against scabies
● Treatment of itching.
   ▲ the worst itching fades in one to two days so treatment may not be necessary
   ▲ crotamiton is somewhat antipruritic
   ▲ antihistamines given at bedtime aid sleep
   ▲ baths (p.318), shake lotions (p.305) are mildly soothing
   ▲ corticosteroids
      ■ potent topical corticosteroids may relieve itching in many cases
      ■ a high dose of systemic (40mg-60mg prednisone) corticosteroid administered for a few days relieves severe itching

Scabies

Treatment (continued)

> ▲ persistent itching and rash may be due to
> - ■ guilt-ridden and disgusted patients greatly irritating skin by repeated application of scabicides and/or compulsive frequent bathing, often with strong soaps
> - ■ reacquisition of scabies from untreated friends and family members
> ▲ treatment failure is rare

- ● Treatment of contacts.
  - ▲ should include
    - ■ all bed-partners for one month before onset of rash
    - ■ children and family members in the household with whom there is intimate contact
  - ▲ may exclude
    - ■ room-mates or housemates with whom there is no intimate skin contact
    - ■ casual acquaintances
- ● Environmental treatment.

> **Note:** remember that the organism is not easily shed from the skin, and it usually lives off the human for only 12 to 24 hours.

  - ▲ upon arising from overnight scabicide treatment
    - ■ wash bedlinen, pajamas
    - ■ don clean clothes or clothes not worn during the preceding two days
    - ■ wash clothes worn during preceding day or set aside for several days
  - ▲ DO NOT
    - ■ wash or dry-clean entire wardrobe
    - ■ fumigate house or try to clean mattress and furniture
- ● Scabies is often sexually transmitted. Look for signs of other sexually transmitted diseases and perform a serologic test for syphilis at the time of diagnosis and again in 6 weeks.

Tinea Versicolor (Pityriasis Versicolor)

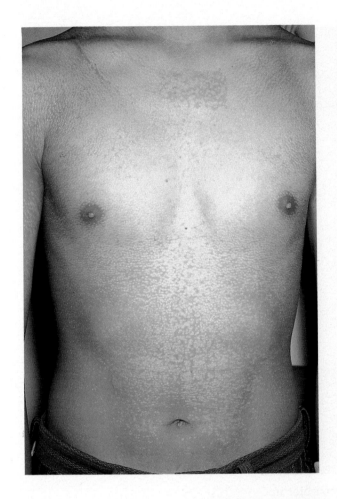

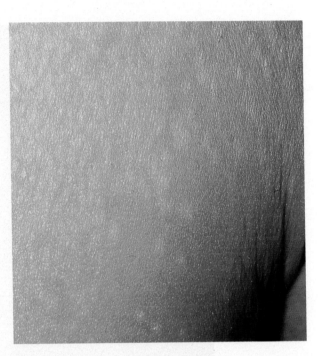

Diffuse hypopigmenting tinea versicolor in a fair-skinned person. Distributed as if "paint poured from above". Close-up shows typical scaly satellite lesions.

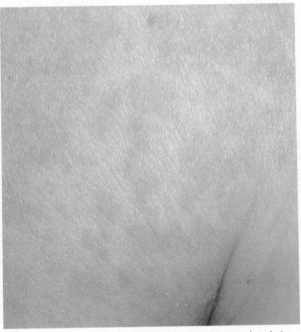

Tinea versicolor in this fair-skinned person is pink-tan.

Tinea Versicolor (Pityriasis Versicolor)

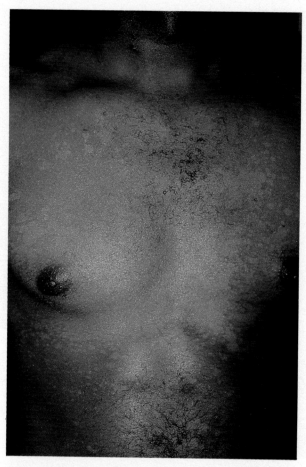

Two shades of hypopigmenting tinea versicolor in
dark-skinned individuals.

Tinea Versicolor (Pityriasis Versicolor)

Clinical
● This condition appears as a discolored scaly eruption in young adults.
  ▲ the eruption consists of sharply-demarcated discrete and confluent macules with a fine, cigarette-ash scale
    ■ the scale is absent for a few hours after bathing
  ▲ it is distributed over the shoulders and upper trunk ('as though paint were poured from above'). Occasionally it occurs in isolated patches
  ▲ it ranges from fawn-tan hypopigmentation to dark brown hyperpigmentation depending on normal skin color *(versicolor means changing colors)*
  ▲ it is more frequent in summer, and in hot, humid climates; it almost never occurs in prepubescent patients and is rare in patients over 40 years of age
  ▲ it is occasionally mildly itchy
● The condition is caused by proliferation of a yeast-like organism *(Pityosporon obiculare)*.
  ▲ it is not known why this normal skin inhabitant proliferates in some individuals and not in others
  ▲ not 'contagious' since all adults carry the organism
  ▲ potassium hydroxide (KOH) examination (p.293) reveals the organism as 'spaghetti and meatballs' with short, curly hyphae and clusters of spores. Will not grow on standard culture media. Scale may be absent for a few hours after bathing and positive KOH identification is then impossible. If clinical diagnosis is in question have patient return without bathing for KOH examination the next day

Tinea Versicolor (Pityriasis Versicolor)

Treatment
- General.
  - ▲ treat for cosmetic reasons only as the organism is not harmful or contagious. Organism is a normal skin inhabitant, so clinical relapse rate is high. Inform patient of its benign nature
  - ▲ treatment clears *scaling* quickly but *color* does not return to normal for two to three months
  - ▲ because various therapies work and relapse is common, treatment is one of the least standardized in dermatology
- Keratolytics. The organism lives on the keratin layer (not in it, as do ringworm fungi) so removal of a superficial layer of keratin is therapeutic.

> Dandruff shampoo is most commonly used. Selenium sulfide 2.5% (p.320) shampoo is applied thinly to the entire trunk with a generous margin of normal skin. Leave on for a period from 15 minutes to overnight, depending on patient tolerance, wash off using more shampoo as soap and scrub briskly with a facecloth. Repeat this procedure once or twice a week for six weeks. Relapses occur months later in one-third of cases and need a repeat course (Patient Guide, p.287).
> **Note:** Other dandruff shampoos are probably equally effective as selenium sulfide, but controlled studies are lacking.

  - ▲ salicylic acid ointment 3%-6% can be applied twice weekly for weeks, or salicylic acid soap may be used several times a week, usually in conjunction with other therapy
  - ▲ sodium thiosulfate solution 25% or acrisorcin cream can be applied twice daily for two weeks
    - ■ onerous, smelly and possibly irritating
- Antifungal agents.
  - ▲ griseofulvin is *not* effective against this yeast-like organism
  - ▲ all topical antifungal agents (p.309) are effective, but must be applied to the entire trunk twice daily for weeks
    - ■ expensive and somewhat inconvenient to use
    - ■ appropriate for a patient on whom a few localized lesions are present

Tinea Corporis

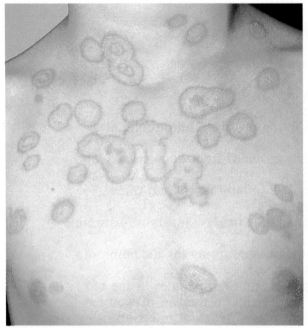

Dramatic widespread tinea corporis in a child.

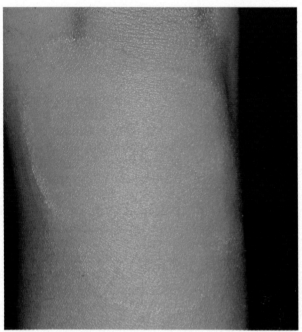

Subtle expanding ring lesion in adult.

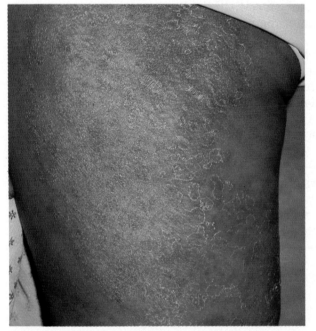

This patient from a hot and humid climate had many large, dry, scaly plaques of chronic tinea corporis.

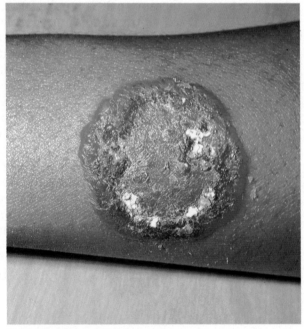

This woman worked in a school where many children had scalp ringworm.

Tinea Corporis

Clinical

- The condition consists of dull red scaly patches on the trunk or extremities.
  - ▲ usually annular or arcuate, with red, scaly border and clearing center
    - ■ more common in children
  - ▲ may be uniform red, scaly patch
    - ■ more common in adults living in warm, humid climates
  - ▲ usually moderately itchy
- In children, the condition is often acquired from dogs or cats, and lesions are inflammatory.
- In adults, the lesions are usually less inflammatory and often preceded by tinea cruris or tinea pedis.
- Both types are fairly rare in temperate climates, and more common in hot, humid climates.
  - ▲ tinea survives best on moist skin, accounting for the common occurrence in the groin and on feet
- Occasionally the lesion will appear as dull red papules in the red patches, or separate from them (especially on the legs of women who shave their legs). In this form it is a *follicular* infection.

Treatment

- If small and localized, the lesions will respond to topical antifungal therapy (p.309), applied twice daily for 10-20 days.
  - ▲ clotrimazole, miconazole, haloprogin, and tolnaftate are probably equally effective
  - ▲ undecylenic acid and iodochlorhydroxyquin are also effective
- If severe, widespread, follicular, or resistant to topical agents, give oral antifungal drugs (p.307) for four to six weeks.
  - ▲ griseofulvin 250mg twice daily
  - ▲ ketoconazole 200mg once a day
- Treat itching with a topical corticosteroid of moderate to potent strength (p.315).

> - ■ this will *not* interfere with healing if topical or oral anti-fungal agents are used with it
> - ■ antifungal agents alone will not affect itching until several days of treatment have elapsed

- ▲ See also tinea capitis (p.6), tinea facei (p.29), tinea cruris (p.85), tinea pedis (p.106) and onychomycosis (p.113)

Impetigo and Bacterial Pyoderma

Superficial bacterial infections may be primary (spontaneous infections
of apparently normal skin) or secondary (infection of broken skin).
Properly, the primary infections are called impetigo, the secondary
ones are called pyodermas.

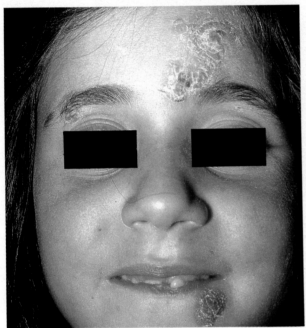
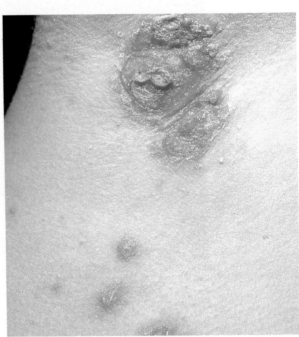

Typical impetigo contageosa: honey-colored crusts on red erosions, on the face and in a fold area (axilla).

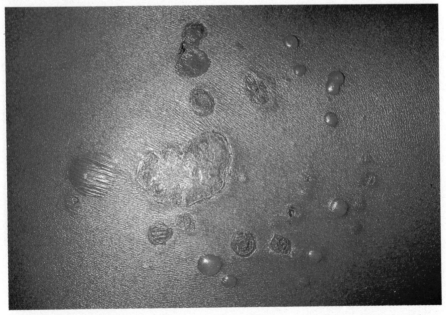

Early localized bullous impetigo in infant. Absence of inflammation in this
infection is striking.

Impetigo and Bacterial Pyoderma

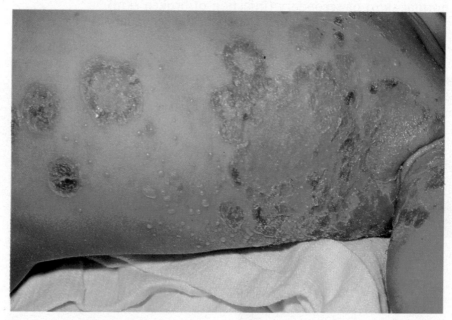

Extensive bullous impetigo in nine-month-old.

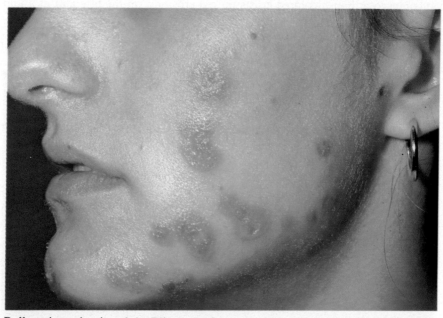

Bullous impetigo in adult. Blister roofs are so thin and fragile that they often are ruptured during routine washing.

Impetigo and Bacterial Pyoderma

Clinical

- Secondary bacterial infections.
  - ▲ the infective organism is usually *Staphylococcus aureus*
    - ■ occasionally *Streptococcus*
  - ▲ any spontaneous or induced lesion may become infected. Common ones are
    - ■ scrapes, cuts, burns, excoriations and insect bites
    - ■ eczemas (especially atopic p.137), stasis dermatitis, bullous diseases
    - ■ other infections, such as tinea and candidiasis
  - ▲ development of infection is signaled clinically by the occurrence of pain, increased erythema, increased weeping, and the formation of thick yellowish crust. In dermatitis, particularly, itching becomes more insistent and the lesions become tender
- Impetigo contagiosa.
  - ▲ a common primary skin infection
  - ▲ typical clinical setting is
    - ■ children
    - ■ hot, humid environment (southeastern US, Central America, or summers in temperate zones)
    - ■ crowded, poor socioeconomic conditions
  - ▲ typical lesions
    - ■ located on face, fold areas (neck and axillae)
    - ■ start as oozing erosion or transient thin-roofed blister, grow rapidly (one to three days), develop honey-colored granular crust. Often after one to two weeks they then dry up. In temperate climates the lesions often heal spontaneously, especially as the weather cools. In tropical climates lesions may persist for weeks and new ones develop
    - ■ lesions may be asymptomatic, itchy, or tender
  - ▲ the primary infecting organism is usually *Streptococcus* (contagious, rapid lesion growth) but often becomes secondarily infected with *Staphylococcus aureus* which becomes predominant (the lesion becomes drier and stops growing)
    - ■ cultures may show *Streptococcus, Staphylococcus,* or both, depending on the state of lesion development
  - ▲ a major cause of *Streptococcus*-induced glomerulonephritis, in endemic circumstances
    - ■ in the US more glomerulonephritis is secondary to impetigo than to pharyngitis

Impetigo and Bacterial Pyoderma

Clinical (continued)

● Bullous impetigo.
- ▲ this is a sporadic and rare primary infection of skin
- ▲ it typically occurs in infants, often in nursery epidemics
  - ■ occasionally in adults, especially on face
- ▲ lesions are vesicles and bullae, on bland, non-inflamed skin. In a few days, dried, collapsed blister roofs cover very superficial erosions. Often heal in a few weeks
- ▲ infecting agent is *Staphylococcus aureus*
  - ■ occurs only in uncommon instance when the strain of *Staphylococcus* produces an epidermolytic toxin which chemically splits the epidermis, causing blister formation

> **Note:** a related condition is staphylococcal scalded skin syndrome, in which a toxin-producing organism inhabits the nose or other internal site, the toxin is blood-borne, causing lysis and denudation of large areas of skin, or of the entire body. The mortality rate is up to 25% in the absence of appropriate medical care.

Treatment

● Secondary pyodermas.
- ▲ keeping an injury or skin lesion clean, especially with use of antibacterial soap, minimizes the likelihood of infection. Use of topical antibiotic preparations (p.307) also probably minimizes infection, but they do not cure established infections
- ▲ topical treatment is adequate for isolated infected lesions
  - ■ soaks (water, astringent [p.318] or antibacterial soap) three times a day for 10-15 minutes
  - ■ gentle debridement with fingers or gauze during soaks
  - ■ keep the lesion dry and non-occluded between soaks
  - ■ some physicians prefer to lubricate lesions after soaks with antibiotic ointment
- ▲ systemic anti-staphylococcal antibiotics are indicated for widespread and resistant cases
● Impetigo contagiosa.

Impetigo and Bacterial Pyoderma

Treatment (continued)

> A major controversy exists in the treatment of streptococcal impetigo because of its high contagiousness and the possibility of glomerulonephritis. Neither systemic nor topical care will prevent glomerulonephritis in a person with established infection. Systemic administration of antibiotics causes lesions to be 'sterile' of *Streptococcus* in 24 hours. Conscientious topical treatment stops the shedding of organisms in only 65% of patients after five days. Impetigo often occurs in crowded poor socioeconomic conditions where contagion is high and likelihood of rigorous topical care is low. Therefore, to prevent spread of disease in the community, treatment is often given in the form of intramuscular long-acting benzathine penicillin, requiring no further participation of the patient or family. Oral erythromycin can be used in reliable patients; it avoids the risk of penicillin allergy. If the parents are conscientious and will isolate the child until the lesions heal, topical care is satisfactory.

- ▲ topical care is the same as for secondary pyoderma
- ▲ systemic antibiotics
  - ■ intramuscular benzathine penicillin 600 000 units to 1 200 000 units, given once
  - ■ oral penicillin-VK 25 000 to 80 000 u/kg per day for seven to ten days
  - ■ for penicillin-sensitive patients, give erythromycin 30mg/kg-50mg/kg per day
- ● Bullous impetigo.
  - ▲ for small, isolated lesions, topical care (as above) is adequate
  - ▲ for resistant or widespread cases, systemic anti-staphylococcal treatment is necessary
  - ▲ if the patient is in a nursery or with other infants isolate and check contacts for infection

> Staphylococcal scalded skin syndrome must be treated by admission to hospital, systemic antibiotics, and close attention to fluid and electrolyte status.

Herpes Zoster (Shingles)

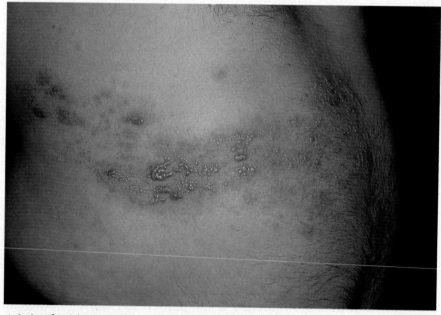

A belt of "shingles" (from Latin: *cingulus*, a girdle), vesicles on an inflamed base. Hemorrhage into vesicles is common.

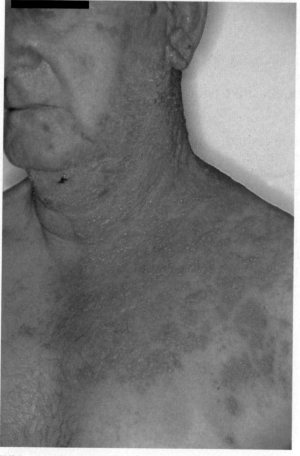

Widespread zoster.

Herpes Zoster (Shingles)

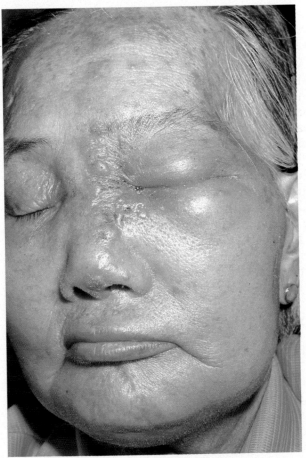

When the tip of the nose is affected, the eye is usually involved, as in this case.

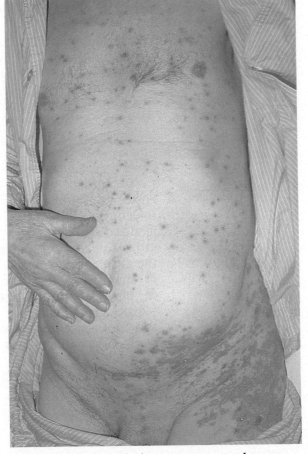

Disseminated zoster in immunosuppressed person.

Herpes Zoster (Shingles)

Clinical

- Rash.
  - ▲ shingles appears as grouped vesicles on bright red edematous plaques
    - ■ these are sometimes pustular or hemorrhagic
    - ■ often the vesicles have ruptured leaving only punctate scabs or erosions on a pink plaque
    - ■ sometimes plaques appear without vesicles
  - ▲ the plaques are distributed unilaterally along the dermatome
    - ■ the entire eruption may be only one small plaque, or may be dozens of large, confluent plaques
  - ▲ it ranges from being asymptomatic to very painful
    - ■ the likelihood of pain increases with age
    - ■ hemorrhagic vesicles are often associated with severe pain
    - ■ the affected dermatome may be hyperesthetic
- Systemic symptoms.
  - ▲ local painful adenopathy may occur
  - ▲ involvement of ophthalmic branch of the facial nerve may include an infection of eye
  - ▲ abdominal involvement may cause two or three days of hypotonic bowel
  - ▲ pelvic involvement may cause two or three days of hypotonic bladder
- Most cases occur without an obvious triggering stimulus.
  - ▲ the condition may follow injury to the spinal or cranial nerve (especially following trigeminal nerve surgery)
  - ▲ there is an increased frequency of incidence in Hodgkin's disease, lymphomas, and immunosuppressive therapy
    - ■ systemic work-up of patients is not necessary unless suggestive symptoms are present
- Oozing erosions or vesicles contain a varicella-zoster virus.
  - ▲ contagious (in the form of chicken pox) by direct contact with people (usually children) who have not had chicken pox
  - ▲ zoster itself probably cannot be acquired by contact with the infecting agent
- Generalized zoster.
  - ▲ at least dozens of vesicles more than a few centimeters beyond the affected dermatome
    - ■ may signify immune suppression – look for the cause
    - ■ may lead to fatal pneumonia or encephalitis
- Post-zoster neuralgia.
  - ▲ this consists of dermatomal pain and hyperesthesia lasting weeks to months after a two week course of acute eruption and pain
  - ▲ the incidence, severity, and duration increase with age

Herpes Zoster (Shingles)

Treatment

- Eruption.
  - ▲ cool compresses or soaks three times a day to wash off serum, and dry up erosions, if present
  - ▲ Castellani's paint (p.306) may be applied after soaks to keep erosions dry
- Acute pain.
  - ▲ appropriate oral analgesics
  - ▲ oral corticosteroids in high doses (50mg-60mg of prednisone) prevent post-zoster neuralgia and probably help relieve acute pain
    - ■ give to patients over 60 years of age in pain
    - ■ taper off over three to four weeks
    - ■ does *not* increase likelihood of viral dissemination
- Post zoster neuralgia.
  - ▲ may be prevented by administration of high-dose corticosteroids during an acute attack (see above)
  - ▲ oral tricyclic antidepressants may be of benefit
    - ■ refer the patient to a neurologist for therapy
  - ▲ nerve root section or ablation with alcohol injections may be necessary in severe cases
    - ■ refer the patient to a pain management center or neurosurgeon
  - ▲ some physicians strongly advocate intralesional injection of corticosteroids. Confirmation of benefit is lacking
- Hyperesthesia.

Frequently a very annoying, persistent symptom.

  - ▲ A tight T-shirt, elasticized underwear or stockings, or wrap provides continuous firm pressure which suppresses hyperesthesia

Molluscum Contagiosum

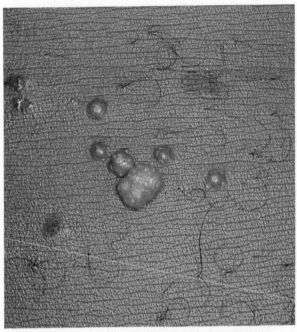

Note multiple cores in large lesion of molluscum contageosa.

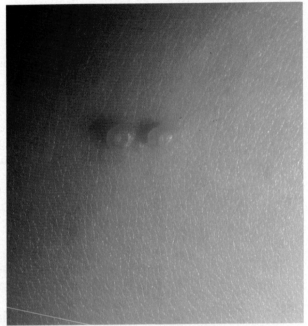

Side light and light freezing highlight the cores of the papules, confirming the diagnosis.

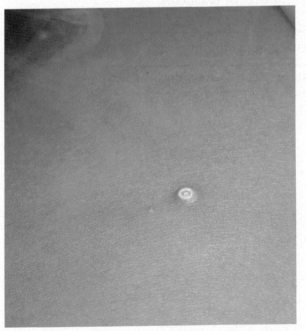

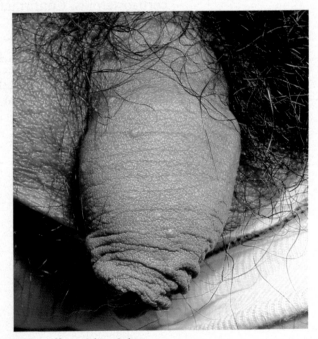

The pubic area is most commonly affected in adults.

Molluscum Contagiosum

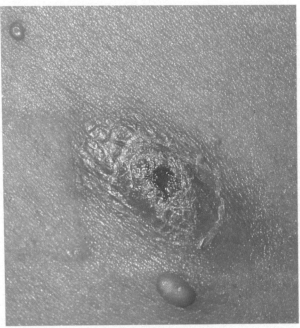

Spontaneous inflammation ("molluscum dermatitis") and resolution may occur.

Clinical
- The condition consists of 1mm-4mm flesh-colored hemispherical papules with a central white core or dimple.
  - ▲ occasionally up to 15mm nodule with multiple cores
  - ▲ occasionally inflamed, with halo of erythema ('molluscum dermatitis')
  - ▲ asymptomatic unless inflamed
- The papules commonly occur in children on the face, arms, and trunk, often in groups. They are acquired by direct contact with other children.
- In adults, the papules usually occur in the pubis and lower abdomen and are sexually transmitted.
- The condition is caused by a virus implanted into the skin.
  - ▲ incubation period two to three weeks
  - ▲ spreads on an individual by autoinoculation, especially by scratching
  - ▲ spontaneously resolves in three to six months (in children) when immunity develops – may last longer in adults. Involution may be accompanied by inflammation

Molluscum Contagiosum

Treatment
- General.
  - ▲ treatment is not medically necessary unless the affected area is very inflamed, but treatment might be preferred for cosmetic reasons or because a school or preschool objects to a contagious disease
  - ▲ minimize scratching and direct skin contact with others
- Destructive treatments must be gentle and not cause scarring, as the lesions will resolve without scarring if untreated.
  - ▲ light liquid nitrogen cryotherapy (cotton swab for 10-20 seconds) is usually effective
    - ■ cryotherapy is of diagnostic help in early papules (where cores are not evident). Freezing greatly enhances the appearance of core
    - ■ avoid excessive freezing, which causes scarring
    - ■ cryotherapy is often impossible in young children with multiple lesions because of pain
  - ▲ an effective treatment is to gently pick out the core with a needle or curette
    - ■ a light anesthetic spray (ethyl chloride, freon) minimizes pain and hardens the core for easier removal
    - ■ this method may be difficult in children because it is slightly painful and requires a steady target
  - ▲ cantharidin (p.324) is a topical agent which causes blisters and inflammation. Apply a tiny amount to each lesion with a blunt wooden applicator stick. Leave uncovered in children and have the patient wash the agent off in four hours. If there is no effect (in 48 hours) apply overnight. If there is still no effect, cover the lesions after treatment with tape for four hours, then wash off
    - ■ not as reliable as cryotherapy or curettage
    - ■ suitable for treatment of young children because application does not hurt, but may be painful later when the blister forms
    - ■ response variable, requiring cautious use at first
    - ■ may require several office visits

> Never give cantharidin to a patient for home use. It is a potent irritant requiring careful application, and severe oral and esophageal burns have occurred after accidental ingestion.

Vitiligo

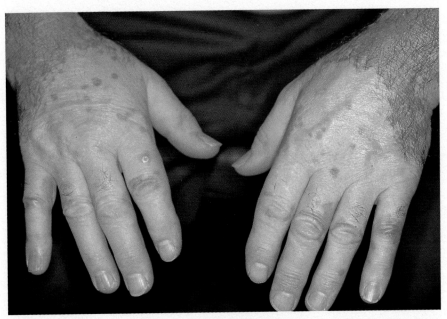

Typical vitiligo with symmetrical sharply-demarcated areas of complete depigmentation.

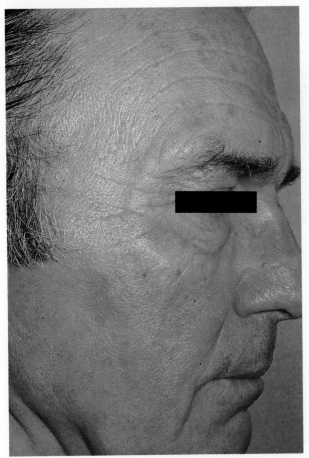

Pigment absence may be subtle in the fair-skinned.

Vitiligo

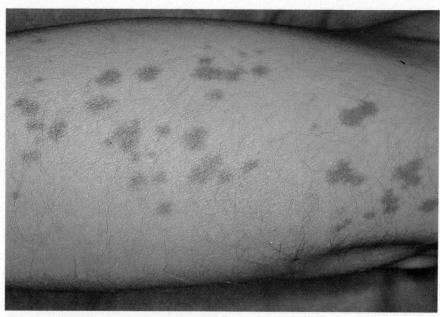

Repigmentation is spreading from follicles.

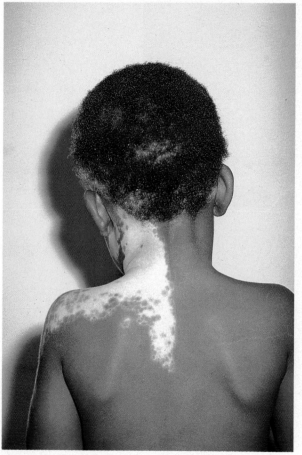

Dermatomal vitiligo. Note "trichrome" quality of inferior margin.

Vitiligo

Clinical
- This condition consists of areas of complete absence of pigment. Two patterns are seen.
  - ▲ dermatomal (linear and zosteriform)
    - ■ infrequent
    - ■ predominantly in children
  - ▲ widespread, but generally occurs in two types of sites
    - ■ areas normally hyperpigmented, such as periorbital, perioral, genital, and flexural
    - ■ areas of trauma, such as knuckles, elbows, knees
- Spontaneous complete disappearance of melanocytes
  - ▲ widespread type on biopsy shows lymphocytes attacking melanocytes
    - ■ can be induced or spread by trauma, including sunburn
    - ■ occasionally the condition is associated with autoimmune diseases such as thyroiditis, pernicious anemia, and diabetes
  - ▲ the dermatomal type is probably not associated with autoimmune lymphocyte attack
    - ■ affected area shows sympathetic nerve dysfunction
    - ■ catechol neurotransmitters probably destroy melanocytes

Treatment

> Treatments for vitiligo are **unreliable, difficult, and time-consuming.** Complete repigmentation can be expected in only 15%-20% of cases, with 75% repigmentation in perhaps another 15%. There is no response in at least 20% of cases. Response is manifested by the development of enlarging pigmented spots (follicular) in the center of the lesions, or as irregular encroachments of pigment at the margins. Facial and genital lesions are the most responsive; lesions over joints are the least. If there is no response after three months of treatment, then continuation of it is unlikely to work. The most recent lesions tend to respond best. Once repigmentation occurs it usually persists.

- Skin dyes and cosmetics are recommended for small areas, especially in very dark-skinned individuals. These are especially useful on the eyelids where potent topical corticosteroids and ultraviolet light should not be used.
  - ▲ an individually prepared cosmetic to match skin color
  - ▲ a walnut-stain or other temporary water-washable dye
- Topical corticosteroids.
  - ▲ potent corticosteroids should be applied twice daily for months
    - ■ examine the patient every month or two for signs of cutaneous atrophy from the treatment
  - ▲ this treatment works only in the widespread type, not dermatomal

Vitiligo

Treatment (continued)

- ● Psoralens and ultraviolet light.
  - ▲ *topical* psoralens easily induce a phototoxic reaction ('sunburn') and should be used only under strict supervision, preferably using only UVA ('blacklight'). The treated areas should be shaded from sunlight for six hours after treatment to avoid sunburn
    - ■ apply 8-methoxypsoralen solution 1% one to three times weekly. If thrice weekly may need to dilute to 0.1% to avoid burning
    - ■ UVA can be administered in gradually increasing doses, the duration depending on bulb intensity and the distance from the skin
  - ▲ *oral* psoralens are unlikely to provoke phototoxic reactions and, most conveniently, are combined with natural sunlight exposure, assuming an appropriate climate. UVA or 'sunlamp' artificial light may be used

> Excessive sun exposure must be avoided for 24 hours after psoralen is taken orally. For that time and *during treatment* the eyes must be protected from ultraviolet damage with opaque goggles or with ultraviolet-screening sunglasses. Few commercial sunglasses filter these wavelengths, so a source of appropriate sunglasses must be identified. In general, grey or green plastic-lens glasses are protective. Blue tint and glass do not protect. Some effective brands available in the US are: American Optical (deep yellow), Sun Vogue Hazemaster, and Cool Ray or Foster Grant polarized green or grey.

  - ▲ trioxsalen 0.6mg/kg *plus* methoxsalen 3mg/kg should be taken two hours before sun exposure
    - ■ for summer sun in a temperate climate, start with exposures of 20 minutes between 10am and 2pm
    - ■ treat three times weekly, increasing the exposure to sunlight for 5 minutes each session until a total exposure of up to 45 minutes is reached

> - ■ the patient may undergo two years of treatment before the maximum benefit is reached

Tumors, Lumps and Marks
Moles (Melanocytic Nevi)

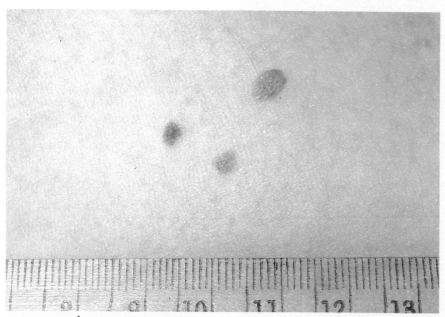

Typical flat "junctional" moles.

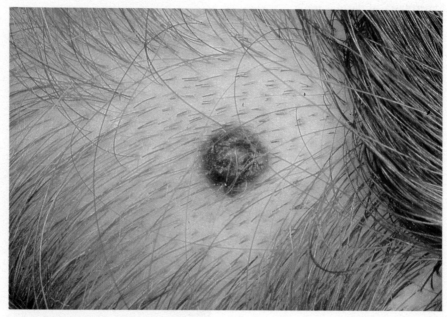

Dermal nevus in scalp.

Moles (Melanocytic Nevi)

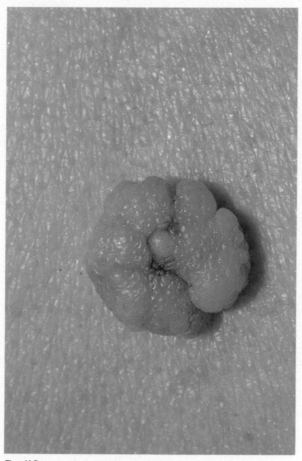

Cauliflower-like hyperplasia of dermal mole.

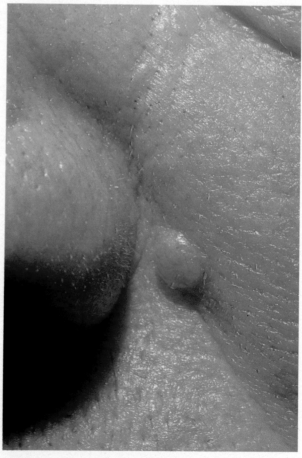

Non-pigmented dermal mole.

Moles (Melanocytic Nevi)

Clinical

- In these lesions there is a proliferation of pigment cells in the epidermis and/or dermis.
  - ▲ genetically determined
    - ■ moles are an inherited tendency
    - ■ the average adult white has about 50 moles; dark-skinned people have few, if any
- Moles are flat to elevated, flesh-colored to dark-brown macules and papules located randomly over the entire skin surface.
  - ▲ onset and course
    - ■ moles are occasionally present at birth
    - ■ they usually start appearing between one to four years of age, and increase in number into adulthood
    - ■ they start flat, but often become elevated in adulthood
    - ■ they may lose pigment (become flesh-colored) in late adulthood
  - ▲ the surface may be flat, smooth, or cerebriform, but never keratotic. Moles in fold and friction areas may become pedunculated
  - ▲ they may contain a few coarse hairs
    - ■ a pimple may develop from a follicle
    - ■ a cyst may develop from a follicle
- Clinical variants.
  - ▲ 'giant hairy nevus', or large, hairy, congenital nevi
    - ■ these are pigmented plaques over one centimeter in size, which are present, and bearing hair, at birth
    - ■ the pigment is often variegated, and is not homogeneous
    - ■ with age, such nevi often become irregularly papular and hypertrophic
    - ■ the rate of malignant transformation (to melanoma) is high (1%-10%) for a large lesion. The rate is less for small lesions, but the risk is still greater than for non-congenital moles
    - ■ a large congenital nevus over the nape of neck may be associated with leptomeningeal melanocyte proliferation, which may block the spinal fluid canals and cause hydrocephaly

Moles (Melanocytic Nevi)

Clinical (continued)

▲ halo nevi
   ■ these usually occur in young adulthood and depigmentation develops around one or several moles. The mole may then fade and disappear, leaving a white macular area, which then may repigment normally
   ■ the process may be arrested at any stage
   ■ in the vast majority of cases halo nevi have no pathological significance. Halos occasionally develop around nevi when the body is fighting a metastatic melanoma
▲ 'blue nevus'
   ■ this is a dark grey-blue or blue-black dermal papule with a smooth surface
   ■ onset is usually young adulthood
   ■ this mole represents pigment cell proliferation deep in the dermis
   ■ there is no malignant potential, but blue nevi are often mistaken for melanoma
● Relationship of moles to melanoma
   ▲ only 20% of melanomas arise in moles–the remainder arise in normal skin
   ▲ moles which are subject to trauma (e.g. waistband) or on the palms and soles are **not** more likely to become malignant

---

■ Clinical signs for melanoma rather than a mole.
  ■ Rapid growth
  ■ Variegated instead of homogeneous pigment (speckles of different color)
  ■ Diffusion of pigment from papule into surrounding skin. Resembles spread of ink on blotting paper
  ■ Inflammation of surrounding skin
  ■ Bleeding, oozing, and crusting of surface

Moles (Melanocytic Nevi)

Treatment

- General.
  - ▲ indications for removal of moles
    - ■ cosmetic
    - ■ the changes listed above, or the conviction of the patient that the mole has suddenly changed
    - ■ remove a large congenital hairy nevus, when feasible
- Surgical removal.
  - ▲ excision
    - ■ this is necessary for diagnosis if melanoma is suspected
    - ■ the preferred method is to allow the linear scar to fall into natural skin folds (e.g. nasolabial)
  - ▲ surgical shave of a papular mole
    - ■ after local anesthesia, shave the mole flat with a scalpel or snip with scissors. Stop the bleeding with stiptic (p.324) or light electrodesiccation
    - ■ do not shave if melanoma is suspected
    - ■ it is possible to achieve a good cosmetic result on the trunk and flat planes of the face
    - ■ shaving may leave residual dermal cells which can grow back or produce pigment. Partial removal does **not** induce melanoma
- Non-surgical methods such as cryotherapy or chemical cautery give unsatisfactory results.

Dermatosis Papulosa Nigra

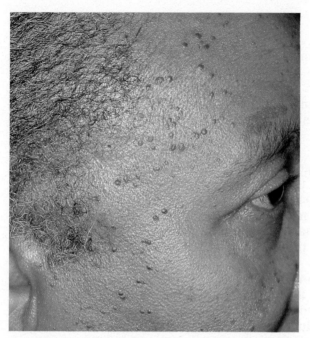

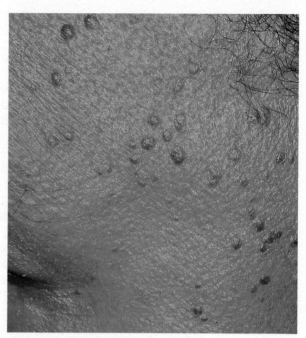

Typical soft, fleshy pigmented papules on the cheeks of dermatosis papulosa nigra.

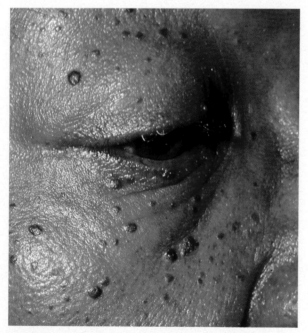

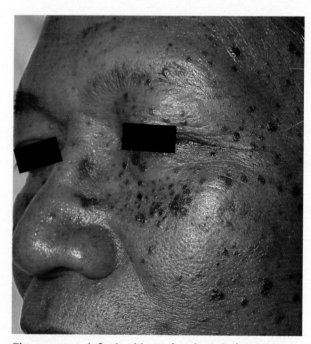

Lesions may occur on eyelids, and may become filiform or verrucous, as here lateral to the eye.

Clear area on left cheekbone is where lesions were shaved off one month before photograph was taken.

Dermatosis Papulosa Nigra

Clinical

- This condition, in at least a mild degree, occurs in up to 40% of adult blacks.
  - ▲ it is less common in mulattos and Asians
  - ▲ it is rare in whites
- The condition consists of soft, fleshy, pigmented papules in a 'mask' distribution around the eyes.
  - ▲ occasionally the papules appear down the cheeks to the neck and on the forehead to the hairline
- A 'delayed birthmark'.
  - ▲ onset is young adulthood, and the extent increases with age
  - ▲ there is a benign proliferation of epidermal cells
- The condition does not become malignant.

Treatment

- Treatment should be for cosmetic reasons only, so avoid scarring and hyperpigmentation.
  - ▲ scalpel shave or scissor snip
    - ■ if the papules are planed flat to the skin little dermal damage or scarring is caused
    - ■ stop bleeding with pressure, Monsel's solution or another mild cauterant if necessary
    - ■ electrocautery increases the chance of scarring and pigmentation
  - ▲ liquid nitrogen cryotherapy
    - ■ hyperpigmentation and hypopigmentation is possible
    - ■ lesions recur if the treatment is too light, and scar if the treatment is too heavy
  - ▲ mild trichloracetic or other acid chemodestruction
    - ■ experience and skill are necessary to get to the right depth and avoid excessive pain and destruction
  - ▲ light electrocautery
    - ■ scarring and pigmentary changes are hard to avoid

Seborrheic Keratoses

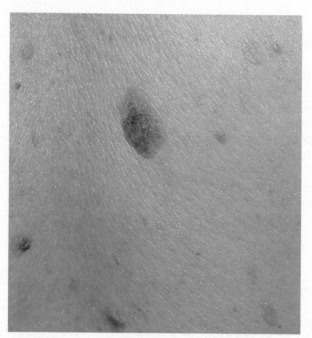

Typical "stuck on" appearance of seborrheic keratoses on the back.

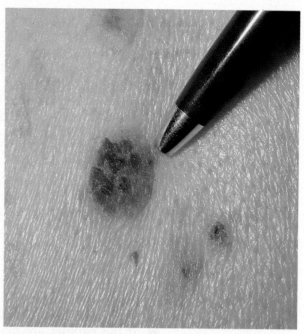

Early lesions are flat, and faint-colored. Older lesion is dark and keratotic.

Seborrheic keratosis covered by belt is softer and less keratotic.

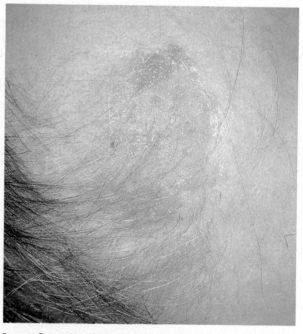

Large flat seborrheic keratoses occur commonly on the face and balding scalp.

Seborrheic Keratoses

Clinical
● This condition consists of rugose or cerebriform tan to dark-brown verrucous plaques and nodules with a 'stuck on' appearance.
  ▲ it may start as granular light tan patches, which slowly thicken and darken
  ▲ the hyperkeratotic cap may repeatedly peel off and a new one accumulate
  ▲ it is found most commonly on the trunk, but the scalp, face, and extremities may be involved
    ■ lesions on the forehead and scalp often remain flat and slightly granular
● This condition occurs primarily in middle-aged to older whites.
  ▲ there is some familial predisposition
  ▲ occurrence seems enhanced by actinic damage
● Lesions are benign proliferation of epidermal cells and keratin piled up above the skin surface (which gives the 'stuck on' appearance).
  ▲ there is no malignant potential
  ▲ the clinical significance is cosmetic, and the possible confusion with potentially harmful lesions
    ■ it may mimic melanoma (p.268) or pigmented basal cell carcinoma (p.263). The major distinguishing feature is that seborrheic keratosis is nearly always surmounted by a keratin cap which can be loosened with a fingernail, and the other growths are fleshy and not keratotic

Treatment.
● General.
  ▲ treatment is cosmetic only
● Since these are growths of epidermis which protrude above the skin surface, destruction of the growth down to the dermal surface will heal by re-epithelialization without scarring. Avoid dermal injury with risk of scar formation. Do not excise.
  ▲ liquid nitrogen cryotherapy
    ■ a light application of from 15-30 seconds is usually curative
    ■ check in one month for residua, which can be treated again
  ▲ light curettage after ethyl chloride or freon spray anesthesia
    ■ the spray freeze imparts stiffness to the skin which facilitates curettage
    ■ spray anesthesia lasts for only 15-20 seconds so quick, firm strokes of the curette are necessary. Curette only to the white, glistening surface of the dermis
    ■ stop bleeding with pressure or chemical stiptic (p.324). Do not stop bleeding with electrocautery, as it causes scarring

Dermatofibroma (Histiocytoma)

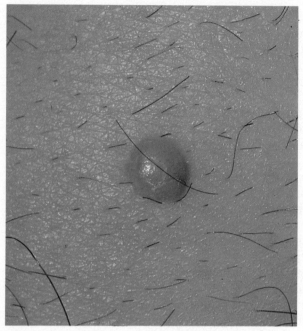

This dermatofibroma is orange because histiocytes in it have phagocytized lipid.

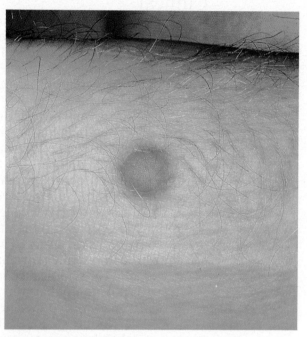

The brown color here is from melanin and hemosiderin.

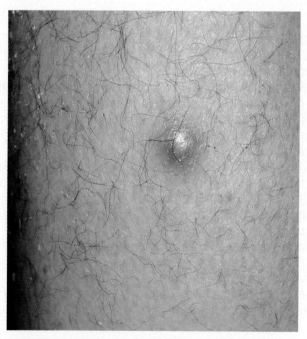

Numerous capillaries in this lesion impart a blue color.

Dermatofibroma (Histiocytoma)

Clinical
- This condition consists of firm, button-like, intradermal papules or nodules.
  - ▲ they are up to one centimeter in size
  - ▲ the color is orange-tan to dark brown
  - ▲ the surface may be smooth or rough and granular
  - ▲ typically, when the surrounding skin is gently squeezed, the lesion puckers down away from the surface
- The papules typically appear on the extremities of young adults and remain throughout life.
- They are a benign growth of fibroblasts and/or histiocytes in dense collagen stroma.
  - ▲ the color depends on presence of phagocytized lipid and/or hemosiderin
  - ▲ fibrosis connects with fiber bundles in subcutaneous fat, which accounts for dimpling behavior when squeezed
  - ▲ there is no malignant potential

Treatment
- Assure the patient of the condition's benign nature, and that no treatment is necessary.
- Excision is definitive but leaves scarring.
  - ▲ location on a leg or arm often tips cosmetic consideration in favor of no treatment – surgical scars on those sites are often wide and unsightly
- Cryotherapy is occasionally employed by experienced physicians, but it must be deep and runs the risk of delayed healing and unsightly scar formation.

Skin Tags (Acrochordon)

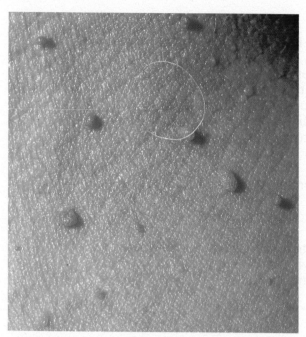

Skin tags often are multiple and on fold areas, as are those on the neck.

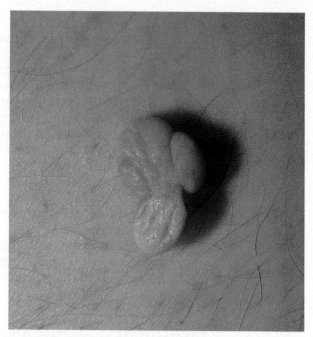

Skin tags can become quite large and pendunculated.

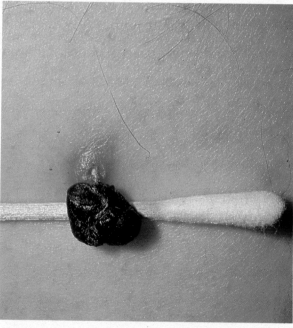

Pedunculated tags may twist on their stalks and infarct.

Skin Tags (Acrochordon)

Clinical
- This condition consists of small (1mm-3mm), fleshy, filiform or pedunculated papules.
  - ▲ they are often hyperpigmented
  - ▲ they are occasionally hyperkeratotic
  - ▲ they are occasionally large (5mm-30mm)
  - ▲ they are located on
    - ■ friction areas (neck, axillae and groin)
    - ■ eyelids
- They occur in
  - ▲ adults
  - ▲ familial tendency
  - ▲ the obese
- They have no medical significance, but occasionally twisting of the stalk causes infarct and inflammation.

Treatment
- Small lesions can be snipped quickly without anesthesia.
  - ▲ grasp the fold of skin between thumb and index finger to position tag on its apex. This allows the tag to be snipped without inadvertently cutting or pinching surrounding skin
  - ▲ a quick snip is practically painless; a slow, pinching snip is painful
  - ▲ stop bleeding with pressure or a dab of stiptic (p.324) (Monsel's solution, aluminum chloride 30%). Bleeding is often delayed for up to 15-30 seconds by arteriolar spasm, so check all sites before the patient dresses
- Larger lesions require local anesthesia and electrocautery to control arteriolar bleeding.

Pyogenic Granuloma

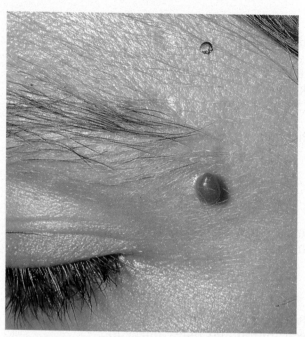

Early (2 weeks) bright red pyogenic granuloma.

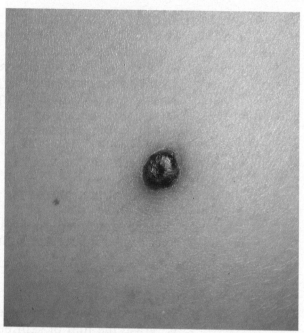

After several weeks fibrosis begins to replace the vessels.

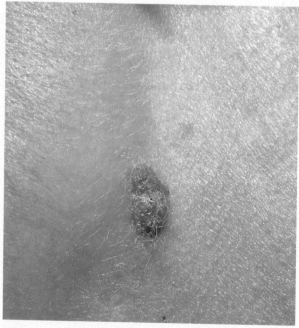

Fibrosis nearly complete.

Pyogenic Granuloma

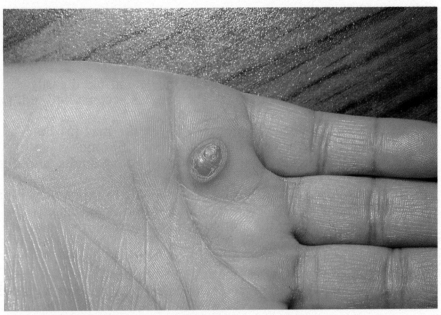

A keratotic collar may be evident, especially on thick-skin areas.

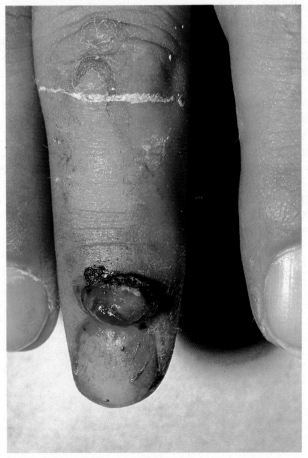

Trauma may cause bleeding. This lesion could easily be mistaken for a melanoma.

Pyogenic Granuloma

Clinical

- This condition consists of the sudden appearance and rapid evolution of
  - ▲ bright cherry-red glistening papules, with fine keratin collar
    - ■ which are somewhat friable, fragile and bleed easily
  - ▲ after a few weeks of growth the papules become dull red, and the surface becomes rougher
  - ▲ after several weeks or months the papules may involute completely or become flesh-colored and fibrotic
- The condition occurs most commonly in young adults, and during pregnancy.
  - ▲ it may arise spontaneously, or at the site of minor skin injury
    - ■ it may occur a few weeks after tattoo or vaccination
  - ▲ during pregnancy the condition may occur on the gums as 'epulis'
- The condition is a growth of granulation tissue ('proud flesh'), consisting of immature capillaries and collagen.
  - ▲ the name is a misnomer. It is neither pyogenic nor a granuloma

Treatment

- Treatment is usually advised because
  - ▲ involution is rarely complete if the condition is untreated
  - ▲ if the condition is not treated early the papules may grow larger
  - ▲ biopsy specimen rules out non-pigmented melanoma (p.268)
- The type of treatment depends on the size and location of the papules.
  - ▲ if they are small, scoop shave (scoop deeply in dermis with no. 15 scalpel blade) or snip them with curved small scissors. Electrodesiccate or cauterize base
    - ■ this procedure leaves a small, flat, round scar
    - ■ the lesion may recur in 5%-10% of cases if destruction is not complete – treat again
  - ▲ if they are large (up to one centimeter) or in a wrinkle line of the face, excision and suture closure have a low recurrence rate and give a good cosmetic result

Cysts

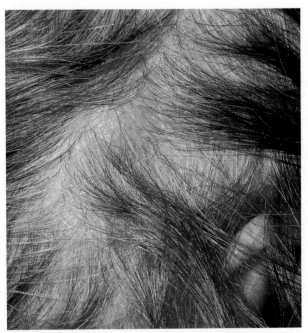

Pilar cyst of scalp. They are more obvious on palpation than on inspection.

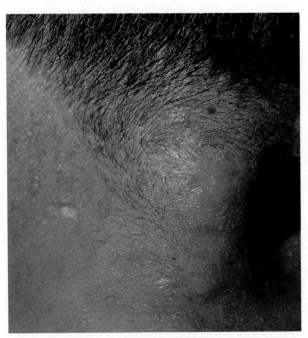

Inflamed and swollen epidermoid cyst at nape of neck.

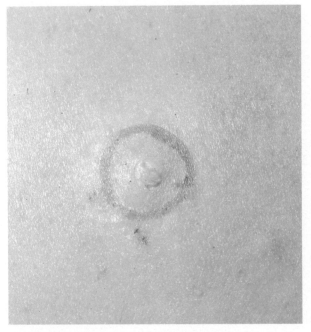

Epidermoid cyst (extent outlined in red) anesthetized and incised by 3mm punch.

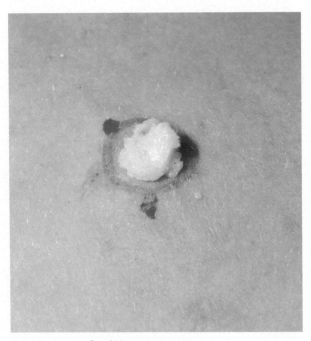

Cyst contents forcibly expressed.

Cysts

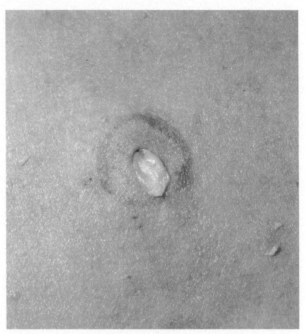

Wiping away debris reveals filmy cyst wall protruding from incision.

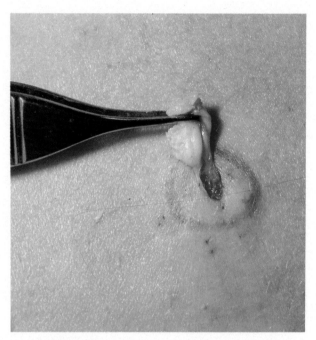

Entire wall is gently teased out, usually using fine curved scissors.

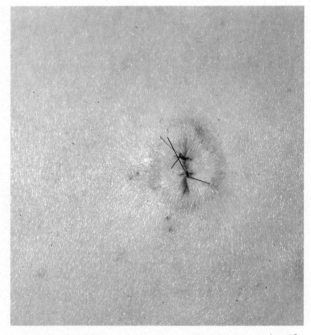

Closure results in scar much smaller than cyst itself.

Cysts

Clinical

● An *epidermoid* cyst is a sac-like growth of the upper portion of a follicle. The wall is like epidermis; the contents are immature keratin and cellular debris.
  ▲ it is a soft hemispherical subcutaneous nodule usually surmounted by a comedo or dilated pore
  ▲ it is usually located on the face, neck, and upper trunk
    ■ it is more common in males and in individuals with large oil glands and acne
  ▲ it occasionally drains cheesy material or the patient expresses such matter through a dilated pore
    ■ the foul odor is rancid lipid and cellular debris, **not** infection
    ■ the lesion will refill after emptying because the intact cyst wall will continue to shed keratin
  ▲ occasionally the cyst will be red, tender, and swollen
    ■ this represents rupture of the cyst wall with leakage of the contents into the dermis provoking an intense inflammatory response like a large pimple
    ■ it is **not** infected but is often misdiagnosed as such. Incision and drainage reveals a soupy, smelly debris which looks like purulence but which is only keratin and cellular debris mixed with tissue fluid and inflammatory cells
● A *pilar* cyst is a sac-like growth of the middle portion of a follicle. The wall is like the follicle; contents are hair-cuticle-like material.
  ▲ it is a hard hemispherical subcutaneous nodule without an overlying pore
  ▲ it is most frequently located on scalp
    ■ may be familial
    ■ often multiple, and/or in clusters
    ■ may develop overlying alopecia
  ▲ it does not drain or become inflamed

Cysts

Treatment

- An inflamed epidermoid cyst.
  - ▲ Do not incise and drain, unless the thinned roof is ready to rupture
    - ■ incision is likely to leave an enlarged pore or sinus
    - ■ the contents will reform because the cyst wall is still present
  - ▲ it is difficult to excise when inflamed because the wall is fragile, hard to differentiate from surrounding tissue, and heals poorly when sutured
  - ▲ the best treatment of an intact inflamed cyst is intralesional or perilesional corticosteroid injection (p.313) Example: triamcinolone acetonide 5mg/ml-10mg/ml, 0.1ml-0.4ml
    - ■ pain and tenderness improve in 12 hours and resolve in two to four days
  - ▲ it may be excised three to six weeks later when it is not inflamed
- A non-inflamed epidermoid cyst.
  - ▲ excision – see below for pilar cyst
  - ▲ if the cyst is not inflamed or scarred from a previous inflammation, make a 3mm-4mm incision into cyst, or, better still, a 3mm-4mm circular punch. Express the contents firmly and the cyst wall will rise to the opening. Grasp gently with forceps and tease cyst wall out, using fine curved scissors to dissect it from surrounding tissue. This manouver is similar to turning a glove finger inside out from within. An absorbable subcutaneous suture may be required to close dead space. Close the skin opening. If cyst had been inflamed in the past, scar tissue may prevent teasing out of the cyst wall
- Pilar cyst.
  - ▲ excision. The wall is thick and the contents hard. Incise over (not into) the cyst and it will often pop above the skin surface. Snip the few fibrous threads attaching it to the dermis and remove the cyst. If the cyst is in hair-bearing scalp, the wound can be closed with absorbable suture. This will leave stitch-mark scars, but they will be hidden by hair, and the patient need not return for suture removal
  - ▲ an *epidermoid* cyst can be excised in similar fashion but the skin over it is thin and the cyst wall is thin and fragile. Care is needed in gently freeing the cyst from the surrounding tissue to avoid rupture

Warts

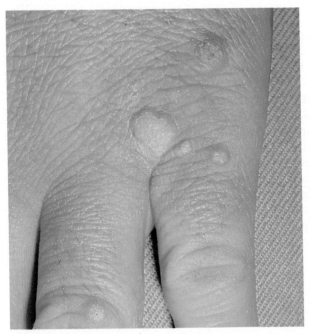

Common warts in a common location.

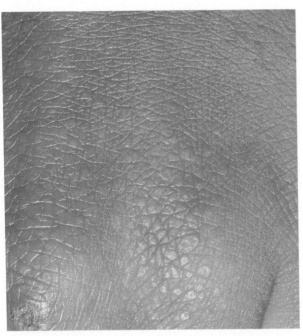

Plane or flat warts often occur as many lesions closely packed.

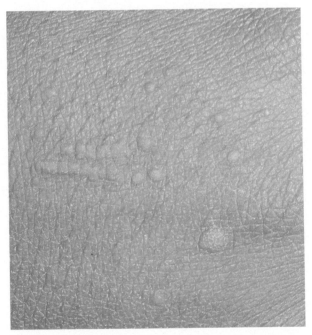

The wart virus can be seeded from one source in sites of trauma.

Exuberant wart growth in scalp.

Warts

Clinical

● Warty keratotic papules and plaques are most common in children on the hands and arms.
  ▲ sometimes they occur in groups or in areas of trauma (e.g. scratches or cuts)
  ▲ they are usually asymptomatic but may crack and bleed
● They are caused by a wart virus implanted in the skin.
  ▲ the incubation period is from two to four months, or more
  ▲ seed into areas of broken skin
  ▲ they will disappear spontaneously when immunity develops. Apart from plantar (p.123) and periungual (p.120) warts, the duration of warts is approximately 6-12 months in children and 12-24 months in adults. In young children warts are particularly capricious and may resolve in weeks while new ones develop

Warts

Treatment
- General (see Patient Guide, p.292).
  - ▲ if they are asymptomatic, no treatment is necessary except for cosmetic reasons
    - ■ if they are untreated there is an unknown risk of spread to new sites
  - ▲ discourage picking or biting of warts, which may cause spread of lesions
- Palliative treatments keep wart tissue soft and flat.
  - ▲ keratolytic agents, usually in a sticky liquid base, are applied daily to soften and reduce keratin. Occlusion with non-porous tape probably enhances the effect
    - ■ salicylic acid 16% with lactic acid 16% in flexible collodion
    - ■ salicylic acid plaster 40%
  - ▲ paring or filing keratin to reduce bulk
- Destructive or curative treatments.
  - ▲ cryotherapy is generally the destructive treatment of choice as it is reasonably effective (over 50% in most areas), easy to perform, only mildly painful (except for periungual and plantar warts), requires no postoperative care, and leaves little scarring. Use liquid nitrogen on a cotton applicator for 15-45 seconds (depending on location), or a cryospray

---

Note: This procedure should only be performed by a trained practitioner, with experience in treating various types of warts.

- ■ young children will often not hold still because of pain. Do not treat
- ■ do not see patient again for three weeks, as inflammation and scab mask site. Re-examine the patient in three to four weeks and treat any tiny residual warts again
- ■ warts may recur at the site of treatment for up to six months. Warn patient of this possibility

Warts

Treatment (continued)

▲ light electrodesiccation and curettage
■ requires local anesthesia
■ insert treatment electrode into the wart and apply the current until wart tissue whitens, swells, and softens (usually 5-10 seconds). Lightly curette
■ skilful use leaves little if any scarring and is effective. Excessive electrodesiccation causes scarring.
▲ cantharidin (p.324) – apply to the wart in the office, cover with non-porous tape for four to 24 hours (with a shorter time for children and thin skin areas). The relapse rate is high if the wart is not curetted (under local anesthesia) within two to three days
■ painless application invites use in children but often forms painful blister at six to 24 hours later, and often recurs without subsequent curettage
▲ hypnosis and suggestion
■ in children, where warts are of short duration, placebos are successful in 30%-40% over a period of a few weeks. There is little evidence that suggestion exceeds this
■ adults have been hypnotized and had treatment focused on specific warts. The rate of those warts resolving is somewhat greater than the resolution of 'untreated' warts in the same person. Five 30-60 minute sessions are required
▲ allergic contact sensitization is under investigation but widely used for difficult warts. The patient is sensitized to a contact allergen (such as dinitrochlorobenzene) and then minute doses of it or an agent the patient is already allergic to (such as *Rhus* plant antigen) is applied to the wart two to three times a week. The low-grade dermatitis which develops often seems to involute the wart. This should be performed only by an experienced practitioner. There is a risk of severe dermatitis
▲ see also facial warts (p.49), genital warts (p.70), periungual warts (p.120), and plantar warts (p.123)

Actinic Damage and Sun Protection

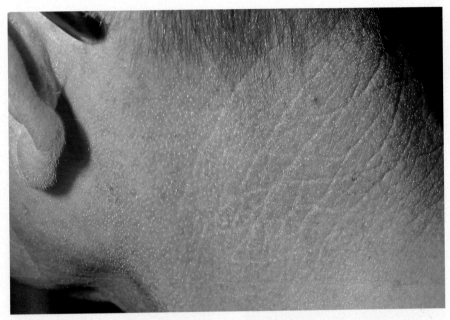

Hyperpigmentation, leathery thickening, and wrinkling from chronic sun exposure.

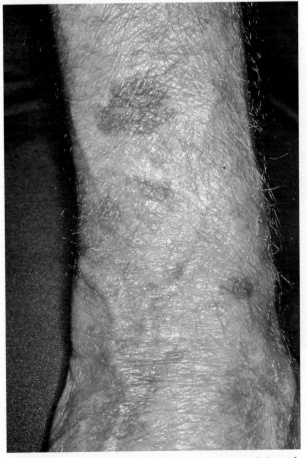

Marked dermal atrophy, loss of normal elasticity of skin. Marked purpura secondary to minor trauma to damaged vessels.

Actinic Damage and Sun Protection

Idiopathic guttate hypomelanosis: small polygonal hypopigmented macules, probably from actinic damage to melanocytes.

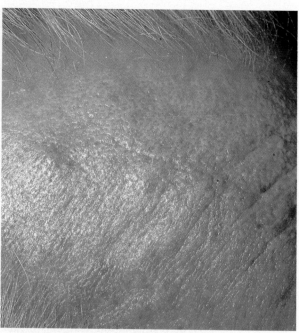

Solar elastosis: yellow dermal plaque is degenerated sun-damaged collagen.

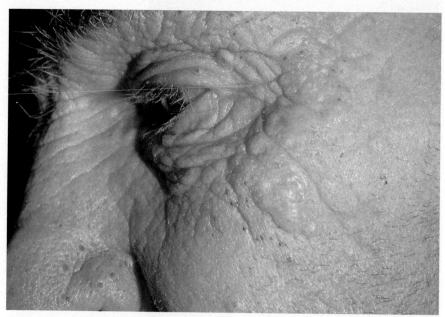

Solar comedos and wrinkling.

Actinic Damage and Sun Protection

Clinical
● In actinic damage penetrating ultraviolet rays damage the epidermal cells, melanocytes, dermal collagen, blood vessels, and even the pilosebaceous structures. Clinical manifestations are
  ▲ epidermal
    ■ dryness and scaling
    ■ epidermal atrophy
    ■ actinic keratoses (p.257)
    ■ epitheliomas (p.263)
  ▲ melanocytes
    ■ freckling, diffuse punctate pigmentation
    ■ lentigo (p.255)
    ■ lentigo maligna and, possibly, melanoma (p.268)
    ■ hypopigmented spots (idiopathic guttate hypomelanosis)
  ▲ dermal
    ■ wrinkling
    ■ solar elastosis (yellow plaques of collagen degeneration on the temples)
    ■ dermal atrophy (thinning of the skin)
  ▲ blood vessels
    ■ telangiectasis (p.253)
    ■ hemorrhage and easy bruising, especially on the dorsa of the hands and arms
  ▲ pilosebaceous
    ■ milia
    ■ solar comedos, or blackheads

Treatment
● Solar damage of the skin is cumulative during a lifetime, so intelligent precautions should be taken during childhood and practised routinely thereafter. Skin changes will occur late in life, even if the skin is then protected, if excessive sun exposure has occurred during childhood and young adulthood. Continued sun exposure worsens the changes.
● Protection.
  ▲ minimize sun exposure
    ■ avoid the sun from 10am to 2pm, the time that 60% of the day's ultraviolet light reaches the earth
    ■ wear protective hats and clothing
  ▲ sunscreens (p.316) – they are ranked for Sun Protection Factor (SPF) usually from 5 to 15, which denotes to what multiple of the regular exposure to sun the wearer can now be exposed before overt sunburn occurs. So, if burning usually occurs after 30 minutes of exposure to the noonday sun, then use of an SPF 5 preparation will safely allow 2.5 hours of such exposure. It is recommended that those who never tan or who burn easily use an SPF 15 product, those who tan after a mild burn use SPF 5-10, and those who are dark-skinned, or who tan deeply and never burn, need not use protection. Products are listed on p.316. They should be applied at least 30 minutes before sun exposure, to allow skin binding, and should be reapplied after swimming or vigorous sweating. Allergy to these materials occasionally occurs

Actinic Damage and Sun Protection

Treatment (continued)

▲ special factors enhancing sun damage
   ■ burning occurs more quickly in a humid environment than in a dry one, and in turbulent rather than still air
   ■ ultraviolet penetration is enhanced by the presence of oil or grease on the skin, as in 'suntan oil'
   ■ reflection from water, sand, and snow is intense, so protection by a beach umbrella may be inadequate
   ■ ultraviolet penetration through wet white cloth is good, so wearing a T-shirt while swimming is only minimally protective
   ■ ultraviolet intensity increases greatly with altitude, due to less filtration by the thinner air. At higher altitudes particular caution must be used, even by individuals who rarely burn
▲ Patient Guide, p.289
● Treatments covered elsewhere.
   ▲ actinic keratoses, p.257
   ▲ epitheliomas, p.263
   ▲ lentigines, p.255
   ▲ lentigo maligna and melanoma, p.268
   ▲ telangiectasia, p.253
   ▲ milia and solar comedos – see p.39 for treatment of comedonal acne. Topical use of tretinoin and comedo removal in the office are effective. Aged, dry skin is easily irritated by tretinoin so begin with alternate day applications and use topical hydrocortisone if necessary to reduce irritation
● Dryness, wrinkling, and atrophy.
   ▲ dryness and fine lines in dry skin can be minimized by the frequent use of emollient oils or creams
   ▲ true wrinkling and atrophy are permanent tissue changes which cannot be prevented, modified, or corrected by lubricants, vitamins, 'skin restorers', or any physical manipulation. Patients should be advised not to waste time or money on their use. Only avoidance of ultra-violet light has any impact on the development of wrinkling and atrophy. Dermabrasion and chemical peeling treatments damage the skin so that flat (unwrinkled) scars form, giving an appearance often cosmetically superior to the original state

Telangiectasia and Spider Angiomata

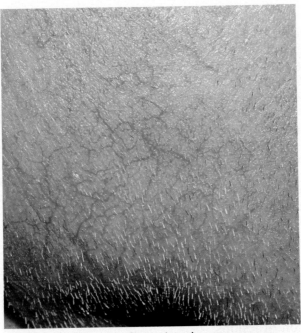

Profuse telangiectasia from chronic sun exposure.

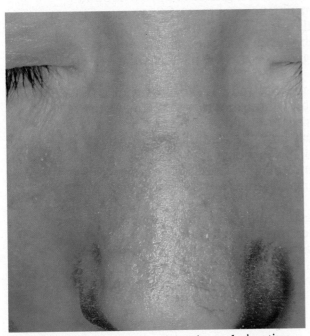
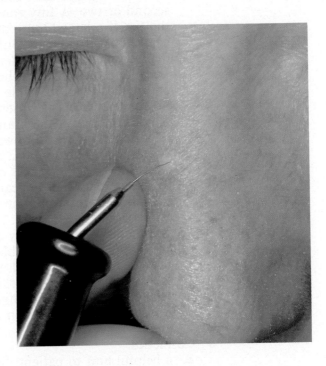

Spider angioma, treated by light electrodesiccation.

Telangiectasia and Spider Angiomata

Clinical

- Telangiectasia are visible dilated capillaries, usually on the nose and cheeks of fair-skinned individuals.
  - ▲ it is a form of chronic sun damage
  - ▲ check for keratoses and carcinomas (p.263)
- Spider angiomata are red dots with dilated capillaries radiating from the center (like legs radiating from a spider's body). They represent dilated arterioles with surrounding engorged capillaries.
  - ▲ they occur in healthy young adults on the face (especially just below the lower eyelid) and the backs of the hands
  - ▲ they occur more frequently and in greater numbers with pregnancy, estrogen therapy, and chronic liver disease

Treatment

- General.
  - ▲ instruct patients in sun protection and avoidance (p.289)
  - ▲ inquire about pregnancy, estrogen therapy, and alcoholism
  - ▲ treatment is for cosmetic purposes
- Destruction of lesions.
  - ▲ electrocautery – use a very fine epilating needle on a treatment probe, set at a very low current. Insert up to one millimeter of electrode tip into the vessel, and tap activating foot switch for a second or two. A tiny zone of blanching should appear around the tip. If a large (2mm-3mm) blanch appears, if there is a spark, or if it is very painful, use a lower setting. The proper dial setting varies considerably from one patient to the next. Local anesthesia cannot be given because it blanches the vessels and makes them invisible
    - ■ for telangiectasia, insert the electrode as far 'upstream' as possible, or at the branch of the tributaries. Treatment there often blanches all downstream outflow
    - ■ for spider angiomata, treat only the central 'body' of the spider. The 'legs' will collapse on their own
    - ■ Note: relapse or appearance of new vessels is common; follow-up examination and treatment in a few weeks is recommended
  - ▲ cryotherapy – moderately deep liquid nitrogen cryotherapy by swab application often ablates tiny telangiectasia and telangiectatic mats. Faint scarring may result but the white scar is less noticeable in fair skin than is the pink blush of the telangiectasia. Perform this on a small trial area and evaluate results with the patient in a few weeks before treating a large area
- Cosmetics.
  - ▲ a helpful hint to patient: the addition of a small amount of green color to the cosmetic greatly enhances its effectiveness in hiding redness

Solar Lentigo (Liver Spots)

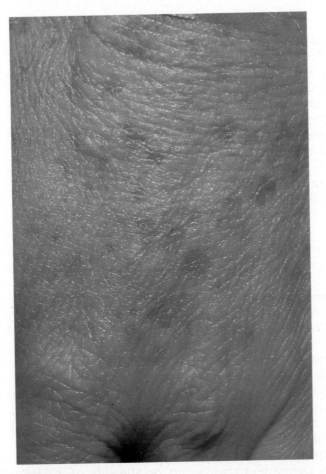

Typical early lentigines.

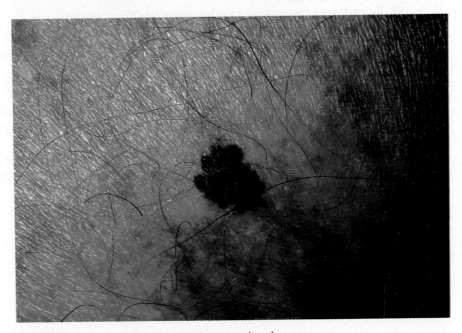

Dark lentigo and mottled hyperpigmentation in
very sun-damaged skin.

Solar Lentigo (Liver Spots)

Clinical
- Solar lentigo consists of flat homogeneous tan or brown spots with well-defined borders 2mm-30mm in size.
  - ▲ they occur on sun-exposed skin of middle-aged to elderly adults
    - ■ face, especially forehead and temples
    - ■ dorsa of forearms and hands
    - ■ less commonly, trunk and legs
  - ▲ occasionally there is slight scale or rough surface
- Lentigo is caused by sun damage and genetic predilection.
  - ▲ it results from increased activity and slight increased number of melanocytes in the epidermis
  - ▲ there is no malignant potential

Treatment
- General.
  - ▲ the appearance of lentigines indicates a certain amount of ultraviolet damage to the skin. Examine sun-exposed areas for solar-induced tumors. Discuss sun protection with the patient (p.289)
  - ▲ removal of lentigines is for cosmetic purposes only
- Epidermal peeling.
  - ▲ inducing epidermal peeling removes the abnormal melanocytes. New epidermis which regenerates from surrounding skin and follicles bears normal melanocytes. Incomplete peeling results in mottled residual pigment, but the treatment can be repeated. Excessively strong attempts at peeling may injure the dermis and produce a permanent scar, so err on the side of inadequate peeling. Agents used are
    - ■ light liquid nitrogen cryotherapy (10-20 seconds). Melanocytes are more sensitive to cold than are epidermal cells, so this method is preferred
    - ■ trichloracetic acid (20%-40%) or phenol (80%) chemodestruction in the office. Apply a thin layer to cause a white frost on the skin
    - ■ phenol (20%-40%) in oil for daily application by the patient for several days. Stop the treatment when mild redness and peeling occurs
    - ■ light electrodesiccation, usually with a fine epilating needle on desiccating current. Control is excellent but it is easy to damage dermis with too much current
- Bleaching agents.
  - ▲ hydroquinone creams are of minimal, if any, value

Actinic Keratoses

Note: Actinic keratoses are also called solar keratoses. These and seborrheic keratoses (p.232) have been called 'senile keratoses', but that term is inaccurate and pejorative.

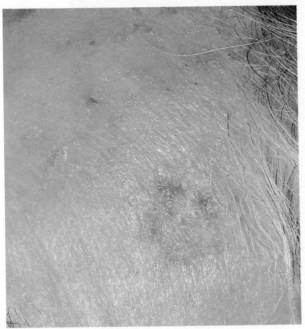

Slightly eroded, scaly actinic keratosis. Higher on the forehead additional granular keratoses could be easily palpated.

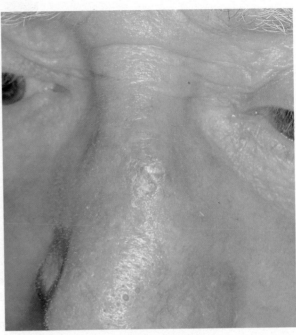

Very keratotic solar keratosis. Note also telangiectasia and dilated pores.

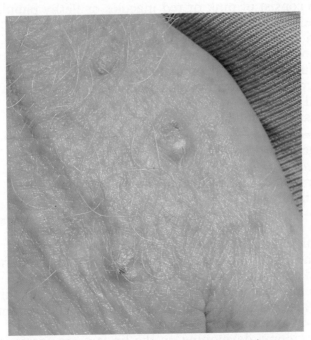

Fleshy actinic keratoses. Squamous cell carcinoma was considered, but biopsy showed that atypical cells were not invading through the basement membrane.

Actinic Keratoses

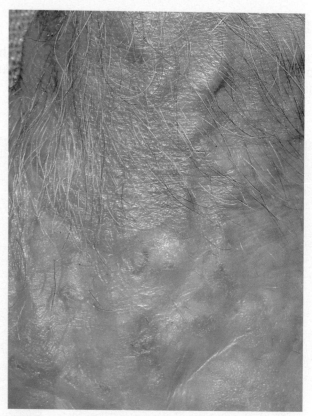

Almost confluent actinic keratoses in area of vitiligo (lower half of photograph), none in area of normal pigmentation.

Clinical

● Actinic keratoses consist of pink or red macules or fleshy papules surmounted by adherent white, grey, or yellow lamellar scale.
   ▲ they occur on sun-exposed areas of the fair-skinned
   ▲ the scale periodically falls off but reforms
     ■ it is painful to remove it prematurely
     ■ the scale may not reform on macular areas, leaving only roughened erosion
   ▲ they are occasionally tender

> ▲ similar changes can occur on the lips, especially on the lower lip, as *actinic cheilitis*. This may be focal or diffuse. Scale is minimal (because of the moist environment), but the lips may fissure

● Actinic keratoses represent focal areas of epidermal cell atypia, forming abnormal keratin. By definition, such keratoses do not extend through the epidermal basement membrane into the dermis, although finger-like projections may protrude into the dermis. Actinic keratoses may become squamous cell carcinoma, but this is uncommon and late. Actinically-induced squamous cell carcinoma (p.263) metastasizes infrequently and late. Actinically-induced squamous cell carcinoma developing on the lip is more aggressive than that on the skin.
     ■ examine all sun-exposed skin for the presence of other sun-induced changes (p.249)

Actinic Keratoses

Treatment

- General.
  - ▲ discuss the significance of the lesions with the patient
  - ▲ advise the patient on sun protection (p.289)
- Symptomatic treatment to prevent malignancy is unnecessary because the development of true malignancy is unlikely and delayed; it is acceptable to treat for redness and scaling, then monitor the patient's progress every six months.
  - ▲ lubricants (p.304) for scaliness
  - ▲ corticosteroids for redness and scale
    - ■ use low-potency (hydrocortisone 1%) cream or ointment once or twice daily
- Physical destruction may be the treatment of choice. Any method which destroys the epidermis is adequate. If dermal injury is avoided, scarring will not occur.
  - ▲ cryotherapy – liquid nitrogen application by cotton-tipped applicator is the preferred treatment, as it causes minimal dermal damage
  - ▲ curettage by a light quick flick with a skin curette after ethyl chloride or freon spray anesthesia. With experience it is possible to avoid significant dermal injury
    - ■ stop bleeding with pressure or stiptic (p.324)
    - ■ such treatment is not suitable near eyes and mouth because of irritation from anesthetic spray
    - ■ such treatment is difficult on soft areas, such as the central cheek, where the skin skates away from pressure of curette
  - ▲ electrocautery and chemodestruction (phenol 88% or trichloracetic acid 60%) are difficult to control and easily cause scarring
- Topical chemotherapy with 5-fluorouracil (p.324) will destroy clinically undetectable incipient lesions as well as visible ones. Apply the drug thinly twice daily to involved areas, and areas suspected of bearing actinic keratoses. Inflammation usually develops in a few days; treatment is continued for two to six weeks, until the lesions are flat and non-keratotic
  - ▲ absorption and response occur more reliably and promptly on the face than on the arms. Usually, inflammation appears in two to five days, and treatment is complete in two to three weeks
    - ■ avoid the eyes, naso-labial fold, and mouth. Material collects in the folds and is irritating to the patient
  - ▲ response is slow and possibly incomplete on arms. Occlusion or the addition of tretinoin cream or gel may be necessary to obtain penetration and effect. Treatment may last for six weeks. Treat the thickest lesions by individual destruction
  - ▲ to minimize irritation from 5-fluorouracil a potent topical corticosteroid may be used. There is disagreement as to whether suppressing the inflammation diminishes effectiveness
  - ▲ a course of treatment may need to be repeated every few years

Keratoacanthoma

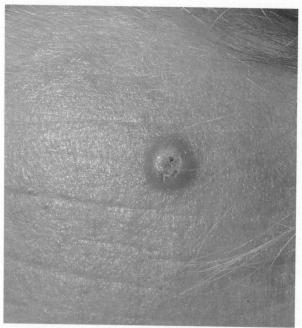

Early keratoacanthoma: a fleshy nodule just beginning to develop a keratotic core.

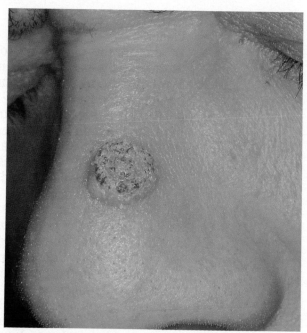

Keratotic core more developed in later lesion (present 3-4 weeks).

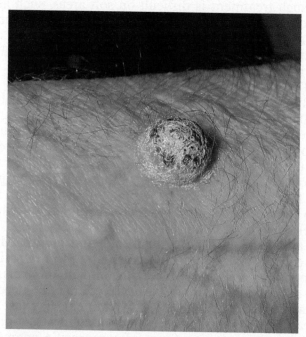

Keratotic cap in keratoacanthoma present 4-6 weeks.

Keratoacanthoma

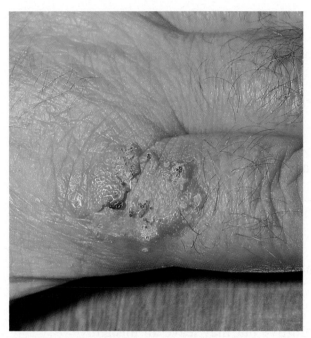

Keratoacanthoma almost completely involuted after 3 months.

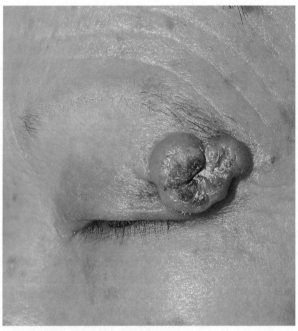

Keratoacanthoma recurrent only one month after presumably complete excision.

Clinical

● Keratoacanthoma consists of a fast-growing nodule on the sun-exposed skin of fair-skinned adults.

▲ it starts as a slightly keratotic fleshy papule, rapidly develops a keratotic core with a fleshy rim; the core may then fall out leaving a fleshy umbilicated nodule. The condition usually resolves spontaneously in about three months, leaving an atrophic scar

▲ it usually reaches maximum size (about one centimeter) in three to four weeks. Occasionally it grows to 3cm-4cm, and rarely to 10cm or greater

▲ it is most common in sun-damaged skin

▲ there are occasional multiple occurrences, sometimes with dozens of lesions

● Histopathologic examination of keratoacanthoma shows quite dysplastic growth of epidermal prickle cells.

▲ biopsy of a piece of the lesion is indistinguishable from squamous cell carcinoma

▲ it is necessary to have a section of the entire lesion or a biopsy specimen from border to border, showing the entire architecture, to confirm the pathological diagnosis

Keratoacanthoma

Clinical (continued)

▲ there are some reports of conversion of keratoacanthoma to squamous cell carcinoma
  ■ if this occurs it is rare
  ■ such reports may reflect the difficulty in making the initial pathological diagnosis

---

Note: diagnosis of keratoacanthoma is clinical, or a combination of history, clinical appearance, and pathological findings.

Treatment

● It is possible to wait for spontaneous resolution but the lesion may grow larger (resulting in a larger scar) and the patient is usually alarmed and wants treatment.
● Biopsy frequently induces resolution, but this is unpredictable.
● Complete surgical excision is definitive but may leave an unsightly scar, depending on the location of the lesion.
● Partial excision, shave removal of a superficial portion, or biopsy sometimes provokes renewed growth of the lesion to a large size (3cm-4cm).
  ▲ this is especially true of lesions on the nose or central face
  ▲ partial removal of these recurrent lesions usually provokes more growth
● Intralesional injection therapy.
  ▲ this usually causes lesions to resolve in a few weeks. Treatment is usually initiated only after clinical diagnosis, so follow-up is essential
  ▲ infiltrate the fleshy portion of the lesion with 0.1mL to 0.5mL of solution at weekly intervals
    ■ 5-fluorouracil 50mg/mL (from vial for intravenous use)
    ■ depot corticosteroid (p.313) such as triamcinolone acetonide 10mg/mL
    ■ 5-fluorouracil is probably the drug of choice as lesions on the extremities are occasionally resistant to corticosteroid
  ▲ the lesions should be smaller in one week and will regress completely in three to four weeks

---

If there is no change, excise the lesions to rule out squamous cell carcinoma.

Basal Cell Carcinoma
Squamous Cell Carcinoma

Basal cell carcinoma (BCC) and squamous cell carcinoma (SCC) are discussed together because of similarities in their biological behavior and treatment.

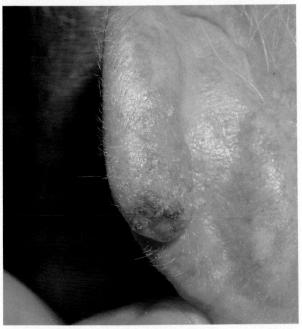

Early squamous cell carcinoma. Surface is fragile and bleeds easily.

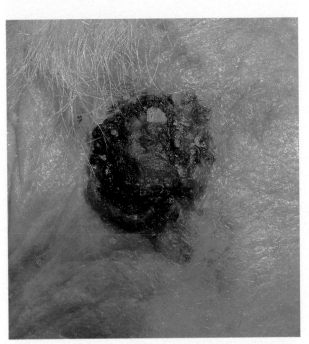

Neglected squamous cell carcinoma.

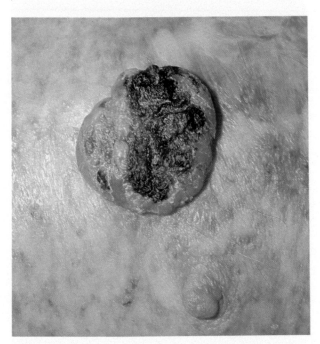

Huge squamous cell carcinoma (note nipple for size comparison) and severely sun-damaged skin. Eighty-year old man had been lifeguard for 40 years.

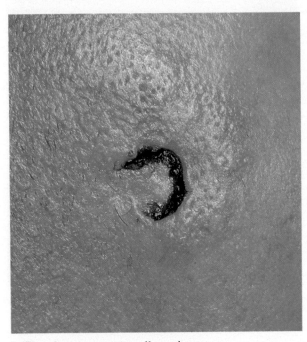

Infiltrating squamous cell carcinoma.

Basal Cell Carcinoma
Squamous Cell Carcinoma

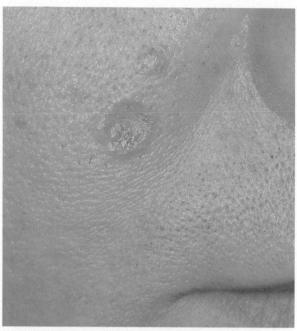

Classic basal cell carcinoma: pearly (translucent) flesh-colored papule with depressed center, rolled edge, and telangiectasia. Lesion above it is non-pigmented mole.

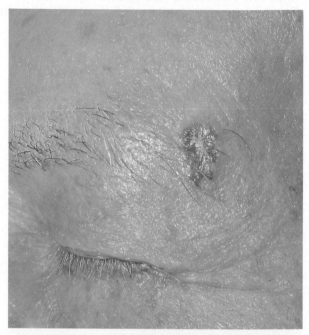

Pigmented basal cell carcinoma still displays pearly quality and depressed center. Note sun-damaged skin.

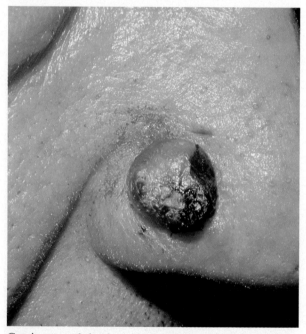

Cystic or nodular basal cell carcinoma.

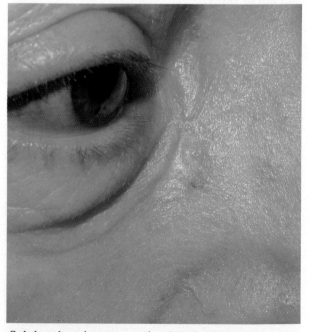

Subtle sclerosing or scarring basal cell carcinoma below indentation from glasses nosepad. Very firm on palpation.

Basal Cell Carcinoma
Squamous Cell Carcinoma

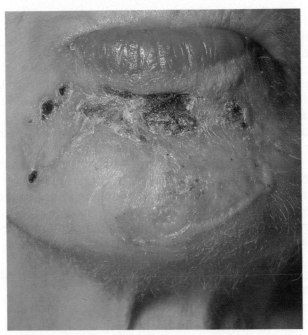

Neglected basal cell carcinoma has enlarged
superficially for years. Note rolled border and
scarred appearance.

Clinical
● Both tumors.
  ▲ are seen mainly on the sun-exposed skin of fair-complexioned
    people
     ■ BCC is occasionally seen in dark-skinned people and on sun
       sheltered skin
     ■ SCC and, to a lesser extent, BCC are occasionally seen at
       sites of chronic inflammation, such as osteomyelitis sinuses,
       old radiation burns, discoid lupus erythematosus, and
       hidradenitis suppurativa. In these locations SCC is more
       aggressive (20% metastasis) than when actinically induced
  ▲ they have a low rate of deep tissue invasion or metastasis
    (except at sites of chronic inflammation)
     ■ they are usually seen in growths neglected for years
     ■ in BCC 'metastasis' is to local nodes; in SCC metastasis
       may be generalized
     ■ the major clinical complication is local extension into
       complex structures such as the orbit, sinuses, or calvarium
● Typically, *basal cell carcinoma* consists of a translucent ('pearly')
  fleshy papule or nodule with an umbilicated or depressed center
  and a rolled border, often containing ectatic capillaries
  ▲ it is not keratin-producing, so the lesions are not scaly or
    hyperkeratotic, but occasionally there is mild oozing and
    crusting

Basal Cell Carcinoma
Squamous Cell Carcinoma

Clinical (continued)

- ▲ clinical variants
  - ■ nodular or cystic – tense and shiny
  - ■ superficial – shiny, thin patch or plaque
  - ■ pigmented – ranges from a few specks of gunpowder gray pigment to complete black pigmentation. Translucent quality differentiates it from melanoma (p.268)
  - ■ 'rodent ulcer' – the central umbilication burrows in to form a pit. This often oozes. It is usually near the nose
  - ■ sclerosing, scarring, or morpheaform – firm, fibrous reaction with subtle tiny pearly papules at the border. This often extends more deeply and is more lateral than it appears on the surface
- ● *Squamous cell carcinoma* consists of an opaque skin-colored fleshy papule, nodule, or plaque which is usually scaly, keratotic, or eroded.
  - ▲ hyperkeratosis may be verrucous, crumbly, or in the form of a cutaneous horn
  - ▲ the tissue is fragile, so oozing and bleeding are common

Treatment

- ● General.
  - ▲ examine all sun-exposed skin for evidence of solar damage (p.249) and other tumors
  - ▲ discuss sun damage and sun protection with the patient (p.289)
  - ▲ if the lesion is small it can be promptly treated by one of the methods discussed below. If it is large or in a difficult site (eyelid, ear or burrowing deep into the nose), perform a biopsy or refer the patient to a dermatologist or an appropriate surgeon
- ● Destructive treatments all have cure rate of over 95% in uncomplicated cases. Each method has advantages and drawbacks. The site, tumor type, patient age, and cosmetic needs all help make a mutual choice.
  - ▲ surgical excision is generally the preferable treatment if the lesion is small, simple, and if the defect can easily be closed. Usually the procedure is quick, postoperative inconvenience slight, cosmetic outcome is good, and, most important, the margins of the surgical specimen can be checked for adequacy of excision
  - ▲ curettage and electrodesiccation are excellent treatments for simple, superficial lesions, and even large ones. An unsightly scab is present for weeks. Residual scarring is usually marked, but may be slight on certain areas of the face. The adequacy of treatment is detected by the 'feel' of the curettage in the hands of an experienced therapist. The surgical specimen is fragmented and useless to determine margins. Curettage and desiccation should be performed only by adequately trained individuals

Basal Cell Carcinoma
Squamous Cell Carcinoma

Treatment (continued)

    ▲ cryotherapy consists of profound tissue freezing with liquid nitrogen spray or metal applicators. A generous margin is selected clinically to insure adequate treatment. Post-therapy pain, swelling, tissue necrosis, and oozing may last for days to weeks. There is suprisingly little scarring. Cryotherapy spares cartilage so it is useful for complex tumors on the nose and ear. It should be performed only by an experienced cryotherapist

    ▲ radiation therapy is appropriate for complex tumors but it is particularly harmful to cartilage. It requires 10 to 20 office visits and is followed by weeks of inflammation. The scar has a good early appearance but looks worse with the passage of years and may undergo malignant degeneration, generally restricting the use of this modality to patients over the age of 60 years

● Topical chemotherapy.

    ▲ limited experience with topical or intralesional 5-fluorouracil has been used with some success in thin superficial tumors, but cure rates are low and patient discomfort is great. This treatment is still under investigation

● Treatment of recurrent and complex tumors.

    ▲ *complex tumors* are treated by wide excision and complex closure, cryotherapy, or radiation therapy. All such cases should be referred to the appropriate therapist

    ▲ *recurrent tumors* have a cure rate of only 50% when treated by curettage, cryotherapy, or radiation therapy. Surgical excision with examination of specimen for margins is the best treatment. For difficult primary or recurrent tumors, the preferable treatment is often 'Mohs chemosurgery', or microscopically controlled serial excisions. The tumor is mapped and excised and the margins are immediately checked on frozen sections. Areas abutting positive margins are immediately excised and checked, and this continues until all specimens are clear. The cure rate for primary and recurrent tumors is over 95%. It is advisable to send patients with complex recurrent tumors to the nearest center where they can obtain this treatment

● Follow-up examinations should be performed at three, six and 12 months, and yearly or semi-yearly thereafter. Look for tumor regrowth, and feel for deep tissue recurrences. The scar is often thick and bulging at six to 12 weeks, so examine the patient a month or two later if growth is suspected then.

    ▲ on each visit examine all sun-exposed skin for new tumors

Melanoma

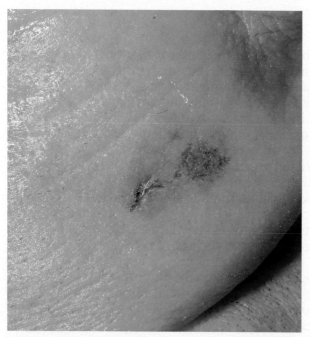 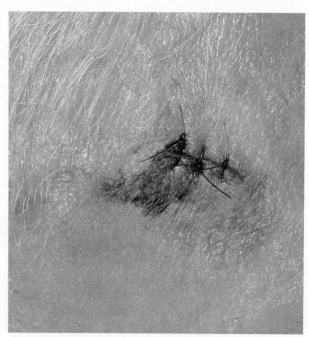

Typical lentigo maligna differs from regular lentigo by having feathered, poorly-demarcated border, and several shades of pigment.

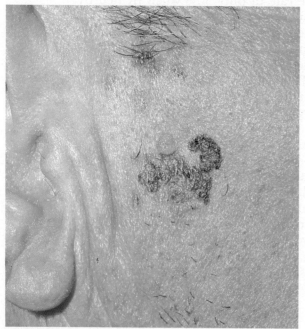 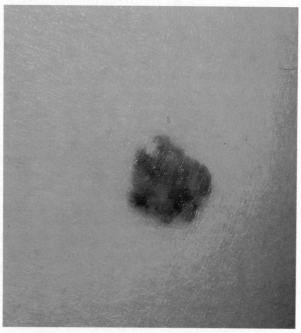

Dark lentigo maligna on cheek and in sideburn. Apparently clear area between two sites was probably involved in past but resolved. Seborrheic keratosis is present at upper edge of lower lesion.

Superficial spreading melanoma: pseudopod-like irregular border and variegated pigment.

Melanoma

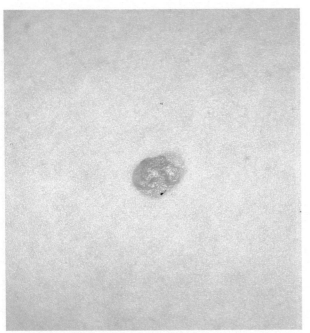

Non-pigmented superficial spreading melanoma, said to be present for 2 years.

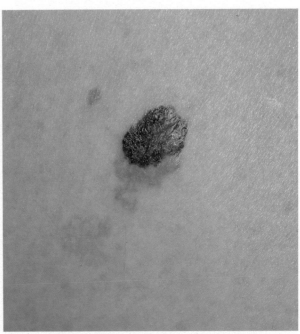

Superficial spreading melanoma still confined to upper dermis.

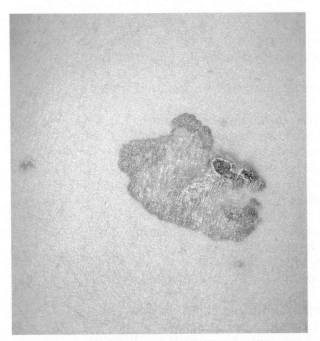

This superficial spreading melanoma was 7x9 cm in size and had been present several years. Healed areas in center were devoid of malignant cells.

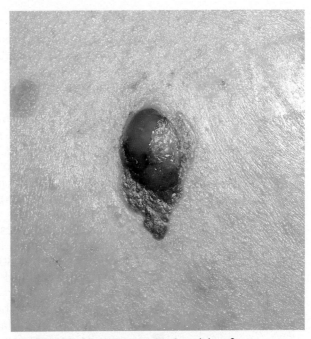

Nodular melanoma apparently arising from superficial spreading type. Fragility and bleeding is common.

Melanoma

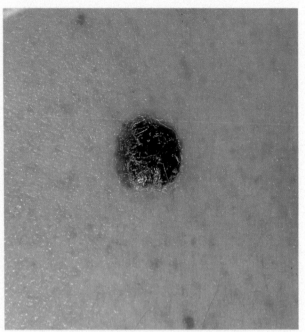

Nodular melanoma. Microscopic examination revealed that it arose in a mole.

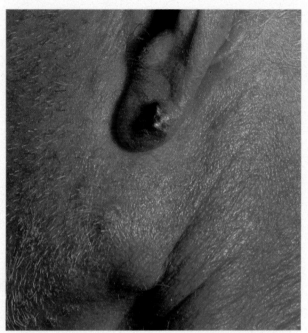

Nodular melanoma and involved cervical lymph node.

Clinical

- Melanoma is a malignant growth of pigment cells.
  - ▲ a large proportion of melanomas (80%) arise from normally-pigmented skin
    - ■ a small proportion of melanomas (20%) arise from moles (p.225)
  - ▲ melanomas are most common in fair-skinned people
    - ■ they are rare in dark-skinned people in whom they occur on less-pigmented palms and soles
  - ▲ they are more frequent in geographical areas of high sun intensity but, except for lentigo maligna, they do not occur on skin sites of great sun exposure
  - ▲ rare familial occurrence
- There are three clinical types of melanoma which differ considerably in appearance, behavior and prognosis.
  - ▲ lentigo maligna (about 30% of melanomas)
    - ■ a slowly-growing dark macule on the face of an elderly white person
    - ■ there is an irregular border, indistinct edges, various shades of brown, tan and black hypopigmentation
    - ■ it may be present for many years as a macule (malignant cells confined to the epidermis) but may eventually develop an invasive nodule (lentigo maligna melanoma) – it may metastasize in the nodular stage, but is less aggressive than the following types

Melanoma

Clinical (continued)

- ■ prognosis is years of slow macular growth, and cure almost 100% if treated in that stage
- ▲ superficial spreading melanoma (about 50% of melanomas)
  - ■ this grows as a slightly elevated plaque anywhere on body
  - ■ it has an irregular border, with areas of blurring of pigment into surrounding skin in various shades of black, brown, white. It may have rim of pink inflammation. The surface is slightly fragile and may bleed or ooze
  - ■ it grows as a small plaque (cells in epidermis and upper dermis) for six to 24 months, then develops a nodule which is highly invasive
  - ■ there is a greater than 90% cure rate with complete excision in the plaque stage, but prognosis is poor after the nodule develops
- ▲ nodular melanoma (about 20% of melanomas)
  - ■ this arises suddenly as a papule or nodule on the skin or in a mole
  - ■ it is a blue-black or brown nodule which bleeds easily, often with a rim of inflammation. It is occasionally flesh-colored
  - ■ it only takes weeks for metastasis to occur (cells spread rapidly into dermis and blood vessels). Occasionally nodular melanoma will involute after metastasis (10% of patients with metastatic melanoma have no remaining primary lesion)
  - ■ prognosis is poor unless there is early and complete excision

Treatment
- ● General.
  - ▲ learn to recognize benign lesions which can look like a melanoma
    - ■ solar lentigines (p.255)
    - ■ moles (p.225)
    - ■ seborrheic keratoses (p.232)
    - ■ dermatofibromas (p.234)
    - ■ pyogenic granulomas (p.238)
    - ■ pigmented basal cell epitheliomas (p.263)
  - ▲ perform biopsy (p.300) or excise suspicious lesions
    - ■ 'suspicious lesions' have the characteristics described above, or have appeared suddenly, or look peculiar to the patient or physicians. A readiness to perform biopsy relieves the concern of patient and physician. Performing biopsy of a melanoma does not increase the incidence of metastasis
  - ▲ the prognosis and treatment depend on the results of pathological examination. In general, thin lesions (less than 0.75mm) have a good prognosis when excised with a small margin. Thick lesions (more than 1.25mm) have a worse prognosis. They are excised with a larger margin, and may require lymph node dissection
  - ▲ except for thin lesions, check for metastasis
  - ▲ refer the patient to a center experienced in melanoma treatment

Melanoma

Treatment (continued)

● Surgical excision is recommended for all melanomas.
   ▲ lentigo maligna is excised with a narrow margin. If a nodule is present, a one-centimeter margin is advised
      ■ large lesions in elderly patient may preclude surgery. Examine the patient every six months and perform biopsy if a papule develops
      ■ radiation therapy and cryotherapy are treatments under investigation, but deep, hidden recurrences (from cells in hair follicles) have occurred
   ▲ superficial spreading melanoma is excised with a one-centimeter margin. If a nodule is present, a larger excision may be necessary, as well as regional node dissection
   ▲ nodular melanoma is excised with at least a two-centimeter margin. Regional node dissection is usually advised if the area drains to one group
● Metastatic melanomas are usually poorly responsive to radiation therapy and chemotherapy. Prognosis is poor. Refer patients to an oncology center.
● Follow-up examinations after excision.
   ▲ sites for lentigo maligna or very thin superficial spreading melanoma should be checked at six and 12 months after excision, then yearly
   ▲ thicker nodular lesions are followed up at six-month intervals with physical examination for metastases

Patient Guides
Seborrheic Dermatitis

It is normal to shed a few flakes of **dander** from the scalp every day, and regular shampooing will keep it from building up in your hair. **Seborrheic dermatitis** is severe scaling, usually with itching and inflammation. It occurs on the scalp and is also frequently seen in and behind the ears, on the face, in the brows, and even in the eyelashes. It often worsens with illness or emotional tension.

Anti-dandruff Shampoos

There are many anti-dandruff shampoos on the market, and they are all effective. Those containing tar are possibly more potent than those without it. Selenium shampoos are probably no more effective than the others. The following points must be kept in mind about the use of anti-dandruff shampoos:

1. The benefit of one shampooing lasts only two to three days, so washing must be at least that frequent.
2. A severe case of dandruff may not respond to repeated shampooing for a week or more, so do not give up after one treatment.
3. The medications in the shampoo must be in contact with the scalp long enough to work. Lathering and rinsing within a few seconds is inadequate. The shampoo should be left on for several minutes, and the longer it is left on the more effective it will be.
4. A severe flare-up of dandruff can occur despite shampoo use. Shampoos are just not strong enough to suppress all natural fluctuations of the disease.

To get the most benefit from a dandruff shampoo you should wash several times a week and leave the shampoo on for several minutes during each wash. If this schedule does not remove all the dandruff, then you may lather the shampoo, rinse it off, lather again, and cover your wet scalp with a plastic shower cap. Leave this in place for 30 minutes to two hours while you perform other activities, then rinse out thoroughly. This may be slightly irritating to the scalp, but will usually remove all the scale.

Try many different brands of shampoo to find the one which is cosmetically acceptable to you. Some lather more than others, or are more drying, or have different odors or textures. If you do not like the way the anti-dandruff shampoo makes your hair feel or smell, then you may perform a final wash with a regular scented cosmetic shampoo, or you may use a conditioner or rinse. This will not reduce the potency of the anti-dandruff shampoo.

Seborrheic Dermatitis

Other Medications

Your doctor may prescribe an oil or gel to apply to the scalp to help remove excessive scaling. These should be rubbed into the scalp sparingly at bedtime, covered with a shower cap and left on overnight. You should then shampoo in the morning, or sooner if this treatment causes burning of the scalp. These treatments usually need to be performed at weekly or less frequent intervals.

Your doctor may prescribe a cortisone solution to help reduce inflammation of the scalp. The easiest way to apply any liquid to the scalp is the following: part your hair along the length of your scalp and apply a drop of medication about every 2cm along the part and rub it in; repart the hair about 2cm parallel to the first part and again apply medication every 2cm; keep reparting the hair and applying small amounts of the medication until the entire inflamed area is treated. This technique provides maximum medication to the scalp, and minimum residue on the hair.

Acne

Causes

Most people have a few pimples during their teenage years; some have severe or long-lasting disease. Acne is predestined in certain individuals and will occur regardless of their physical, social or cultural upbringing. The sensitivity of the oil glands to plugging (to form blackheads and whiteheads) and to rupture (to form pimples) is inherited.

Here are things known about acne

Oil glands are inactive in childhood, and develop at puberty. This explains why the face then becomes oily, pores become visible (pore size is related to oil gland size), and acne may develop. Pore size is unchangeable, and is not affected by astringents, massage, saunas, facial packs, or cosmetics.

Blackheads or pore plugs, the basic culprit in acne, are composed of dead skin produced by the cells lining the pore. The plug is not made of dirt or hardened oil. It is deep and cannot be scrubbed out. Its formation cannot be prevented by washing or the use of astringents.

A pimple is an inflamed area of tissue reacting to the rupture of an oil gland and/or hair root. The hair root ruptures at least partially because it is plugged. A pimple may contain a few bacteria, but it is not a true infection, and is not the result of touching the face with dirty fingers.

The occurrence of acne in some people may be influenced by
1. Stress, illness, or exhaustion.
2. Sunlight. Sun exposure often improves acne, but may worsen it in some individuals (especially those who sunburn easily).
3. Hormonal changes. There are often slight flares of acne related to the menstrual cycle. Pregnancy usually improves acne. Birth control pills may or may not improve acne depending on the estrogen content.
4. Cosmetics. Certain cosmetics irritate the cells lining the oil gland pores so that they make dead skin plugs. The thickness of the cosmetic, or whether it is 'hypoallergenic' is not related to this effect.

The occurrence of acne is NOT influenced by
1. Diet. Chocolate, junk food, greasy food, vitamins and minerals do not affect acne.
2. Cleanliness.
3. Sexual activity.

Scarring is the natural result of significant skin inflammation. It is not caused by picking. However, picking may worsen the inflammation of a pimple so that it is more likely to scar. The type of pimple especially sensitive to manipulation is the deep red bump not surmounted by a pus head. This type has nowhere to drain and is fragile, so manipulation of it is likely to cause more rupture and inflammation in the tissues.

Acne

Treatment

There is no 'cure' for acne, but modern treatments help keep acne under control until it clears with time. Your doctor will select the treatments which work best and have the fewest side effects, and will follow you and change treatments if your response to treatment changes. Below are general rules about acne treatments; your doctor will tell you specifically how to use various medications.

Except for cortisone treatments given by doctors, all treatments for acne primarily work by preventing the formation of new pimples, and do little to hasten the healing of existing pimples. As a result, at least two to four weeks of constant treatment are necessary before improvement begins. Things will continue to improve even more for up to 12 weeks before levelling off. Also, treatment must be given constantly to all acne-prone areas, and not just to individual existing pimples.

Washing excessively with regular soap, special acne soaps, or with abrasives has little impact on acne. More often they dry out, chap, and irritate the skin. Then when effective anti-acne creams or lotions are used they are likely to burn and irritate more. Just washing once or twice a day with a mild soap is best. If parts of the face feel oily during the day, they can be wiped with a mild alcohol-and-water astringent.

Acne treatment with topical antibiotic, benzoyl peroxide and/or tretinoin

These are external anti-acne medications. All are applied regularly to the areas likely to break out with acne. They work slowly to stop the appearance of new pimples. No benefit may be seen for a month or more, and the benefit may increase over two to three months. About two-thirds of patients get a good response.

Benzoyl peroxide and tretinoin, especially, may be irritating. To minimize irritation they should be applied thinly, with care taken to avoid puddling in folds around the eyes, nose and mouth. They are more irritating to moist skin, so they should not be applied within 15 minutes of washing. Washing should be infrequent (twice a day) and with mild soap. Strong acne soaps tend to increase irritation. Your doctor may prescribe a soothing medication if irritation cannot be avoided.

Benzoyl peroxide

This helps reduce inflamed pimples and will also reduce blackheads. It should be applied twice a day – to the point that the skin feels slightly dry and tight, but not to the point of redness or irritation. Some people can use it only once a day, and some can tolerate it more often than twice a day. Find the schedule that suits your skin. Occasionally an allergy to it will develop, so if an itchy red rash occurs, stop treatment. Also, benzoyl peroxides have a mild bleaching action on dark clothing.

Topical antibiotic

Like benzoyl peroxide, topical antibiotics help prevent new pimples. They have no effect on blackheads. Most are in alcohol solutions and may be slightly drying, but usually do not irritate as benzoyl peroxides might. They do not bleach clothing. They are applied twice daily to acne-prone areas.

Tretinoin

Tretinoin, or vitamin-A acid, works best against blackheads, but also reduces pimples. It can usually be used only once a day, or even

Acne

Treatment (continued)

every other day. After a few weeks your skin may be able to tolerate it more often. Mild redness often occurs. It may make your skin more sensitive to the sun, so be cautious when getting your first sun exposure of the year. Sunscreening lotions should be used if you are outside a lot.

Using tretinoin with benzoyl peroxide or topical antibiotic

Benzoyl peroxide or topical antibiotic and tretinoin together are often more beneficial than either alone. Tretinoin is used at night, and the other medication is applied in the morning or afternoon. They must not be put on at the same time, as such mixing could neutralize the tretinoin.

Isotretinoin Therapy for Acne

Isotretinoin is a derivative of vitamin A which is taken orally for severe acne. It works by greatly reducing oil gland output, and possibly by decreasing inflammation and pore plugging. It completely clears facial acne in almost all patients, and usually clears acne of the chest and back. It is unique among all acne medications in that its effect continues for weeks, months, or even years after its use is discontinued.

Isotretinoin is generally taken for three to five months. The dose (number of tablets per day) varies depending on body weight and side effects. The drug is very expensive. If the first three to five months' treatment is not completely successful, then it may be given again after a two month rest period.

Side effects are numerous and common, but none is permanent. Because oil gland output is reduced so much, skin dryness is a common problem. Up to 80% of people taking the drug get dry, chapped skin, or itching, dry nose and/or mouth, or even nose bleeds; 90% get dry, cracked lips, and 40% get dry or irritated eyes. Fewer than 10% experience dry, lifeless hair, and breaking or thinning of hair. Fewer than 5% experience peeling of the palms and soles.

Other symptoms which may be caused by the drug include muscle or joint aches and pains (15%), and occasionally there are headaches or fatigue.

Isotretinoin is probably harmful to unborn babies, so it should not be taken during pregnancy nor while nursing. Women taking the drug should use reliable birth control methods, and should have at least one normal menstrual period after stopping therapy before becoming pregnant.

Up to 25% of persons taking isotretinoin develop elevated blood fats, and 10% may have mild liver test changes, or changes in blood cells. The practical significance of these findings is unknown, but blood tests should be taken before therapy and at two to four week intervals during treatment.

Because these side effects are similar to those of vitamin A overdose, vitamin supplements containing vitamin A should *not* be taken during isotretinoin therapy. Other medications may also exaggerate side effects so be sure to clear those medications with your doctor.

Isotretinoin is an effective, exciting new drug for severe acne. Because of side effects and expense, however, it should not be used casually, and close supervision by a physician is necessary.

Herpes Simplex

Herpes simplex is a viral infection unique in its ability to recur repeatedly. It can do so because virus particles lie dormant in the nuclei of nerve cells located near the spinal column, where your natural immune reaction cannot destroy them. The dormant virus may awaken spontaneously, or be provoked by fever, illness, sunburn, injury, or stress.

In an individual, herpes simplex occurs repeatedly at the same site, the most common sites being the lips, genitals, and buttocks. The virus causing the lip eruption is usually a slightly different one than the one causing the genital rash, so it is possible, but rare, to get fever blisters in both places.

The frequency and duration of attacks is difficult to predict. Fewer than one in four persons has recurrent episodes. Attacks may occur as often as a dozen times yearly, or as rarely as twice in a lifetime. The attacks are more frequent in young adulthood, and diminish with age. Attacks often start with a tingling and burning sensation for a few hours before the skin breaks out. A red, swollen area appears which usually becomes studded with tiny blisters after one or two days. After another few days the blisters dry up to become scabs, which are shed in a few more days. There may be redness without blisters, or tiny ulcers without blisters. The attack may last two or three days one time, and seven to 10 days the next, with varying amounts of discomfort.

Herpes simplex is passed by skin-to-skin contact, and is contagious during the blistering phase, until dry, hard scabs are present. During that time, skin contact should be avoided. A condom probably prevents spread of infection during intercourse. Herpes simplex present in the vagina during childbirth may be dangerous to the newborn infant, so the obstetrician should be informed if attacks occur there so that precautions can be taken at birth. Brimmed hats and sunscreen lotions for the lips may prevent fever blisters induced by sunburn. You should avoid touching fever blisters and then rubbing your eye, because occasionally the eye will become seriously infected.

With time, attacks of herpes simplex diminish and die out on their own. There does not now exist a medical cure for the condition. Various medications, vitamins and vaccines have been tried but have proven to be ineffective in preventing recurrent attacks. Accelerating the drying and healing of a current attack is possible, and your doctor may recommend a lotion, cream, or compress for that purpose.

Pubic Lice (Crabs)

Crabs are tiny insects which live on humans in the pubic area, and occasionally on body hair on the trunk or in the armpit. Occasionally they even inhabit eyelash hair. They grasp the hair firmly with a pincer, periodically bite the skin for food, and attach eggs (nits) to the hairs. The organisms are small (three millimeters), gray, flat, and slow-moving. They are often mistaken for flakes of dry skin. Itching may be non-existent to intense.

Site of Infestation
The pubic area is by far the most common site of infestation. The organisms are passed between humans who sleep together. Less frequently the organisms fall off the host and they may survive in bedlinen or clothing for up to four days, and can possibly infest other people from those sources, but rarely.

Treatment
To treat crabs, use the shampoo or lotion prescribed by your doctor, and follow his or her instructions: some types of shampoo or lotion are left on for minutes, others are left on for hours. Usually the area from the waist to the knees is treated, to ensure adequate coverage. One treatment kills the organism and the eggs, but itching from bites may last for a few more days. The dead nits may remain tightly attached to the hairs after treatment but are usually of no further concern.

After treatment, you should dress in clean clothes, and put fresh linen on the bed. The old bedlinen and clothes worn during the last day should be washed, cleaned, or hot-ironed. It is not necessary to clean your entire wardrobe, or to clean the mattress and the bedroom. Persons sleeping together should be treated simultaneously to prevent reinfection.

Eyelash Infestation
If the eyelashes are infested then your doctor will prescribe an ointment which should be applied thinly with a cotton swab twice a day. Your doctor may gently remove the organisms from the lashes with fine tweezers. Do not attempt to do this yourself as absolute stillness, good light, and magnification are needed.

Head Lice

This infestation occurs in epidemics among children, and is often passed to adults in their families. The tiny insect bites the scalp and attaches its eggs (nits) to the hairs with a strong glue. A person with head lice may have no itching at all, or may have a lot of itching, especially toward the back of the scalp and the nape of the neck. He or she may be aware only of the tiny nits beading the hairs. The infestation is passed from one person to another by close personal contact (kids wrestling, or sleeping together), or on infested hats, collars, pillows, upholstered furniture, or combs and brushes.

To kill the lice, use the shampoo or lotion that your doctor prescribes or recommends. The shampoo is generously lathered in, and left on for five minutes, then rinsed. The lotion is generously rubbed in and left on for 15 minutes, then washed out. Avoid contact with the eyes, and make sure that children do not have the opportunity to drink the materials, as they are strong poisons. The bites may itch for several days after successful treatment so do not treat again unnecessarily, and do not refill the prescription until you have consulted with your doctor. All individuals in the family possibly infested should be treated at the same time.

The shampoos and lotions kill the nits, but do not remove them from the hairs. If the dead nits do not comb out easily and are annoying then:

1. Soak the hair thoroughly with a solution made up of equal parts of water and white vinegar.
2. Wrap the wet scalp in a towel or put on a shower cap for at least 15 minutes to soften the attachment of the nits to the hairs.
3. Comb gently but thoroughly with a fine-toothed comb. Flea combs, available at pet stores, are well-suited to this task.
4. Thoroughly rinse or shampoo the hair.
5. Repeat periodically if necessary for stubborn nits.

Note: After adequate treatment, the lice and nits are dead and the infestation is no longer contagious. Children may return to school even if nits are still present.

To prevent spread of or reinfestation by head lice certain measures should be taken at home. Wash combs and brushes in hot, soapy water. Hats, coat collars (especially fur), sheets and pillow-cases should be washed, dry cleaned, or pressed with a hot iron. Vacuum or clean possibly infected pillows, mattresses and upholstered furniture. The adult lice can live away from humans for only a few days, so cleaning of all articles of clothing and furniture is unnecessary.

Hand Dermatitis

The hands of some people are sensitive to normal daily activities and easily become dry, cracked, and scaly. Water, soap, detergents, and cleansers are the most common culprits in triggering this problem, so 'dishpan hands' occur in housewives, nurses, cooks, beauticians, bartenders, waiters and others whose hands are repeatedly wetted. The rash caused by these exposures is a mild to severe irritation, not an allergy.

Blistering eczemas, psoriasis, and other rashes may occur on the hands. They may look like dishpan hands, and are irritated and worsened by water and cleanser exposure. The treatment of these 'hand eczemas' of whatever cause is the same.

Treatment
Prevention of Further Irritation
1. Decrease exposure to water and cleansers as much as possible. This might mean asking another household member to do some of these chores, or being temporarily transferred to another sort of job at work. Frequency of wetting and drying is more important than the duration of wetting, so washing, say, one large load of dishes a day is better than doing several small ones during the day. If you can use tongs and long-handled brushes when practical, this decreases water exposure. Unfortunately, rubber or plastic household gloves are not of great benefit in protecting you from common household exposures because it is the wetting which is most damaging, and gloves trap sweat and make the hand completely wet after a few minutes of wearing. Gloves flocked with cotton take only a few more minutes to do this. A truly protective system is to use a thin cotton glove under a loose vinyl one and to change to a fresh dry cotton glove whenever the current one becomes moist. This is so complicated and bulky as to be impractical for many activities. Avoiding wetting is much more effective than trying to protect against wetting.
2. Lubricating the skin is important to replace natural skin oils leached out by wetting. You should stop using all commercial hand lotions and moisturizing creams and use only the products your doctor recommends, because many of the commercial products contain fragrances and other chemicals which are irritants. Plain greases, such as mineral oil or vaseline, are the safest. These should be rubbed in thinly very often: after every water exposure; and whenever the skin feels dry. This may require applications as often as 10 times a day, especially at the beginning, but overlubrication is impossible, and underlubrication is harmful.
3. Treatment of the inflamed skin itself is by cortisone creams. Potent ones are usually necessary because penetration through thick palmar skin is poor. The cortisone cream or ointment is applied thinly two or three times a day, especially after water exposure. If the cream alone does not suppress redness and itching then a much greater effect can be obtained by covering the cream with a disposable plastic glove.

Hand Dermatitis

Treatment (continued)

This 'occlusion' greatly increases penetration of the medication, and softens and humidifies dry skin. After wearing the gloves overnight, for a few hours, or as long as possible, the hands should be rinsed and a cortisone cream or lubricant applied to prevent drying. If only the palm of the hand has a rash then the glove fingers can be cut off to make wearing the glove more comfortable.

After the rash has improved, or is under control, a mild cortisone cream is used instead of the potent one. Prolonged use of potent cortisone creams, especially under plastic gloves, may cause thinning of the skin. Lubricants alone will suffice if the rash has resolved, and cortisone creams can be used again if a relapse occurs.

If the hand inflammation does not respond to external therapy then your doctor may recommend cortisone pills or shots. These usually improve the rash but may have internal side effects, and the rash may reappear when they are stopped, so they are used with caution for only short periods.

Atopic Dermatitis

Atopic dermatitis (also called atopic eczema) is an inherited condition. It often occurs in individuals who have allergic hay fever or asthma, or in whose families those conditions occur; but atopic dermatitis itself is not an allergy. It is a condition of sensitive skin which is easily provoked to itch, and when the skin is rubbed or scratched, an itchy rash quickly appears. Dry weather, soaps, bathing, sweating, rough clothing, and common industrial agents (automotive greases, ceramic clays, and so on) may provoke severe itching in an atopic person, whereas they usually have less effect on other people. Similarly, most people can scratch, for instance, an insect bite for a few days with no lasting consequences, but an atopic person may scratch for only a day or two and develop a stubborn, itchy rash.

Atopic dermatitis usually starts in childhood and flares and subsides repeatedly for several years before resolving. The trend is for the rash to improve before adolescence, but it may flare in adulthood, especially on the hands when they are exposed a lot to water, detergents, and chemicals. Occasionally, atopic dermatitis appears only briefly in a lifetime, and occasionally it lasts unremittently into adulthood.

Treatment

Until it improves spontaneously, atopic dermatitis can be controlled by medication. Treatment has two goals; the prevention of itching; and treatment of the rash itself.

Prevention of itching is important. Try to determine what conditions in your life stimulate itching. In temperate climates, dryness of the skin is a major provoking cause. Dryness is often worst in the winter when central heating causes low humidity in buildings. Bathing, even with mild soap, removes natural lubricating oils from the skin and makes it drier. It is nearly impossible to make interior winter air humid (huge central humidifiers are necessary; pans of water on radiators have no effect). Therefore, the only practical way to minimize skin dryness is to bathe relatively infrequently (every other day) with a mild soap and then to immediately lubricate the skin with an oil or cream. Lotions are pleasant to use but contain too little oil to be effective, and are occasionally even more drying. Applications of lubricants once or twice a day on particularly dry skin (usually the arms and legs) may be necessary.

Heat and humidity make some atopic persons itch. If that is true of you, wear lightweight, loose clothing and **avoid** thick greases and oils, as they may plug your sweat pores. In general, most atopic people itch when they wear heavy unlined wool or polyester clothing. They are not allergic to wool, but the rough fibers of those materials often provoke sweating, which may cause itching. Wear cotton and cotton blend clothing as much as possible to minimize such irritation.

Atopic Dermatitis

Treatment (continued)

Atopic persons are not allergic to soap but they are often irritated by exposure to soaps, detergents, cleansers, and chemicals. Wearing plastic gloves is recommended when using strong cleansers, but they provoke sweating which itself may be irritating. Minimize exposures to water, detergents, and cleansers as much as possible and apply your medication immediately after each exposure.

Your doctor will probably give you a cortisone-type cream or ointment to treat and prevent your eczema. Rub it in thinly to all susceptible areas about twice daily, and use it more often if frequent water exposure occurs. Your doctor will tell you if certain creams are too strong to use on thin-skinned areas, such as the face and groin. Do not apply them to the eyelids without specific recommendation from your doctor.

People inaccurately say that atopic dermatitis is caused by nervousness, and much guilt can result from such statements. Eczema is inherited, not 'caused' by anything. However, as dryness and detergents can provoke itching, so tension can provoke it. Such provocation of disease by tension is not peculiar to atopic eczema; it occurs in almost all diseases, it's just that in eczema the consequences are apparent. Itching and scratching can occur subconsciously and during sleep. Your doctor may prescribe an 'itch pill', usually an antihistamine, to reduce the urgency of itching. Such medications often cause drowsiness, so they are best taken at bedtime. If you take them during the day, do not drive or operate dangerous equipment until you know how you react to the medication.

Dry Skin

Dry skin afflicts many people. It can be annoying because of its rough, scaly appearance, and it can cause severe itching. In dark-skinned individuals, 'chapping' can cause vague areas of decreased pigment (light color). This is particularly common on the face in children. After puberty, heavy oil production on the face usually corrects that dryness. Adults usually find that their legs and arms are the driest areas; the tendency to dryness increases in the elderly.

Warm, humid weather will usually completely control dry skin. Hot, dry weather is moderately drying to the skin, but the most drying occurs in cold climates. When cold air is heated in buildings, its humidity drops drastically, drawing water from the skin, lips, and nasal membranes, and from plants and wood (doors become loose in their frames). It is difficult to make such indoor air humid again; gallons of water must be added (by a central humidifier on the furnace) to each room each day. Putting open pans of water on the radiators is useless.

The only ways to treat dry skin are to avoid removing normal skin oils, and to add oil (lubrication) to the skin. Putting **water** on the skin is actually **drying** because water leaches out the natural skin oils which keep the skin soft and smooth. Soaps and detergents leach oil out even more. Bathing thus can result in 'dishpan body', with dry, rough skin. In dry weather, bathe only once a day or less, and avoid long, hot baths or showers with lots of soap. Oilated or superfatted soaps are probably less drying than regular and deodorant bath soaps.

After bathing, and at other times if necessary, apply a lubricant to dry skin areas. Lotions are pleasant to use, but contain a lot of water and little oil, so usually are not adequate for lubrication.

Oils, such as mineral oil, bath oil, or vegetable oil (such as olive oil) are good lubricants, and are pleasant to use if applied lightly. Use caution in adding oils to the bath. They provide less lubrication to the skin and make the tub very slippery. Creams and ointments are good lubricants but are more difficult to apply. Creams containing urea are commonly used as lubricants and work well, but they may temporarily cause a burning sensation on dry, cracked skin. All lubricants are best applied immediately after bathing and toweling; there is no advantage to applying to wet skin before toweling.

Certain myths about dry skin should be laid to rest. Dryness of the skin does not lead to permanent wrinkling, and lubricants (moisturizing creams) will not prevent wrinkling. Dryness occurs only on the top, dead skin layer, and is seen as fine lines. The dead skin layer is constantly shed and renewed, so no surface dryness lines are permanent. Wrinkles are due mostly to sun exposure (which damages deeper skin layers) and aging. Another myth is that diet affects dry skin. It does not. Short of starvation, the skin's oil glands make the same quantity and type of oil regardless of diet, and eating less or more oil has no impact on them.

Pityriasis Rosea

Pityriasis rosea is a mysterious condition which erupts on the skin, lasts a short period, and disappears. It is unsightly and may itch, but it does no harm. Its characteristics are:

- It occurs mostly in young adults, but may appear in children or older adults.
- It often starts with one large patch, which is followed in a few days by increasing numbers of smaller spots.
- It usually lasts about six weeks and then clears. Occasionally, it lasts eight to ten weeks. Many spots occur during the first few weeks; few spots appear during the last two to three weeks.
- The spots are usually concentrated on the trunk and the upper portions of the arms and legs. The rash rarely occurs on the face, wrists and hands.

The cause of pityriasis rosea is unknown, but a virus is considered the most likely culprit. The condition occurs in a certain age group, erupts suddenly, lasts a certain length of time, clears completely, and rarely occurs again in the same individual. There is also a slight 'epidemic' quality to the occurrence of pityriasis rosea; it is more frequent in the spring and autumn. However, against a viral cause of this disease is the fact that it is not contagious (it is rarely seen in family or school groups), and no viruses have been found.

There is no treatment that shortens the duration of pityriasis rosea. Ultraviolet light temporarily suppresses or heals some of the rash, but effective treatment with it is impractical. Itching is usually sporadic and mild. When it is bothersome it can be soothed by baths, lotions, or creams which your doctor will recommend. Antihistamine pills may relieve itching but often cause drowsiness, so they are best used at bedtime. In cases of severe itching your doctor may prescribe cortisone pills for a week or two.

All in all, the appearance of pityriasis rosea is at first alarming, but you can take comfort in the knowledge that it will not last long, it will not harm internal organs or leave scars, it is not contagious, and it is unlikely to recur.

Tinea Versicolor

This is a harmless, non-contagious mild fungal infection of the skin. The organism which causes this condition normally lives on everybody's skin in small numbers, but in young adults it occasionally grows profusely and causes a discolored rash. We do not know why this sudden growth and rash occurs, but it does not mean low resistance or internal disease.

The rash may last for years, worsening and improving over the months. It often becomes more noticeable during the summer with sun exposure and tanning of the skin. Washing with regular soap will abolish the scaling of the rash for a few hours, but the rash itself cannot be washed away that easily. However, the fungus is on the surface of the skin, not in it, so treatment with medication which causes mild peeling of the top dead skin layer will remove it.

The most commonly used medication is a dandruff shampoo (sometimes only available by prescription) such as Selsun or Exsel (Selsun Blue is weaker) which softens and removes the 'dandruff' or top dead layer of skin, found on everyone. Apply this lotion thinly over the entire trunk from neck to waist and down the arm to the elbow. Put it on a generous margin of normal skin around the rash, just to be sure you get all the fungus. Leave this on a few hours or overnight, if you can, but remove it sooner if your skin begins to burn or itch. Then wash in a bath or shower using more of the shampoo as a soap, and rub the area briskly with a facecloth to help remove the loosened dead skin. If you have a tendency to dry skin then apply a lubricating oil or lotion after bathing.

This treatment should be repeated once a week for six weeks. The ashy scale of the rash will disappear after a few treatments, but it may take months for your skin color to return to normal. This slow return of color is a normal healing process and does not mean that the treatment has failed. The rash may return in months, and a repeat treatment may be necessary. If the rash does not seem to respond well to this treatment, or if it returns immediately after each treatment, then return to your doctor for another medication.

You will outgrow this condition eventually, but usually it is easy to cure or keep under control. Your skin is not harmed or scarred by this infection, and you cannot give it to other people, so do not let tinea versicolor blemish your peace of mind.

The name tinea versicolor means 'fungus which changes color'.

Scabies

Scabies is caused by the human itch mite, which is too tiny for most people to see with the naked eye. When one organism gets onto human skin it burrows into the top layer of dead skin and lays eggs. The eggs hatch in five days; those mites burrow in and produce more eggs. During this initial phase of reproduction, while a few hundred mites are produced, the human host experiences no itching or rash, but is contagious to others. Finally, after two or three weeks the person becomes allergic to the mites and an itchy rash develops. Paradoxically, only a dozen or so mites are now present, as the allergic response kills many of them.

The rash is usually extremely itchy, especially at night. Dozens to hundreds of tiny bumps are present all over the body, with greater concentrations in the fold areas, such as finger webs, wrist folds, armpits, bellybutton, under the breasts, and between the buttocks. There is often a rash on the nipples and genitals. Older children and adults almost never have rash above the neck and on the palms and soles, but infants frequently have rash at those sites. Some people have only a mild allergic reaction and develop only a few faint bumps with only mild itching.

Scabies is passed by skin-to-skin contact, usually among people sleeping together, and to children who are hugged and carried by adults. Casual contact such as handshaking or contact in crowds does not pass the organism. Mites live in the skin and do not come off easily, but occasionally an organism is shed into clothing or bedding where another human may contract it; such passage is rare, partially because the organism can survive off a human host for only 12 to 24 hours (usually less).

Treatment of scabies is simple and effective. Children and adults apply a cream or lotion (prescribed by the doctor) to their entire skin surface below the neck. Do not apply just to rash or itchy areas, and do not skip the buttock folds, genitals, toe webs or other difficult treatment areas. The medication is applied at bedtime and washed off in the morning. One or two treatments are adequate, depending on the medication prescribed. Bed partners should be treated simultaneously. Infants may be given a different medication than that used by adults; they should be treated on the face and scalp as well as elsewhere.

Itching usually persists for a few days, or even for a week or two after treatment, because it takes time for the allergic reaction to subside. Your doctor may prescribe creams or pills to relieve the itching. Do not increase your frequency of bathing or repeatedly use the anti-scabies cream because that further irritates the skin and can increase itching. If you think that you still have scabies or have acquired it again you should return to the doctor for examination.

Simple precautions should be taken to prevent the spread of scabies in the home. All occupants who are in intimate contact with each other should be treated at the same time (whether or not they are itching). The morning after treatment the bedlinen and night clothes should be washed, as well as the clothes which were worn the previous day. No other clothes or furnishings need be cleaned. Don't forget, scabies mites are rarely shed into the environment and survive less than 24 hours, so just setting aside clothing (which might be difficult to clean) for a day or two ensures that it is safe to use again.

Sun Protection

The considerable energy in the sun's rays can significantly penetrate and damage skin. The effect can occur immediately after exposure, as a sunburn, but the more common and serious damage is that which accumulates over years of repeated exposure. Many late changes occur as a result of exposures experienced years before, even if the skin is more recently protected. These late effects of sun exposure include wrinkles, freckles, light spots, coarsened surface texture, dilated capillaries, scaly growths, and tumors. Worst affected are fair-skinned individuals; somewhat affected are darker persons who tan easily, and almost immune to the effects of the sun are the very dark-skinned. Some skin changes mentioned above can be treated, but the results are never as satisfactory as just avoiding their development. Simple precautions greatly reduce sun damage without really interfering with work or recreational activities. A few facts about sun intensity form a basis for these precautions:

- Almost two-thirds of the sun's energy strikes the earth between 10am and 3pm. At other times the rays come to the earth at such a sharp angle that the atmosphere filters out much of their energy.
- Less energy is filtered out by the thin air at high altitudes. About 5% more energy is present for each 300 meters increase in altitude. For this reason even short sun exposures at high altitudes can be damaging.
- Much energy is reflected by water, sand and snow. So even being in the shade at pools, beaches, and in the snow can result in significant exposure if the reflection goes under a sun-shade.
- Sun penetrates through water and wet, white clothing, so being in the water or wearing a T-shirt while swimming is not completely protective.

Knowledge of these facts about the sun can help minimize sun damage. If convenient, plan outdoor activities before 10am and after 3pm, and take extra precautions between those hours, or at high altitudes and around water, sand and snow.

The best precaution against sun damage is complete shading from the sun by clothing and hats. The frequent wearing of a hat is a simple way to greatly reduce sun damage to the face, ears, and back of the neck – areas most commonly affected by the sun. Even a very lightweight long-sleeved shirt or blouse will protect the arms and trunk.

When fixed shade and clothing are impractical, sun-screening lotions should be worn. These materials filter out 70%-95% of the damaging energy of the sun. Do not confuse a sun screen with a sun-bathing oil or cream. The latter are merely lubricants to minimize drying and, if anything, they actually **increase** sun penetration into the skin.

Sun screens are ranked by a Sun Protective Factor (SPF), usually from 4 to 15. Those close to 15 are most protective and should be used by fair-skinned persons, or at high altitudes. Darker skinned

Sun Protection

(continued)

individuals and those who tan quickly can use the lower SPF preparations, which allow a little tanning. Most preparations are clear, easy to apply, and effective. Since they are available in creams, gels, lotions, and alcohol solutions, anyone should be able to find a cosmetically convenient preparation. These materials are safe to use but those which contain para-aminobenzoic acid (PABA) or its esters may stain white clothing faintly yellow, and they occasionally cause an allergic skin rash.

All in all, you can enjoy the sun but, by taking a few simple precautions, you can greatly minimize its consequences. Learn to do this now and teach your children so that they can wear still-young skin for the rest of their lives.

Psoriasis

Psoriasis is a red, scaly rash which often occurs on the scalp, over joints (elbows, knees, knuckles), and on the lower back. It generally appears first in teenagers and young adults, and in common mild cases waxes and wanes with a few patches here and there over many years.

Psoriasis is not an infection or allergy; it is familial. One-third of people with the condition know that it runs in their families and, in another third, examination of relatives reveals mild cases. In the remaining third, inheritance cannot be proven and it is possible that these people represent new genetic cases. Nonetheless, psoriasis is inborn and is not 'caught' or caused by certain foods or emotional behavior. However, its development or severity may be influenced by several things. A profuse eruption, for example, may occur a week or two after a streptococcal throat infection. Fortunately, this type often heals by itself in a few weeks. Patches of psoriasis may occur at sites of skin injury, such as scrapes or bruises. Sunlight tends to improve the rash; illness or emotional upset may worsen it.

Occasionally psoriasis is severe. The scalp may become inflamed and caked with thick scale. The palms and soles may erupt with scales and cracks, or even blisters. The nails may become pitted, thickened, and crumbly. A rash may occur on the genitals. So much rash may develop on the body that flakes are shed profusely, and the person may feel chilled from loss of body heat. Occasionally an arthritis may develop, especially in the fingers and back.

Several effective treatments exist which control psoriasis. Prolonged cures are not expected, but the condition tends to wax and wane, so there are often periods when no treatment is needed. Most treatments require a doctor's supervision. Cortisone, tar, and anthralin creams are easy to use at home. Tar and ultraviolet light treatments are an old and excellent treatment combination. They are usually administered in hospitals or clinics, but sunlight can be used, or an ultraviolet 'light box' can be built and used at home under the doctor's supervision. In severe cases, an oral antimetabolite, methotrexate, may be carefully administered, but it may have serious side effects and needs to be chosen and supervised closely. PUVA is a new treatment involving a drug taken orally (psoralen) and a special-wavelength ultraviolet light. It is available only in clinics and doctors' offices.

In summary, psoriasis is an inborn condition which can manifest itself in different ways and in varying severity. It can be controlled fairly well with treatment, but a doctor's supervision is necessary for many cases. Much research is being conducted on new treatments and they can be expected to appear as experience with them develops.

All About Warts

Warts are benign growths of the skin caused by a virus. The virus gets into the skin from the outside, through cuts, scratches, or cracks, and does not go into the bloodstream. The time elapsed between the penetration of the virus and the appearance of the wart (the incubation period) is a few months.

As with most virus infections, warts occur more commonly in children, and they go away when immunity develops. In young children, warts may last just a few months, in older children they may last about a year, and in adults they may last for months to years. Some people never develop complete immunity to warts and may have them intermittently for most of their lifetime. However, most warts do go away and heal without scars.

Warts may behave differently in different locations. Warts around the fingernails and on the palms and soles are particularly long-lived and stubborn. Warts on the beard area of men who shave are particularly troublesome because shaving often spreads them around, as does shaving of the legs in women. In the same way, picking or chewing of warts on the hands may spread them, especially under the fingernails. Warts may grow profusely on the genitals of adults and be passed back and forth between sexual partners.

Treatment of warts is not always satisfactory. Genital warts often respond to an antiviral liquid (podophyllin) applied in the doctor's office, but repeated treatments are often necessary. The callous-like dead skin on the wart surface can be reduced with repeated applications of wart softeners or corn plasters. They reduce the bulk of the wart and may speed healing.

'Cure' of the wart can be achieved by destroying it by freezing, burning, or surgical removal, but all of these treatments may leave scars. Freezing is the preferred method, as a rule, because it tends to be least scarring.

However, these treatments are painful and are not infallible. Regrowth of warts occurs probably 30% of the time on the hands, and up to 70%-90% for warts around the nails and on the soles. Repeated treatments usually produce a cure, but in many cases the wart disappears on its own. With an incubation period of several months it is common that a 'cure' becomes a relapse as time goes on, requiring more treatments. What treatment, if any, is selected for warts depends on the age and needs of the patient and on the location of the wart.

You may have heard that warts can be charmed or hypnotized away. Most of these reports concern children and probably reflect the rapid spontaneous disappearance of warts expected at that age. Adults have been treated by intense hypnotism and it does have some effect, but it takes several 30 to 60 minute sessions to produce a 50%-60% success rate; not a very practical or effective approach. Research is in progress on treatments with vaccines, allergy production, injection of anti-cancer drugs, and other ideas, and it is hoped that our success rate with this pesky problem will improve.

Note: Warts on the soles are called plantar warts because they occur on the plantar surface of the foot (similar to the palmar surface of the hand). They are not 'planter's warts'.

Diagnostic Procedures

The Potassium Hydroxide (KOH) Examination and Culture for Fungi

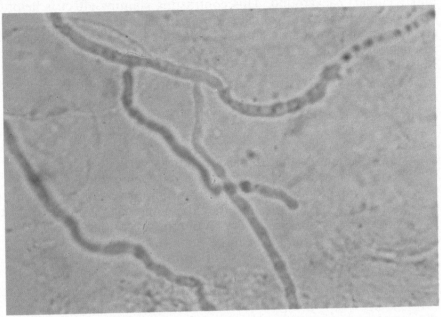

Branching hyphae of dermatophyte fungus on skin scraping.

Fungi live on or in the keratin of the skin, hair, and nails. On the skin and nails they exist mainly as hyphae, but on hair they produce hyphae and spores. Direct examination of scale, nail, or hair may reveal their presence, thus immediately confirming a clinical diagnosis. Culture of the material may also confirm their presence, but cultures take two to four weeks to grow, and they require training and experience to interpret.

The **absence** of fungi on examination and culture does **not** rule out the diagnosis of a tinea infection. Even in experienced hands, direct examination and cultures may often be negative in a single examination of nail infections (p.113), and some cases of vesicular tinea pedis (p.106). Tinea cruris (p.85) and corporis (p.207), however, are usually positive. The correct ways to do each examination so that it is most likely to yield positive results are discussed below.

Direct examination is usually called a 'KOH exam' because the keratin specimen is treated with an alkali, usually 10% potassium hydroxide solution. The alkali 'clears' the material by dissolving oils and cellular debris, but it leaves untouched the fungal hyphae and spores, thus making them more prominent. The KOH solution is usually aqueous, and to accelerate its effect the specimen is heated gently over an alcohol burner. KOH dissolved in dimethyl sulfoxide (DMSO) is popular because it does not require heating.

A useful modification of the KOH solution is the Swartz-Medrik stain. With it, you apply a few drops of a blue solution, and then a red

The Potassium Hydroxide (KOH) Examination and Culture for Fungi

(continued)

one; on examination the hyphae are seen stained a faint blue against a pink (cellular) background. This contrasting staining effect is helpful to novices who may have trouble spotting hyphae in unstained specimens. Stain and specific instruction for its use can be obtained through: Muro Pharmacal Laboratories Inc., 121 Liberty St., Quincy, Mass. 02169, USA.

KOH solutions crystallize and evaporate and should be replaced once or twice a year.

Scale

- Arrange patient so that the lesion skin is vertical.
- Place a microscope slide against the skin below the lesion.
- Gently scrape (do not cut) scale from flaky areas of the lesion. In an annular or arcuate lesion, the advancing edge is most likely to yield a positive specimen. Try to obtain several large flakes.
- Add KOH on stain. This can be done in two ways.
  - ▲ put one to two drops of solution on specimen, then add coverslip
  - ▲ place coverslip on dry specimen, then carefully add solution at edge, allowing capillary attraction to spread the fluid. This method ensures that there is no excess solution to mar the microscope stage
- Heat slide gently over alcohol burner for 10-15 seconds (except DMSO). Do not boil solution.
- Place slide on microscope stage. **Rack condenser way down.** This is essential to heighten detail of the specimen. If the condenser lens is up under the stage fungal hyphae detail is lost.
- Scan under ten times magnification objective and locate a piece of scale. Examine it with ten times magnification for hyphae. Look for a narrow, straight, sometimes branching, walled structure which crosses epidermal cell walls (epidermal cell walls are in a honeycomb pattern and are not straight). Focus up and down to examine all levels of the specimen. If necessary, examine with 43 times magnification to confirm parallel hyphal wall structure (like garden hose sliced end-to-end).
- Pitfalls and novice mistakes.
  - ▲ get adequate scale
  - ▲ warm KOH and allow time for clarification
  - ▲ rack condenser down
  - ▲ **examine scale.** Most novices hunt futilely for hyphae floating free in solution between scales. The hyphae are embedded in the scale
  - ▲ focus up and down in all fields
  - ▲ learn to recognize oil droplets, dirt, and epidermal cell walls
- Culture (see below for interpretation).
  - ▲ slice no.15 blade into agar. This makes blade sticky.
  - ▲ loosen scale from lesion, carry on blade to agar, slice it into the agar
  - ▲ plant several scales

The Potassium Hydroxide (KOH) Examination and Culture for Fungi

(continued)

Hair

- Fungal infections of hair are at scalp level and slightly into the follicle. The scalp, usually flaky, should be examined as above. Hairs often break off a few millimeters above scalp level. Examine those broken stubs.
- With forceps, **gently** pluck stubble or intact hair. Try to remove hair with the bulb at the end. If it breaks you might leave the fungal-bearing portion behind.
- Place the stubble or snipped-off proximal 1cm-2cm of hair (the distal portion is negative and clutters the slide) onto the slide. Add KOH and coverslip, or infiltrate KOH under dry coverslip (see above). Warm the slide and let sit a few minutes.
- Place on microscope stage, **rack down condenser**, and examine under ten times magnification objective.
- Hyphae are rarely seen. Look for clusters of small walled spores coating the hair shaft (ectothrix) or packed in the hair shaft (endothrix).
- Pitfalls are numerous.
  - ▲ obtain a deep proximal portion of hair
  - ▲ learn to distinguish between spores and epithelial cells clinging to bulb of hair
  - ▲ learn to distinguish hyphae from edges of cuticle plates on surface of hair (not long, straight, branching)
  - ▲ examine several hairs
  - ▲ **kerion** is usually negative (inflammation kills fungi)
- Culture.
  - ▲ with tweezers, obtain specimen as above and embed on agar surface
  - ▲ plant several hairs. Be sure **proximal** end is embedded.

Nails

- The rate of obtaining positive KOH or culture results on a single specimen is low. Also, saprophytic fungi often colonize infected nails and confuse the evaluation. Much skill is needed to obtain and interpret results. Repeat the examinations three times before considering the results negative.
- Wipe distal nail and toe surface with alcohol, to remove dirt and oil. Allow the surfaces to dry.
- With no.15 blade or the edge of a pointed forceps, scrape crumbly debris from under the distal nail edge. If the nail is long, clip a generous portion off, scrape debris from the undersurface of the fragment and of the remaining nail.
- Place debris or nail clipping on the slide and add KOH; add the coverslip. The thick nature of the specimen holds the coverslip off the slide. Gently heat. Add more KOH if necessary. Allow the specimen to soften for five minutes or longer. As it softens, gently compress coverslip onto specimen, flattening it as much as possible.

The Potassium Hydroxide (KOH) Examination and Culture for Fungi

(continued)

- Place the slide on the microscope stage. **Rack condenser down.** Examine as above for scale. The thickness of the specimen makes examination of the center difficult, but the edges are thinner and may show hyphae. Focus up and down to examine all levels of specimen.
  - ▲ if negative, re-examine in 30 minutes (may need to add more KOH), after further softening of specimen
- Pitfalls are numerous. The debris is 'messy' with dirt, keratin, and fibers. Hyphae are sparse.
- Culture.
  - ▲ plant debris obtained by above method on agar
  - ▲ interpretation is difficult since saprophyte overgrowth is common (see below).

Culture

- Dermatophytes will grow out on Sabouraud's agar generally as dry, folded white colonies in two to four weeks.
- The organism of tinea versicolor (p.203) can be identified on KOH examination but will grow only on special media.
- *Candida* (yeast) will grow out on Sabouraud's agar in two to six days as a creamy smooth colony.
- Saprophytic fungi ('contaminants') grow out as dry, folded colonies, often in one week. They are often black or brown.
- Identifying true dermatophytes from contaminants requires training and experience. One fairly reliable shortcut is Dermatophyte Testing Medium (DTM). Specimens are placed on this yellow agar as described in the preceding sections. If a colony grows the entire agar may turn red. This almost always indicates that it is a dermatophyte colony. If the agar stays yellow, it is most likely a contaminant (the test is based on the pH of the organisms).
- Pitfalls.
  - ▲ keep the media fresh – do not allow them to dry out
  - ▲ interpreting results is often difficult
  - ▲ **do not tightly cap culture after implantation.** Dermatophytes are aerobic and will not grow in sealed bottles. Novices often forget this and tighten caps too snugly. Leave the cap loose enough to rattle.
  - ▲ do not declare a specimen negative until after four weeks of incubation at room temperature. However, with DTM, late color conversion may yield a false positive result.

Scabies Prep

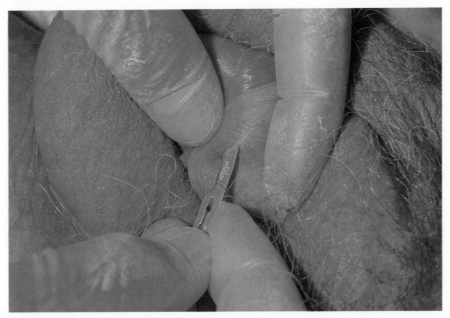

Specimen for scabies examination is obtained by superficial shave, not scrape.

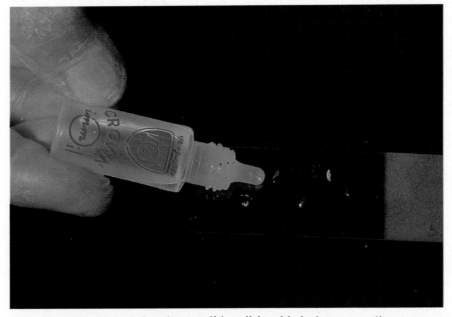

Several specimens are placed on a slide, oil is added, then coverslip.

Scabies Prep

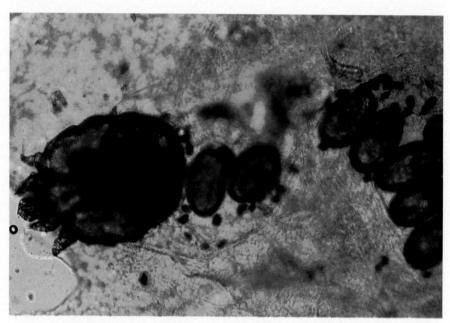

Adult mite, eggs, and feces in burrow in skin shave specimen.

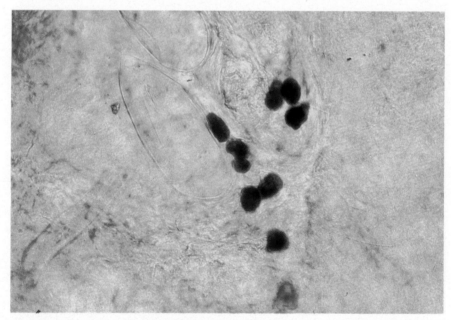

The diagnosis can be confirmed just by finding the small, oval, honey-brown feces alone.

Scabies Prep

Most of the lesions in scabies are allergic in nature and do not contain organisms. In a full-blown rash perhaps only 10 living mites are present, although dozens of lesions may contain eggs or feces. Identifying mites, eggs, or feces in a skin specimen confirms the diagnosis.

Selection of an appropriate lesion for examination is all-important. Infested lesions are likely to be in fold areas and are rare on open surfaces such as the arms, legs, and trunk. Examine the finger webs, wrist folds, axillae, nipples, umbilicus, and penis for intact (unscratched) papules, especially those surmounted by a 1mm-5mm white line (burrow). Often no lesions with burrows can be found because scratching has destroyed them. To help identify burrows, the suspicious areas can be wiped with a gauze soaked with black ink, then dry-wiped. Burrows take up the ink and stand out as distinct black lines.

Two techniques can be used to obtain a specimen for examination. Most commonly, a no.15 scalpel is used to carefully **shave** a paper-thin 3mm-5mm wafer off the top of the papule. Scraping (instead of shaving) results in a rolled, crumpled specimen which is difficult to interpret. Many practitioners prepare the lesion before shaving by placing a drop of mineral or immersion oil on it. The oil sharpens the appearance of the lesion and makes the specimen adhere to the scalpel blade for safe transport to a microscope slide. Shavings should be obtained from several lesions to increase the likelihood of a positive result.

Place the shaving on a microscope slide, add a drop or two of mineral or immersion oil, then cover with coverslip. Oil mounting the specimen in this manner sharpens the microscopic image and does not kill mites which may be present (as potassium hydroxide (KOH) would), so that their movement can be observed. Examine each shaving under ten times magnification objective. Mites are easily recognized as oval, slightly spiny organisms with several fine, short legs. The eggs are egg-shaped and large (one third to half the size of the mites) with thick walls. Feces are usually plentiful and are seen as small (about 1/10 the size of the eggs), oval golden-brown objects. Brief experience will enable the viewer to identify feces or eggs in a specimen, even if only one example is present, thus confirming the diagnosis.

The other method of examining a scabies lesion requires much experience. The examiner identifies a burrow and places a drop of oil on it. Using a hand lens he or she locates a tiny dark dot at one end of the burrow. Still using the lens for magnification, the dot is gently teased out with the point of a 16-22 gauge hypodermic needle and it is placed in a drop of oil on a microscope slide. Examination with a ten times magnification objective shows the adult mite.

Skin Biopsy

Histopathological examination of some skin eruptions is helpful in confirming a diagnosis, but the main utility is in classifying growths, granulomas, and infiltrates. A small biopsy is simple, quick, and usually leaves little scarring. There are three techniques for doing small skin biopsies.

Shave biopsy is applicable only to elevated lesions. A papule or a portion of a plaque is anesthetized with an injection of local anesthetic. The papule or a portion of the edge of the plaque is shaved off with a no.15 scalpel, or snipped off with small, curved scissors. It may be possible to control bleeding with pressure or a styptic (Monsel's solution, aluminum chloride, p.324), but light electrocautery or electrodesiccation may be required. The resulting scab may be covered or left open, and it will come off in one to three weeks. The patient need only keep the area clean with routine bathing.

> **Note:** shave biopsy should **not** be performed on a suspected melanoma (p.268). Shave biopsy yields a partial specimen which is not adequate for determining prognosis and method of treatment.

Punch biopsy is an easy way to obtain a full thickness specimen. Biopsy punches are available in sizes from 2mm to 10mm, but 3mm or 4mm punches usually yield an adequate specimen with minimal scarring. The anesthetized lesion is cut with forceful repeated turning of the circular biopsy punch. It is easy to feel when the soft subcutaneous fat layer is reached. The specimen is gently elevated with a fine forcep, and fine, curved scissors are used to snip the restraining subcutaneous fat. For best cosmetic results, close the defect with one or two sutures. However, in many cases, hemostasis with styptic or electrocautery and healing by secondary intention yields an acceptable appearance, and saves the patient a return visit for suture removal.

Good punch biopsy specimens require the use of sharp punches. A dull punch excessively compresses the skin and produces a cone-shaped specimen with inadequate deep tissue mass. Reusable punches should be resharpened as often as necessary. Disposable punches (Chester A. Baker Labs, 50 N.W. 176th Street, Miami, Florida 33169 USA) in individual sterile envelopes are sharp, easy to store, and particularly practical for physicians who perform few biopsies.

> **Note:** the round defect left by a punch biopsy may heal with an unsightly, depressed scar. To encourage healing as a linear scar along fold lines, forcefully stretch the skin at right angles to the intended scar line when making the biopsy. When the skin is released the round hole assumes an oval shape oriented in the intended direction.

Skin Biopsy

(continued)

Incisional scalpel biopsy requires more time and skill than does a punch biopsy and it almost always requires suture closure. However, incisional biopsies can be carefully aligned for good cosmetic closure, and they close with no dog-ear or depression (as punch ovals often do). They also allow angling of the incision edge outward to obtain a generous biopsy of deep dermal and subcutaneous tissue, which is important in certain conditions (e.g. erythema nodosum).

Biopsy Tissue Processing
The biopsy specimen should be placed in 10% buffered neutral formalin solution, in a volume which is 10 to 20 times greater than that of the specimen. Small specimens are often difficult for the pathologist to orient for cutting. This should be discussed with your pathologist so that an identification system can be agreed upon. A common one is to press the deep part of the specimen onto a small piece of filter paper or paper towel before placing them (stuck together) into the formalin. Dyes can also be painted onto certain surfaces.

Formulary
Principles of Topical Therapy

- Topical therapy is usually used to combat
  - ▲ inflammation
    - ■ acute – redness, edema, vesiculation, oozing, and crusting
    - ■ chronic – lichenification (epidermal thickening and scaling)
  - ▲ infection – by bacteria, yeast, fungi, viruses
- Agents used for this purpose are
  - ▲ soaks, compresses, baths (p.318)
  - ▲ paints or tinctures (p.306)
  - ▲ powders (p.305)
  - ▲ shake lotions (p.305)
  - ▲ lubricants (emollients) (p.304)
  - ▲ active topical medicaments (p.304) in
    - ■ solutions
    - ■ lotions
    - ■ gels
    - ■ creams
    - ■ ointments
    - ■ pastes
    - ■ occluding tape or glazes (benzoin or collodion)
  - ▲ The proper prescribing is detailed on the indicated pages; other agents (bleaches, styptics, soaps, shampoos, and so on) will be covered.

The Dermatologic Prescription
- A typical prescription for a topical agent is as follows

---

hydrocortisone cream 1%
Dispense: 60g
Sig: apply thinly to itchy rash on face b.i.d.

                                                    Signature

---

Writing such a prescription requires knowledge of several components.

The **first line** describes the agent, the vehicle, and the concentration. The choice of the agent is discussed throughout this book. Vehicles determine the ease of application and delivery of the active agent; they are discussed in the clinical sections, and below (p.304). The concentration of the active agent in the topical preparation is usually fixed or standard, but sometimes is variable, in which case the concentration must be carefully stated for the druggist.

Principles of Topical Therapy

(continued)

The **second line** directs the volume to be dispensed, expressed, depending on country, in ounces, grams, milliliters, cubic centimeters, pints, and so on. One ounce = 28.5g (approximately 30g) = approximately 30mL. Deciding on a volume to dispense requires experience and knowledge of the surface area and length of time to be treated, but it depends greatly on how the medication is applied by the patient, which must be directed by the physician.

For almost all topical medications, **the thinnest application possible provides maximum therapeutic effect.** Applying two or three times more material does **not** increase therapeutic effect. If the medication is a cream or ointment, applying more of it may be more lubricating, but a less expensive way to achieve the same lubrication is by applying a thin layer of the medicated cream and then later applying a bland lubricant (p.304) as necessary.

The patient should be instructed in how to apply a medication. Typically, the patient applies a large bolus from a tube or jar and then tries to rub it in. This results in a layer of medication which is too thick at the center and thin at the edges. The correct way to apply a topical medication is discussed below and should be demonstrated for the patient in the office. Tiny amounts are dabbed on over the area to be treated and then rubbed in as a thin layer. The resulting treatment film is usually not unpleasantly sticky, even if an ointment is used, and it uses the medication most efficiently. When a cream or ointment is applied in this manner, 20g to 25g can be made to cover the entire body.

Estimates of coverage for specific sites can be made using the 'rule of 9s', in which the approximate surface area of the body is divided into 11 equal parts, each comprising 9% of the total surface area. The areas are: head; arms; half of each leg; half each of the anterior and posterior chest; abdomen; and lumbar/buttocks. Each area can be covered with about 2g of cream or ointment. Lotions and solutions go further per ounce.

The **third line:** the *'Sig:'* determines the labelling instructions. Directing that the patient 'apply thinly' reinforces the above instructions. Most medications need to be applied only twice daily for maximum benefit; exceptions are discussed in the clinical sections.

The instructions should state what skin condition the medication is for, in terms the patient understands. The direction of only 'apply twice daily' or 'apply as needed' may not be adequate for the forgetful patient. More importantly, as creams and lotions accumulate in the patient's medicine cabinet, mention of the disease being treated becomes important. If that rash on the face returns, the patient goes to the medicine cabinet and finds a collection of tubes, some perhaps for acne or athlete's foot, but all labelled only 'apply twice daily'. This possible confusion is avoided by labelling for 'athlete's foot', or 'eczema on legs'. Also, use understandable terms; do not use labels such as 'tinea pedis', or 'pityriasis rosea'.

Principles of Topical Therapy

(continued)

Vehicles

In each clinical section there are recommendations for the form (vehicle) in which the appropriate medication is best prescribed. What follows is a general discussion of each vehicle.

Ointments

An ointment is a simple, lubricating vehicle. It is basically a pure grease, like petrolatum, or a grease with a small amount of water suspended in it. Ointment medications are best used on dry skin rashes, such as chronic dermatitis of the legs. The greasy ointment film is lubricating and enhances penetration of the active ingredient through a mild occlusive effect. A disagreeable greasy feeling is minimized by thin applications (as described above). Lipid-soluble medications, such as corticosteroids, are stable in ointments and require few or no stabilizers or preservatives. If some water is present in the ointment, then stabilizers are required.

Sometimes propylene glycol, an oily liquid, is added to an ointment as a solvent to make it somewhat thinner and easier to apply. However, propylene glycol may irritate the skin and cause a slight stinging on application, especially noticeable in dry, cracked skin. If your patient complains of such a reaction, try an ointment free of propylene glycol, as indicated on the label list of ingredients. Ointments are objectionable and unnecessarily greasy to use in moist skin areas such as folds (axillae or groin) and in the scalp.

Creams

Creams are ointments into which more water is whipped, or, as in thin 'vanishing creams', water into which a lipid is whipped. A cream is easier and more pleasant to use than an ointment, but is less occlusive and requires preservatives and stabilizers. Creams are good for dry skin areas (arms, legs, trunk) in humid climates, and for semi-fold areas (antecubital and neck) even in dry weather. Creams are also appropriate for use on the face, which is rarely very dry. Still, for the scalp and moist fold areas creams are unnecessarily greasy. Propylene glycol or other alcoholic stabilizers may make creams somewhat irritating.

Lotions

Lotions are mostly water with some lipid whipped in. They leave little residue and are suitable for use in moist folds and the scalp. Lipid-soluble drugs, such as corticosteroids, are difficult to blend into lotions and are generally less potent than in ointment or cream vehicle. Lotions are pleasant to use but contain so much water and so little lipid that they are not very lubricating, and are even drying in dry skin. A better vehicle, even for the scalp and moist folds, which are the best sites for lotions is discussed next.

Solutions

Solutions consist of alcohol or alcohol and propylene glycol. A more precise term for a pure alcohol solution is a **tincture.** These materials predominantly or completely evaporate, to leave the active ingredient on the skin. Since they leave little or no residue, they are ideal for use

Principles of Topical Therapy

(continued)

in hair areas and in moist folds (groin, toe webs and so on). See page 3 for instructions on the best way to apply solutions to the scalp, leaving the least residue on the hair. They cause a temporary burning sensation on cracked or open lesions, and are very drying and should not be used on dry skin areas. Solutions containing antimicrobial dyes which dry to leave a stain on the skin are sometimes called **paints** (Castellani's paint, gentian violet).

Aerosols and Sprays

Aerosols and sprays are basically solutions in a propellant system. They are easy to apply to large areas but may be drying and irritating (partially because of the presence of propellant chemicals), and the complexity of the vehicle compared to simpler formulations may result in suboptimal release and penetration of the active ingredient. With a fine tubular applicator nozzle aerosols may be particularly elegant for use on the scalp, where tiny amounts of medication can be directly sprayed onto the scalp under the hair.

Gels

Gels are essentially gelled propylene glycol solutions. They are easy to apply and leave little residue. However, they are drying and possibly irritating on dry skin; in moist areas the propylene glycol may be irritating, and true solutions would leave less residue. Their best uses may be under occlusion, or on the face (tretinoin gel, p.306, or with keratolytics (tars p.323, salicylic acid p.323) because the propylene glycol itself is keratolytic (keratin-softening).

Shake lotions

Shake lotions are lotions to which a powder has been added, and they must be shaken to temporarily suspend the powder. Calamine lotion is a typical example. The powder forms a mat on the skin which retards evaporation of the water in the lotion, prolonging a mild cooling and soothing effect. Mild alcoholic antipruritics (camphor, menthol and phenol) are sometimes added to give this effect, but active medications are usually not used in this vehicle.

Pastes

Pastes are creams or ointments to which powder has been added. They are thick and stiff and are usually used to form a protective shield over the skin (zinc oxide paste) or hold a medication on a specific site.

Powders

Powders are occasionally used as vehicles for antifungal agents or other medications, but delivery of the active ingredient to the skin in this form is poor. The best use of a powder is to dry a moist, sweaty fold area, and to reduce friction (in moist folds, or in rubber gloves). To deliver active medication to a moist fold, it is best to use a solution, and then use a bland powder (talcum) as necessary to reduce friction and chafing.

Acne Medications

Benzoyl peroxide

- Available in various vehicles, concentrations, and by prescription or over-the-counter.
- In general.
  - ▲ gels are more stable and more pleasant to use than are solutions, and are far more popular
  - ▲ water-based gels are less drying and less likely to be irritating than are alcohol- and acetone-based gels
  - ▲ concentrations of 2.5% and 5% are adequate to sterilize follicles, so a 10% concentration is probably unnecessary, and is often irritating
- Some proprietary preparations of benzoyl peroxide are: 'Benzac', 'Desquam-X', 'PanOxyl', 'Xerac' (water based); 'Benoxyl', 'Benzagel', 'Loroxide', 'Vanoxide' (alcohol or acetone-based); 'Vanair' (cream).

Some Commercially Available Topical Antibiotics

- Erythromycin – 'A/T/S' 2%, 'EryDerm' 2%, 'Staticin' 1.5%
- Clindamycin – 'Cleocin-T'
- Tetracyclines – 'Meclan' 1% [1], 'Topicycline'

1. Cream (all other formulations are liquids).

Tretinoin (vitamin A acid)

- Tretinoin is available in solution (most drying), gel, or cream (least drying). In approximate order of decreasing potency
  - ▲ solution 0.05%
  - ▲ cream 0.1%
  - ▲ gel 0.025%
  - ▲ cream 0.05%
  - ▲ gel 0.01%
- See acne p.33.

Some Topical Antibacterials and Paints

- Gentian violet (methylrosaniline chloride).
  - ▲ usually 1%-3% solution
- Castellani's paint (carbol-fuchsin solution).
  - ▲ contains: boric acid 1%; phenol 4.5%; resorcinol 10%; fuchsin 0.3%; acetone 5%
- Thymol.
  - ▲ dissolved 2%-4% in chloroform or alcohol (95% ethanol, or isopropanol)

- Aluminum chloride.
  ▲ usually 10%-20% in alcohol
- Bacitracin ointment.
- Neomycin ointment.
- Gentamicin cream.
- Polymyxin-bacitracin-neomycin ('Neosporin', 'Mycitracin').
- Polymyxin-bacitracin ('Polysporin').

Treatment of Fungal Infections
See clinical sections for specific recommendations

- tinea capitis p.6
- tinea facei p.29
- tinea corporis p.207
- tinea cruris p.85
- tinea pedis p.106
- onychomycosis p.113
- tinea versicolor p.203

Small, uncomplicated fungal infections respond to **topical antifungal agents** listed below. General guidelines for use are

- apply thinly twice daily
- the usual duration of therapy is one to two weeks. Treat until the lesions flatten and stop scaling, then treat a few days longer
- creams are best for dry areas
- solutions, lotions, and aerosols are best for moist areas (groin or toe web) or hairy areas, because they leave little residue, and are drying
- powders are poor vehicles for antifungal agents. It is better to use solutions in moist areas, then use a bland powder (talcum) if necessary to reduce chafing. Antifungal powders are effective for prophylaxis of interdigital tinea
- topical antifungal agents will not stop itching the first few days. Use a topical corticosteroid (p.311) for itching. It will **not** interfere with the antifungal agent.

Systemic antifungal agents are indicated if the infection is

- on the scalp or in a very hairy area
- widespread
- resistant to topical therapy
- in the fingernails

Griseofulvin is the standard oral antifungal agent. The original preparation was of large particle size; doses required were 1g-2g daily. It has been superseded by materials of smaller particle size which are absorbed better and are taken in smaller doses.

- micronized, microsize, or ultra-fine form is taken in a dose of from 500mg to 1000mg daily (usually divided in a twice daily dose)
- ultramicronized form is taken in a dose of 125mg twice daily

Treatment of Fungal Infections

(continued)

Response to griseofulvin is slow; clinical improvement is not seen for one to two weeks. Most infections require treatment for four to six weeks, or one to two weeks after apparent clearing. Topical corticosteroids may be given to relieve itching. It was originally thought that griseofulvin should be taken with fatty foods to enhance absorption, but absorption occurs just as completely on an empty stomach, though it is somewhat slower (which is not important to therapy). Fungal resistance to griseofulvin does exist.

Side effects to griseofulvin are common and numerous. They include

- gastrointestinal upset (common) which can be severe
- a headache, which is usually unresponsive to aspirin
- mood changes, anorexia, insomnia, and nightmares
- peripheral paresthesias
- allergic rashes

Bone marrow supression and photosensitivity were originally reported, but are inadequately documented. Griseofulvin induces liver microzymes and increases the metabolism of coumarin, phenobarbital, and other drugs. Chronic administration in rats has produced hepatoma.

Ketoconazole is active against systemic fungal infections, *Candida,* and dermatophytes, but it is approved in the US only for candidiasis and deep fungal infections. The adult dose is 200mg (one tablet) daily. Pediatric doses are: up to 20kg, 50mg (quarter tablet); 20kg to 40kg, 100mg (half tablet).

Side effects are said to occur in fewer than 5% of patients, and the most common problems are gastrointestinal upset and pruritus. Transient rises in liver enzyme levels have been observed in some patients, and care should be taken in prescribing ketoconazole for patients likely to be at risk of intolerance, i.e. older women, those with a history of liver disease, those having other drugs which may affect the liver.

Antifungal Agents

See individual clinical sections for administration. Creams and solutions are most effective; powders are least effective

	Derma-tophytes	Yeast	Tinea versico-lor
Topical agents			
clotrimazole (Lotrimin, Mycelex)	+	+	+
haloprogin (Halotex)	+	+	+
miconazole (Monistat-Derm)	+	+	+
tolnaftate (Tinactin, Naftate, etc.)	+		+
undecylenic acid (Desenex, etc.)	+		
amphotericin B (Fungizone)		+	
nystatin (Candex, Mycostatin, Mycolog)		+	
iodochlorhydroxyquin (Vioform)	+	+	
acrisorcin (Akrinol)			+
sodium thiosulfate (Tinver)			+
Systemic agents			
griseofulvin (Grisactin, Grisovin etc.)	+		
ketoconazole (Nizoral)	+	+	+

Pediculocides and Scabicides

- Gamma benzene hexachloride ('Kwell' – lotion, cream, shampoo; 'Scabene' – lotion)
- Crotamiton ('Eurax' – cream, lotion)
- Pyrethrin ('A-200 Pyrimate' – solution, gel; 'Barc' – liquid, cream; etc.)
- See discussions of head lice (p.10), pubic lice (p.80) and scabies (p.198) for selection and administration of these agents.

'Mycolog' ('Kenacomb') – Use and Abuse

- Mycolog contains
  - ▲ nystatin
  - ▲ gramacidin
  - ▲ neomycin
  - ▲ triamcinolone 0.1%
    - ■ an upper-medium potency corticosteroid (p.315)
- It is effective in
  - ▲ yeast and yeast/bacterial mixed infections
    - ■ intertriginous candidiasis (p.88)
    - ■ diaper dermatitis (p.91)
    - ■ chronic angulocheilitis
- It is not effective in
  - ▲ dermatophyte (tinea, ringworm) infections
    - ■ **does not contain anti-dermatophyte medication**
  - ▲ 'yeast' chronic paronychia
    - ■ cream or ointment is occlusive and macerating, which often counteracts anti-infective effects
- Caveats
  - ▲ triamcinolone 0.1% is potent enough to cause atrophy and striae with prolonged use in thin-skinned intertriginous areas
    - ■ limit use to two weeks
    - ■ be especially careful in infants (diaper dermatitis) as the effect is more pronounced in them
  - ▲ neomycin frequently causes allergic contact dermatitis
    - ■ stop treatment if rash worsens
  - ▲ the cream (but not the ointment) contains the preservative ethylenediamine, which may cause allergic contact dermatitis
    - ■ stop treatment if rash worsens
    - ■ use ointment only
  - ▲ do not use in tinea (ringworm) infections
    - ■ it will not work

Corticosteroids

Choosing a topical corticosteroid is daunting because of the vast selection of brands, concentrations, sizes, and vehicles. The process is actually fairly simple if one adopts a method of classification such as used in this book. However, when you choose a preparation for a particular patient you should consider:

vehicle – see p.304
size–see p.303 for 'rule of 9s'
directions – see p.302 for 'how to write a dermatologic prescription'
    Emphasize a thin application. This gives maximal therapeutic effect, least residual stickiness, and minimal cost. Twice daily applications are usually adequate, especially just after bathing (to lubricate, and get maximal penetration). More frequent applications are permitted to relieve itching.
    The list below gives the main corticosteroids grouped according to relative potency. Preparations within groups are comparable in therapeutic effect, but may vary considerably in cosmetic qualities. Creams may very immensely in thickness, for example, and may contain various amounts of propylene glycol, alcohol, or other additives which may be irritants in some people. Try to accumulate samples of these products and set aside a time to apply each of them to your skin to compare their properties.

For simplicity, we group the materials only by name. As a rule, corticosteroids in the ointment form are more potent that the same material in a cream or lotion form. The difference may be so great that they fall into a lower group. However, modern vehicle formulations are so sophisticated that this rule is variable.
    Selection of a potency is determined by the severity of the rash and its location. Rashes in a moist fold or on thin-skin areas (axillae, groin or eyelid) usually require only mild or moderately-potent corticosteroids, because absorption there is good. Rashes on dry, thick skin (back or extremities) or which are scaly or lichenified usually require potent corticosteroids. It is believed that corticosteroids behave more potently on the skin of children, especially in infants, but experimental proof is lacking.
    Mild rashes on moist or thin-skinned areas may be treated initially with a mild corticosteroid (group IV, hydrocortisone 1%). More severe rashes, or rashes on other sites, may require a potent corticosteroid for initial therapy but then a milder preparation may be used for maintenance. Prescriptions for both strengths can be given during the initial visit.
    In some countries some corticosteroids, such as hydrocortisone, fluocinolone acetonide, and triamcinolone acetonide are available as generics; however, vehicle compounding can have a great impact on potency, and some casual preparations are less active than branded products.
    For maximum efficiency of corticosteroid use, do not forget that **occlusion** greatly increases potency, thus saving money. It is difficult and messy, but can be simplified. Instead of adapting sheet plastic wrap for all uses, try disposable plastic gloves for hands, shower caps for the scalp, and plastic bags for other areas. The midportion of an extremity can be covered with a long, slender bag (such as used for bread) with the end cut off. Holding the plastic on with socks, T-shirts,

Corticosteroids

(continued)

or gauze wraps is often more comfortable than using tape. It is often most convenient to use occlusion only during sleep, or for a few hours in the evening.

Occlusion may cause adverse effects. Patients may experience heat rash or even overheating if large areas are covered. This increases cardiac demand and can be dangerous in the elderly or in patients with heart disease. Occlusion encourages or worsens bacterial infection in moist, oozing lesions. It is best used only on dry eruptions. Lastly, occlusion of a corticosteroid increases the risk of systemic absorption or cutaneous atrophy.

Side effects

Side effects from topical corticosteroids are rare, and can be avoided if the preparations are used correctly.

Systemic absorption is rarely a problem. Only small amounts of the applied material actually gets into systemic circulation. Total body application of even group II corticosteroids (moderately potent, see below) only occasionally results in lowered morning cortisol levels, and even then clinical changes are rare; the adrenals still respond to stress with endogenous cortisol production. A similar response can be seen with application of group I corticosteroids to 25%-50% of the body. Actual Cushingoid changes can result from prolonged application of group I materials to the entire body, or from application of less potent corticosteroids with widespread occlusion (total body), or group I materials with less than total body occlusion. Children and infants are probably somewhat more sensitive to these effects, particularly with respect to growth retardation. It is emphasized that systemic effects are rare and require prolonged and widespread application of strong corticosteroids. Skin conditions calling for such therapy are severe and are probably best managed by a dermatologist.

Cutaneous side effects from topical corticosteroids are somewhat more common, but still unusual. They almost always result from incorrect use of corticosteroids, often from unauthorized refills or in persons borrowing medications from friends. Basically they occur from the prolonged (over six weeks and often six months) daily application of corticosteroids which are too potent for the area to which they are being applied, such as the face, eyelids, genitals, and flexors (in the groin particularly). *These side effects are related to the potency of the corticosteroid and not to whether or not the steroid molecule is fluorinated.* Fluorine or chlorine atoms are present in many potent corticosteroids, but some are not halogenated and 'fluorinated' should not be used to imply potency.

Chronic application of potent (group I and II) corticosteroids to thin skin on the face, genitals, and flexors can eventually cause dermal and epidermal atrophy (this can occur on thick-skin areas if occlusion is used). Atrophic skin appears thin, shiny, and pink, with visible blood vessels. Even marked atrophy usually resolves in a few weeks or months when corticoid therapy is stopped. Chronic potent corticosteroid applications on stretch areas, such as the upper thighs, axillae, and antecubital fossae, may eventually cause permanent striae.

Corticosteroids

(continued)

Chronic potent corticosteroid application to the face can provoke a 'steroid rosacea' (see rosacea, p.42) which has atrophy, telangiectasia, and acne-like papules and pustules. Another manifestation of this is 'perioral dermatitis', which consists of many tiny acne-like papules around the mouth and on the chin. Inexplicably, young white women are most susceptible to these conditions. Steroid rosacea and perioral dermatitis clear when application of potent topical corticoids is discontinued, but often there are days or weeks of rebound flare before the eruption fades. Potent topical corticosteroids will suppress the flare, an effect which may seduce the desperate patient into starting them again. Cool soaks, lubricants, and mild topical corticosteroids (hydrocortisone 1%) may relieve the symptoms until they fade.

One last complication of topical corticosteroids is the possible development of glaucoma or cataracts if the material is applied on the eyelids. A few cases have been reported; most involved the use of potent corticosteroids, but in one case hydrocortisone was used. Experience with ocular corticosteroid drops suggests that this rare side effect would tend to occur in persons predisposed to their development. If chronic therapy to the eyelids appears to be necessary, it is probably wise to obtain an ophthalmological examination first, with slit lamp examination and pressure determinations to identify susceptible individuals.

Use of potent corticosteroids is appropriate even on the face, genitals, and flexural areas, if the clinical situation calls for it and its use is monitored. Severe rashes require potent therapy, but usually one can switch to a less potent preparation in a few days. The patient should be cautioned against prolonged (over three weeks) therapy, and the possible consequences should be explained. Fortunately, it requires almost outrageous abuse of the medications to produce adverse reactions.

Technique for Giving Intralesional Corticosteroids

Materials

For most lesions one uses triamcinolone acetonide (Kenalog®) 10 mg/ml, from a 5ml multidose vial. Many physicians dilute this to 3.3-5.0 mg/ml with sterile saline or lidocaine. When injecting keloids or hypertrophic scars one may use the more concentrated 40 mg/ml form. All of the above are suspensions which must be shaken before use.

A small syringe allows accurate dosing and provides for injection into firm lesions with ease. Our favorite is a 1ml insulin syringe with a swaged-on or integrated needle. A 1ml tuberculin syringe is similar but the needle is attached only with a compression fitting which may pop apart if the injection is given under more pressure.

Corticosteroids

(continued)

A 30-gauge needle is most comfortable for the patient, and the suspension can be injected through it, but it is almost impossible to draw the material into the syringe through it. The suspension can be drawn through a larger needle, and then the needle can be changed. If an insulin syringe is used then the attached 27-gauge needle must be used for both functions.

Technique
Intralesional corticosteroid injection is an invaluable treatment for many conditions. Correct technique is learned by doing. It is strongly advised that you initially perform the procedure with an experienced physician to get a feel for the subtlties of volume and depth of dosing.

Conditions in which intralesional steroids are frequently used include acne, alopecia areata, psoriasis, lichen simplex chronicus, scars and keloids.

In all conditions the suspension is injected directly into the lesion. In acne, injections go right into nodules, and into the bases of cysts or pustules (injecting into the pus-filled cavity would yield no benefit). Psoriasis and dermatitis are treated by injection into the dermis of the lesions. In alopecia areata the injections go into the junction of the dermis and subcutaneum. To minimize the number of injections required in large lesions the needle is angled sharply beneath the lesion and a trail of triamcinolone is injected as the needle is withdrawn.

If a 10 mg/ml concentration is used, then tiny doses will suffice, and pain is minimal. A volume of 0.05 ml would be typical for an acne nodule, or 0.1 to 0.2ml for a one-centimeter patch of alopecia areata. The more dilute preparations would require commensurately larger volumes, and would be somewhat more painful.

Injection of excessive material may result in atrophy or depression of the skin, but this complication resolves in a few months. In general, it is better to under-treat rather than over-treat, and give a repeat injection if necessary. For acne and inflammatory conditions benefit starts in 1-3 days, and benefits last at least 3 weeks. In alopecia areata, injections are given monthly and regrowth is usually not seen until 6-8 weeks, and the shots are continued for several more months.

Corticosteroids

(continued)

The principal topical corticosteroids are grouped below according to potency (Group I strongest to Group IV mildest).[1]

Group I
Amcinonide 0.1% ('Cyclocort')
Beclomethasone dipropionate 0.5% ('Propaderm-Forte')
Betamethasone dipropionate 0.05% ('Diprosone')
Clobetasol propionate 0.05% ('Dermovate')
Desoxymetasone 0.25% ('Topicort')
Diflorasone diacetate 0.05% ('Maxiflor')
Diflucortolone valerate 0.3% ('Nerisone')
Fluocinolone acetonide 0.2% ('Synalar-HP', 'Synalar Forte')
Fluocinonide 0.05% ('Lidex')
Halcinonide 0.1% ('Halciderm', 'Halog')
Triamcinolone acetonide 0.5% ('Aristocort', 'Kenalog')

Group II
Beclomethasone dipropionate 0.025% ('Propaderm')
Betamethasone benzoate 0.025% ('Benisone', 'Uticort')
Betamethasone valerate 0.1% ('Valisone', 'Betnovate')
Fluclorolone acetonide 0.025% ('Topilar')
Flucinolone acetonide 0.025% ('Synalar', Fluonid)
Fluprednidene (fluprednylidene) acetate 0.1% ('Decoderm')
Flurandrenolide (flurandrenolone) 0.05% ('Cordran', 'Drenison'),
   ('Haelan')
Hydrocortisone butyrate 0.1% ('Locoid')
Triamcinolone acetonide 0.1% ('Aristocort', 'Kenalog')

Group III
Clobetasone butyrate 0.05% ('Eumovate')
Desonide 0.05% ('Tridesilon', 'Apolar')
Desoxymetasone 0.05% ('Topicort')
Fluocortolone 0.25% ('Ultralanum')
Fluocinolone acetonide 0.01% ('Synalar')
Flurandrenolide (flurandrenolone) 0.025% ('Cordran', 'Haelan')
Halcinonide 0.025% ('Halciderm', 'Halog')
Hydrocortisone valerate 0.2% ('Westcort')
Triamcinolone acetonide 0.025% ('Aristocort', 'Kenalog')

Group IV
Hydrocortisone 1-2.5% ('Hytone', 'Cort-Dome', 'Efcortelan' etc.)
Flumethasone pivilate 0.02-0.03% ('Lorcorten')
Methylprednisolone 0.25% ('Medrol')

1. This list reflects the authors' experience. An accurate ranking would require rigorous testing under conditions of standardized clinical and pharmaceutical conditions.

Sunscreens and Agents
Which Affect Pigmentation

Sunscreens

See page 251 for discussion of selection and use. The most common sunscreen ingredient is para-aminobenzoic acid (PABA) and its esters. It blocks ultraviolet rays in the wavelengths of 280nm-320nm, which are the sun-burning rays. Longer wavelength ultraviolet light (UVL) (320nm-400nm) penetrates through PABA and stimulates some tanning. Sunscreens with a sun protective factor (SPF) of 4 to 10 may contain just PABA.

Benzophenones block a broader spectrum of UVL, from 250nm to 400nm, but their filtering of the burning rays is less effective than is that of PABA. Some pure benzophenone preparations are available, but it is more commonly combined with PABA to make the very effective sunscreens with protective factors of 10 to 15, or higher.

PABA and benzophenone compounds are clear, lightweight, and cosmetically pleasant to use. Red veterinary petrolatum (RVP) is very protective, but it is in a greasy base, or even in a white paste, so it is noticeable on the skin. Titanium dioxide or zinc oxide pastes are sometimes used as physical sun blocking agents, and they do block all ultraviolet and visible rays, but they are thick, unsightly pastes. RVP and sunblocking pastes are used only in the rare individuals who are allergic to PABA and benzophenones, or in those with sunburns or exquisite photosensitivity who must protect their skin from all light. All preparations can be purchased without prescription.

PABA and Benzophenone Sunscreens

SPF of 15 or more
 Block Out cream lotion
 Total Eclipse (Eclipse 15) (creamy lotion)
 Elizabeth Arden Suncare Sun Blocking Cream
 Bain de Soleil Ultra Sun Block Creme
 Clinique 19 SPF Sun Block (cream)
 Estee Lauder Sun-Cover Creme
 Presun 15 solution
 SolBar Plus 15 cream
 Super Shade 15 (Coppertone) cream

SPF between 8 and 14
 Almay Sun Tanner Full-Filter Sun Lotion
 Avon Sun Seekers Sun Safe Lotion
 Bonnie Bell Sun Bloc cream
 Bain de Soleil Sun-Filter Lotion
 Block Out clear lotion
 Clinique Sun Block cream
 Deleal Sun Cream
 Eclipse 10 cream lotion
 Elizabeth Arden Suncare Sun Shading Cream
 Estee Lauder Ultra-Violet Screening Cream
 Pabafilm 10 gel
 Pabafilm 10 lotion
 PabaGel

Sunscreens

(continued)

    Pabanol lotion
    PanUltra lotion
    Presun solution
    Princess Marcella Borghese LaRiviera Sun Screening
      Cream
    SolBar cream
    Sundown 8 lotion
    Ultima II Scientific Sun Block Lotion
    Uval Sunscreen Lotion

SPF between 4 and 7
    Block Out gel
    Hawaiian Tropic Dark Tanning Lotion
    Pabafilm Sunscreen Gel
    Sundown 4 Sunscreen Cream
    Sundown 6 Sunscreen Cream

RVP and Titanium Dioxide Paste

RVP paste
    RVPaque (RVP + zinc oxide)
    RVPlus (RVP + titanium)
    Solar (PABA + titanium)

Sunscreens and Blocks for Lips

Eclipse Sunscreen Lip and Face Protectant (SPF 6,
    PABA only)
Pan Ultra Sun Stick (benzophenone)
PreSun Lip Protection
RVPaba Lipstick (RVP + PABA)

Pigmenting Agents

For a discussion of the use of these materials see the section on
Vitiligo (p.221).
    Note: Some cosmetic preparations are purported to gave a 'tan' by
application or ingestion. They are either topical dyes or oral carotene
derivatives. They usually impart an unnatural orange hue to the skin.
    Psoralens (which require prescription) are available as methoxsalen
('Oxsoralen') 1% lotion, 10 mg tablets, and trioxsalen ('Trisoralen'),
5mg tablets.

Hypopigmenting Agents

See discussion of Melasma (p.59). The only agent which effectively
produces temporary pigment reduction is hydroquinone.
    Monobenzone ('Benoquin') produces *permanent* destruction of
melanocytes and permanent depigmentation. Its uses are very limited
and it should be administered only by a physician experienced in its
use.
    Hydroquinones are available in a range of strengths (2 to 4%) and
vehicles (lotions, creams, pastes) ['Artra', 'Eldoquin', 'Melanex' etc.]
some containing PABA and/or benzophenone as well ('Nudit',
'Solaquin' etc.).

Soaks, Baths, Compresses, and Astringents

Wet dressings and soaks are generally used in acute oozing or infected dermatoses, erosions, or ulcers. They soften and remove serum, debris, and bacteria, and are soothing. For this debriding, flushing action to occur, the solutions should be washed over the lesions, or wet dressings changed frequently, rather than just leaving dressings on for long periods of time (which macerates surrounding tissue).

Soaks and **baths** can be performed in a washbowl, pan, bucket, or bathtub. The affected part, such as the foot, is placed in the partially filled container for five to 15 minutes. The solution is gently agitated over the lesion or repeatedly splashed up onto it, and debridement is gently encouraged with the fingers, cloth, or gauze pad.

Wet dressings are used when it is difficult to get the patient to a tub, or it is difficult to immerse the affected area, or facilities are not available for soaks. Soft cotton cloth or gauze is used to apply the solution. The material is dipped in the solution and gently wrung so that it is still nearly dripping wet. The sopping dressing is applied to the lesion for a few minutes, to soften the debris, perhaps rubbed gently across the lesion, and then removed, rinsed out in solution, gently wrung, and reapplied. By repeating this cycle several times in 15 to 30 minutes, serum and debris are loosened and carried away from the lesion. Merely applying and removing a wet dressing once is usually inadequate for debridement.

If the goal of a soak or dressing is to dry oozing tissue and prevent infection, then one may use an **astringent** or **antiseptic** solution. However, nearly equal results can be achieved with plain tap water, which many dermatologists routinely recommend. Prescribing astringents or antiseptics has some risks. They normally are dispensed as tablets, powders, or liquid concentrates which the patient adds at home to a large volume of water. Unfortunate accidents have occurred where the tablets were ingested, the liquid concentrate was used directly, or the tablets burned the skin in the bath before they dissolved completely. It is perhaps better to recommend saline solution or Epsom salts, which are relatively safe even if ingested.

Astringents
- Saline solution is made by dissolving one teaspoon of salt in 500mL of water.
- Epsom salts (magnesium sulfate) are added to water in a proportion of 60g per 500mL.
- Acetic acid, approximately 1%, can be made up by diluting vinegar half-and-half with water.
- Aluminum acetate (Burow's solution) is a widely available astringent and antiseptic. It is usually diluted to a 1:20 or 1:40 solution. It is commercially available as tablets or as powder ('Demboro', 'Blueboro') in individual foil envelopes. Adding one tablet or one envelope of powder to 500mL of water yields a 1:40 solution.

Soaks, Baths, Compresses, and Astringents

(continued)

- Aluminum chloride is made up as a 2% solution from powder in foil packets ('Aluwets') with one packet per 375mL water.
- Potassium permanganate 1:5000 to 1:25000 is sometimes used as a soak or bath, but stains the skin purple. Find out from your local pharmacist how he or she dispenses it (it is available in generic tablets, crystals, or liquid concentrate of various strengths).
- Silver nitrate 0.25% solution is a strong astringent made up by adding one teaspoon of 50% aqueous solution to one liter of water. It stains skin, clothing, and (especially) metal utensils black.

When soothing and cooling baths or soaks are desired, but the skin is dry and astringency would be irritating, then oil, protein, and carbohydrate substances are used. **Beware that all oil-containing products make the tub so slippery that it becomes dangerous for even young, agile patients.** Oils in baths leave little residue on the skin. If lubrication of the skin is required, bathing in plain water is strongly recommended; apply the bath oil to the skin after bathing.

- Cold milk (not skim or low-fat) may be used as a soothing, non-drying soak for irritated areas such as first-degree burns or herpes simplex.
- Starch colloids apparently have a soothing effect, of unknown mechanism. Starch baths are made by adding two cups of starch to a tub of water. Sometimes two cups of baking soda (sodium bicarbonate) are added as well. Oatmeal bath colloid is commercially available in powder form, plain or with oil added ('Aveeno', 'Oilated Aveeno').
- Bath oils contain mineral or vegetable oil with surfactants. Many preparations are commerically available
  'Alpha-Keri'
  'Domol'
  'Jeri-Bath'
  'Kauma'
  'Lubath'
  'Lubrex'
  'Lubriderm'
  'Nutraderm'
  'Surfol'
  'Syntex'

Soaps and Shampoos

Soaps help remove oil and dirt from the skin. Antibacterial or deodorant soaps reduce the bacterial population of the skin.
Soaps which are low in detergent properties or which have oil added may be less drying to the skin and may be used in people with a tendency to dry skin (p.146).

Contributing more to skin dryness than soap are the frequency and duration of bathing, water temperature and lubrication after bathing.

Shampoos remove oil, dirt, and scale from the scalp. Dandruff shampoos are perhaps keratolytic (soften scale) and/or suppress inflammation and epidermal turnover (scale formation). More important than the specific shampoo chosen is the frequency and duration of use (see p.2 for treatment of seborrheic dermatitis).

Four ingredients known to help control seborrheic dermatitis are: chloroxine; selenium sulfide; sulfur/salicylic acid; and zinc pyrithione. Some brands are listed below. Chloroxine and selenium sulfide 2.5% require prescriptions. There is no evidence that they are superior to the over-the-counter preparations, although the 2.5% selenium sulfide is possibly more effective than the 1% form, which is available over the counter.

The addition of **tar** to a shampoo is thought to make it more effective, although conclusive studies are lacking. Tar shampoos are particularly popular for psoriasis of the scalp, but thorough rinsing (which is recommended) removes all or most tar residue. Tar shampoos can stain white and light blond hair slightly yellow.

Some 'dandruff' shampoos contain none of the above ingredients and their effectiveness is questionable.

Some commercially available shampoos

Chloroxine shampoos: 'Capitrol'
Selenium sulfide shampoos (1-2.5%): 'Exsel' 'Iosel' 'Selsun'
Sulfur and/or salicylic acid shampoos: 'Ionil' 'Meted' 'Sebaveen'
    'Sebulex' 'Tiseb' 'Vanseb' 'Xseb'
Zinc pyrithione shampoos: 'Danex' 'DHS Zinc' 'Head & Shoulders'
    'Zincon'
Tar shampoos: 'DHS Tar' 'Ionil-T' 'Pentrax' 'Polytar' 'Sebutone'
    'T-Gel' 'Tegrin' 'Tersatar' 'Vanseb-T' 'Xseb-T' 'Zetar'

Antihistamines

Antihistamines are often prescribed to counteract **itching,** but they are effective in that role only in histamine-mediated conditions, such as hives (urticaria) and some drug reactions. For non-histamine-mediated itching (dermatitis, dry skin, jaundice) they are no better than a placebo. However, the placebo effect in itching is enormous (usually over 40% of patients respond).

In **sedative** doses antihistamines diminish the perception of itching, as would any central nervous system depressant. They are particularly useful to take at bedtime to encourage sleep in an itchy individual. Significant scratching occurs during sleep, and antihistamines in sedative doses reduce it.

Individuals vary considerably in their response to specific antihistamines, so various ones should be tried to find one which is effective, but which has minimal side effects. Listed below are the antihistamine families from which specific agents should be chosen. There is some experimental evidence, and it is generally believed by dermatologists, that hydroxyzine is the most effective single agent against hives (p.180). If all agents fail, sometimes a combination of two antihistamines from different families will succeed.

Antihistamines often cause drowsiness, unco-ordination, gastrointestinal upset, dry mouth, or blurred vision. These side effects may vary considerably in prominence at different times when the same agent is taken. There may be gradual development of tolerance to the benefits and side effects of an antihistamine when taken regularly. Because of the common occurrence of drowsiness and diminished coordination, patients must be warned of their occurrence and be advised not to drive or to operate dangerous machinery when taking antihistamines, especially at the onset of therapy, when the response is unpredictable.

Some important antihistamines by chemical class

Ethylenediamines
Hydroxyzine hydrochloride	'Atarax', 'Vistaril'
Tripelenamine hydrochloride	'Pyribenzamine'

Ethanolamines
Diphenhydramine	'Benadryl'
Carbinoxamine	'Clistin'
Doxylamine succinate	'Decapryn'
Clemastine fumarate	'Tavist'

Antihistamines

(continued)

Alkylamines

Chlorpheniramine maleate	'Teldrin' 'Chlor-Trimeton'
Brompheniramine maleate	'Dimetane'
Dexchlorpheniramine maleate	'Polaramine'
Triprolidine hydrochloride	'Actidil'

Phenothiazines

Promethazine hydrochloride	'Phenergan'
Trimeprazine tartrate	'Temaril'
Methdilazine hydrochloride	'Tacaryl'

Propylamines

Cyproheptadine hydrochloride	'Periactin'
Azatidine maleate	'Optimine'

Keratolytics, Tars, and Destructive Agents

Keratolytics

Keratolytic agents soften and/or remove keratin and scale. For the treatment of scaling disorders (e.g. psoriasis, p.169), warts, callouses, and so on.

1. **Salicylic acid** is used alone or in combination with other medications for the treatment of psoriasis, seborrheic dermatitis, tineas, warts, and acne. Most preparations are sold over the counter.
   A. Salicylic acid 3%-6% ointment.
   B. Whitfield's ointment contains salicylic acid 6% and benzoic acid 12%. Half-strength Whitfield's ointment (3%/6%) is used so commonly that many pharmacies routinely dispense it when Whitfield's (unspecified) is ordered.
   C. Propylene glycol is a keratolytic and, used as a vehicle, enhances the effect of salicylic acid. Tars and other compounds are also sometimes added. Salicylic acid 3%-6% in propylene glycol may be prescribed or one of the proprietary equivalents ('Keralyt', 'Saligel').
   D. Salicylic acid 5%-20% in flexible collodion, often with equal parts of lactic acid, is used to treat warts and callouses. It may be prescribed as such or as a branded equivalent ('Duofilm', 'Salactic' film).
   E. Salicylic acid plasters (40% on adhesive moleskin) are used for warts and callouses ('corn plaster', 'Dr Scholl's Zino pads').
2. **Urea compounds** are purported to be softening to keratin, and are hydroscopic (draw water from the atmosphere) so they are used for dry skin (p.146). Urea is sometimes combined with corticosteroids to enhance penetration. Urea creams can be compounded by a pharmacist, but are relatively unstable, so commercial preparations are usually dispensed ('Aquacare', 'Carmol', 'Calmurid').
3. **Lactic acid** is a potent keratolytic when in an ointment base in 5%-20% concentration, made up by a pharmacist. It is combined with salicylic acid in flexible collodion for the treatment of warts and callouses (see above). In a 5% lotion form it is used for dry skin ('Lacticare').
4. **Tar** preparations are possibly keratolytic, antimitotic (slowing epidermal cell division of psoriasis), anti-inflammatory, and a phototherapy enhancer. Tars are derived from petroleum, coal, shale, and wood. The most commonly-used ones are coal tars.
   A. Crude coal tar can be compounded in ointment, (1%-5%), cream, oil, gel or shampoo. The most common commercial preparations are 'Pragmatar', 'Estar', 'Psorigel' (the latter are pleasant gels).
   B. Tar emulsions or bath oils are added to the bath or applied directly to the skin. Some brands available are: 'Balnetar', 'Doak' oil, 'Lavatar', 'Polytar', 'Tarsum', and 'Zetar'. All are sold over the counter.
   C. Tar shampoos are listed under shampoos (p.320).

Keratolytics, Tars, and Destructive Agents

(continued)

      D. Liquor carbonis detergens (LCD) is an extract of tar which is less dark and, probably, less potent. It is used in 5%-10% concentrations in creams, oils and shampoos, often in combination with corticosteroids, sulfur, or salicylic acid.

5. **Anthralin** (dithranol) is a specific molecular substance extracted from coal tar. It inhibits epidermal mitosis and is used primarily in psoriasis. It is often mixed with salicylic acid in a stiff paste containing 0.1% to 1% anthralin. Commercially available preparations are 'AnthraDerm', 'Lasan Unguent', 'Drithocreme'.

Destructive Agents

1. These are either caustics (which chemically burn tissue) or styptics (chemicals which stop bleeding). Mild caustics are often used as styptics.

      A. Monochloracetic, dichloracetic, or trichloracetic acid can be compounded for use in the office. It is in 20%-80% solutions, 30%-50% being the most common.

      B. Silver nitrate solution below 1% is used as a compress, but above 5% it is a cauterant. Silver nitrate sticks have a wad of nearly 100% silver nitrate at the end and are used as cauterants and styptics after moistening the wad.

      C. Ferric chloride solution 3%-5%, or ferric subsulfate 40% (Monsel's solution) are used as styptics.

      D. Aluminum chloride is the active ingredient in antiperspirants in 1%-3% concentrations, and in a 20% solution is a potent antiperspirant and drying paint (p.306). In a 30%-80% alcoholic solution it is a styptic, and does not stain, as the iron salts might.

      E. Negatol ('Negetan') is a styptic which coagulates blood by enzymatic action.

2. Cantharidin is a vesicant (produces vesicles), originally extracted from the blister beetle (Spanish fly), which is used to destroy warts and molluscum contagiosum (p.218). It is used in the office and should not be prescribed for home use. The commercial preparations are in flexible collodion ('Cantharone').

3. Podophyllin is a plant extract which inhibits viral replication in genital warts (p.70). It rarely affects non-genital warts. It is usually compounded in a 25% solution in benzoin, for application in the office.

4. An anti-cancer drug, 5-fluorouracil, interferes with DNA synthesis. It is used topically as a cream or solution ('Efudex', 'Fluoroplex') to treat actinic keratoses (p.327).

Potency of Oral Contraceptives
(modifed from: Int J Obs Gynaec 16: 1979)

Name	Estrogenic Potency[a]	Progestational Potency[b]	Androgenic Potency[c]
Therapeutic indication only			
Enovid 10	438	0.94	0.00
Enovid 5	240	0.48	0.00
Norinyl/Ortho-Novum 10	NA	3.71	3.35
Ortho-Novum 5	76	1.90	1.67
Contraceptive-combination (more than 50mg of estrogen)			
Enovid E (21)/Novinol	80	0.25	0.00
Ortho-Novum 0.5	68	0.53	0.21
Ovulen (21)	46	0.74	0.67
Ovulen 0.5	42	0.38	0.34
Norinyl/Ortho-Novum 2	64	0.26	0.10
Norinyl/Ortho-Novum 1/80	77	0.19	0.17
Contraceptive-combination (50µg of estrogen)			
Anoryl	50	0.26	0.10
Ovcon 50	50	0.36	0.34
Ovral	42	0.50	0.80
Logest/Nortestrin/Zorane 1/50	39	0.44	0.52
Norinyl/Ortho-Novum 1/50	32	0.38	0.34
Demulen	26	0.53	0.21
Norlestrin 2.5	16	1.02	1.25
Contraceptive-combination (less than 50µg of estrogen)			
Brevicon/Modicon/Moda Con	42	0.19	0.17
Ovcon 35	40	0.15	0.14
Lo-Ovral/Min/Ovral	25	0.30	0.48
Loestrin/Logest/Zorane 1.5/30	14	0.65	0.79
MinEstrin/Loestrin/Zorane 1/20	13	0.44	0.52
Contraceptive-progestogen only			
Nor Q.D./Microner	6	0.80	0.16
Ovrette	0	0.10	0.16

a) micrograms of ethinyl estradiol equivalents per day
b) milligrams of norgestrel equivalents per day
c) milligrams of methyl testosterone equivalents per day

Subject Index